Information Systems Outsourcing

Wiley Series in Information Systems

Editors

RICHARD BOLAND   Department of Management and
Information Systems, Weatherhead School of
Management, Case Western Reserve University,
699 New Management Building, Cleveland,
Ohio 44106-7235, USA
RUDY HIRSCHHEIM   Department of Decision and
Information Systems, College of Business Administration,
University of Houston, Houston, Texas 77204-6283,
USA

Advisory Board

NIELS BJORN-ANDERSEN   Copenhagen Business School,
Denmark
D. ROSS JEFFERY   University of New South Wales,
Australia
HEINZ K. KLEIN   State University of New York, USA
ROB KLING   University of California, USA
TIM J. LINCOLN   IBM UK Limited, UK
BENN R. KONSYNSKI   Emory University, Atlanta, USA
FRANK F. LAND   London School of Economics, UK
ENID MUMFORD   Manchester Business School, UK
MIKE NEWMAN   University of Manchester, UK
DANIEL ROBEY   Florida International University, USA
E. BURTON SWANSON   University of California, USA
ROBERT TRICKER   Hong Kong University, Hong Kong
ROBERT W. ZMUD   Florida State University, USA

Information Systems Outsourcing

Myths, Metaphors and Realities

MARY CECELIA LACITY
University of Missouri, St Louis, USA
RUDY HIRSCHHEIM
University of Houston, USA

JOHN WILEY & SONS
Chichester · New York · Brisbane · Toronto · Singapore

Published 1993 by John Wiley & Sons Ltd,
Baffins Lane, Chichester,
West Sussex PO19 1UD, England

Other Wiley Editorial Offices

John Wiley & Sons, Inc., 605 Third Avenue,
New York, NY 10158–0012, USA

Jacaranda Wiley Ltd, G.P.O. Box 859, Brisbane,
Queensland 4001, Australia

John Wiley & Sons (Canada) Ltd, 22 Worcester Road,
Rexdale, Ontario M9W 1L1, Canada

John Wiley & Sons (SEA) Pte Ltd, 37 Jalan Pemimpin #05–04,
Block B, Union Industrial Building, Singapore 2057

MB

Library of Congress Cataloging-in-Publication Data
Lacity, Mary Cecelia.
   Information systems outsourcing / Mary Cecelia Lacity, Rudy
      Hirschheim.
      p.   cm. — (John Wiley series in information systems)
   Includes bibliographical references and index.
   ISBN 0-471-93882-3 (cloth)
      1.   Electronic data processing departments—Contracting out.
   I. Hirschheim, R. A. (Rudy A.) II. Title. III. Series.
   HF5548.2.L227   1993
   658'.05—dc20   92–41996
                                                              CIP

British Library Cataloguing in Publication Data

A catalogue record for this book is available from the British Library

ISBN 0-471-93882-3

Typeset in 10/12 pt Palatino from authors' disks by Photo·graphics, Honiton, Devon
Printed and bound in Great Britain by Biddles Ltd, Guildford, Surrey

Contents

Series Preface

The information systems community has grown considerably since 1984, when we first started the Wiley Series in Information Systems. We are pleased to be part of the growth of the field, and believe that the series books have played an important role in the intellectual development of the discipline. The primary objective of the series is to publish scholarly works which reflect the best of research in the information systems community.

As the information systems field matures, there is an increased need to carry the results of its growing body of research into practice. Hence, after consultation with our editorial board, it was decided that the series should also place an emphasis on publishing research results that speak to important needs in the development and management of information systems. Beginning with this volume, therefore, we are broadening our editorial mission to recognize more explicitly the need for research to inform the practice and management of information system. This is not so much a dramatic altering of direction as a change in emphasis. The present volume, *Information Systems Outsourcing: Myths, Metaphors and Realities*, is a case in point. It is a serious treatment of the outsourcing phenomenon, firmly rooted in empirical research involving thirteen organizations and seventeen outsourcing decisions. The lessons learned from this research are of direct consequence to information systems practitioners, and managers generally.

To reflect the broadening of our editorial mission, and the increased emphasis on how research can affect the practice of information systems, we have instituted a change in book layout and cover design. We hope readers will enjoy these changes.

Rudy Hirschheim   Dick Boland
University of Houston, Texas   *Case Western Reserve University,*
Ohio

Preface

Ever since Eastman Kodak announced their outsourcing contracts with IBM, Businessland and DEC, large companies have found it acceptable (some might go so far as to say "fashionable") to transfer their information systems (IS) assets, leases and staff to third party vendors. Companies that have followed Eastman Kodak's example include Continental, Enron, First City, Freeport McMoRan, Hibernia, American Standard, National Car Rental, First Fidelity, American Bankshares, Farm Credit Bank, Copperweld, and Cypress Minerals to name a few. Many more companies are likely to follow suit as is evidenced by a Yankee Group report which estimates that every Fortune 500 Company will evaluate IS outsourcing and 20% will sign outsourcing deals by 1994.

As the outsourcing trend gains momentum, it is prudent to stop and reflect on several poignant questions: What are organizational members' intentions for evaluating outsourcing decisions? What problems are they attempting to solve with outsourcing? Do vendors really provide solutions to these problems? In this book, we describe a research project whose purpose was to explore questions such as these by investigating the information systems outsourcing phenomenon from individuals who have already gone through the evaluation process. Through a series of in-depth interviews with participants in thirteen companies who have gone through formal IS outsourcing evaluations, many insights were gained about the intentions, motivations and consequences of information systems outsourcing. The following four seem particularly cogent.

First, organizational members may initiate outsourcing for reasons other than cost efficiency. Participants identified a variety of motives for initiating outsourcing decisions: react to the efficiency imperative, acquire or justify additional resources, react to the positive outsourcing media reports, reduce uncertainty, eliminate a burdensome function and enhance personal credibility.

Second, an outsourcing vendor may not be inherently more efficient than an internal IS department. The theory of economies of scale states that large-sized companies achieve lower average costs than small-sized companies due to mass production and labor specialization efficiencies. In the outsourcing arena, however, the applicability of the economies of scale model may be challenged. Small shops may have lower costs per MIP than large shops by employing older technology, offering below market wages, and maintaining tight controls and procedures. A vendor's hardware discount advantage, in many cases, is insignificant when compared with the discounts available to the potential outsourced company. Changes in software licensing agreements diminish a vendor's advantage. Labor expertise is largely a myth since clients are usually supported by the same staff that transitioned to the vendor.

Third, the internal IS department may be able to achieve similar results without vendor assistance. When vendors submit bids that indicate savings, companies may question whether they can achieve similar results without vendor assistance. Perhaps the company can reduce their own IS expenses through data center consolidation, resource optimization, chargeback implementation, and other sundry methods.

Fourth, if a company decides to outsource, the contract is the only mechanism to ensure that expectations are realized. When some companies decide that outsourcing is the preferred mechanism for achieving IS objectives, they often like to view their vendors as partners. This assumption, however, is dubious: vendors are not partners because profit motives are not shared. An outsourcing contract is the only way to ensure an equitable balance of power. Service level measures, provisions for growth, and penalties for non-performance must be stipulated prior to outsourcing commencement.

In this book, we describe in some detail how these four conclusions have been reached, as well as other lessons and recommendations which emerge from our analysis of the thirteen case studies. We note that under specific circumstances, such as when companies cannot control IS costs on their own or need to sell IS assets to generate cash, it may well be appropriate for companies to outsource. If so, to ensure that outsourcing expectations are realized it is prudent that organizations follow the stringent contract negotiation strategies presented in this book.

EXECUTIVE SUMMARY

This book's purpose is to help organizations understand the growing trend in information systems outsourcing. The book will be particularly helpful to those organizations yet to face outsourcing evaluations. A summary of the book is presented below.

1. Introduction

This chapter briefly defines IS outsourcing and explains why the interest in outsourcing is unlikely to wane. The reader is also introduced to the primary research questions:

1   *What do we understand about IS outsourcing prior to this research?*
2   *How is senior management's view of the IS function related to IS outsourcing decisions?*
3   *What are organizational members' intentions for evaluating outsourcing alternatives?*
4   *How should practitioners about to face outsourcing decisions conduct their evaluations?*
5   *What overall lessons can we learn from the successes and failures of practitioners who have already evaluated the outsourcing alternative?*

The first question is answered by reviewing outsourcing reports contained in public information sources (i.e. the trade and academic literature). To answer the remaining questions, 36 individuals who have conducted outsourcing evaluations from thirteen firms were interviewed. Their outsourcing successes and failures provided significant insights into each of these questions.

2. Public Outsourcing Reports

1   *What do we understand about IS outsourcing prior to this research?*

This chapter reviews the information practitioners receive about outsourcing from the trade press and other public information sources. Most notably, outsourcing is portrayed as a panacea for IS problems. Throughout the outsourcing literature, the topic of IS for competitive advantage is abandoned in favor of the view that IS is merely a utility. As a utility, public reports suggest that IS is most efficiently handled by an expert.

Compared to the research findings, public outsourcing reports are often overly optimistic. The optimism stems from the fact that no company wishes to offer an outsourcing failure for public scrutiny. Therefore, the literature misrepresents the spectrum of outsourcing experiences by focusing only on the success stories. This book is unique compared with other outsourcing reports because firms that decided NOT to outsource as well as firms that regretted their outsourcing decisions were included in our study.

3. Theoretical Foundation

Two theories of organizational decision-making were used to help guide this research: Williamson's transaction cost theory (TCT) and Pfeffer's political model. Williamson's theory was adopted because it represents the widely-accepted view that organizational members make outsourcing decisions based solely on an economic rationale. Pfeffer's model was selected because it offers an alternative interpretation that focuses on the power and politics associated with outsourcing. Together, these models offer two alternative ways of interpreting outsourcing decisions.

4. Case Descriptions

This chapter discusses the thirteen case studies in detail. Each case is described in terms of the key players involved in the outsourcing evaluation, an historical background as to why outsourcing was considered in the first place as well as the eventual outcome, a brief overview of the company, and an interpretation of the actual processes surrounding the outsourcing decision. The outsourcing decision process is analyzed from two different perspectives outlined in the previous chapter.

The thirteen cases demonstrate the diverse circumstances that prompt outsourcing decisions. Some decisions were initiated by IS managers, others by senior executives. Some decided to outsource nothing, others decided to outsource everything, and two others decide to outsource then bring the function back in-house. Some decisions appear rational, others political, most both. Some companies were pleased with their outsourcing vendors, others displayed vile repulsion. Some companies saved money, some companies lost money, and some companies appeared to do nothing as a result of their outsourcing evaluations.

These individual cases provide the "raw data" for the analysis of outsourcing evaluations discussed in subsequent chapters. Despite the apparent uniqueness of the cases, common themes do arise.

5. Senior Management's View of IS

2 *How is senior management's view of the IS function related to IS outsourcing evaluations?*

This chapter explores senior management's view of their IS functions in the participating firms. Their perceptions are important to scrutinize since research findings are best understood by exposing the relationship between outsourcing evaluations and senior management's view of IS. In particular, outsourcing evaluations seemed to be couched in the larger problem of demonstrating the value of IS to senior management. With little top management support, IS managers had difficulty acquiring resources, demonstrating efficiency, and gaining personal credibility. Outsourcing evaluations were often initiated to temper these and other pressures.

6. Reasons for Initiating Outsourcing Evaluations

3 *What are organizational members' intentions for evaluating outsourcing alternatives?*

Participants in this research identified many motives for initiating outsourcing evaluations. In addition to the cost-efficiency imperative, some participants stated they initiated outsourcing investigations to acquire or justify additional resources, to react to the positive outsourcing reports, to reduce personal risk associated with uncertainty, to eliminate a burdensome function, and to enhance personal credibility. These motives represent a variety of economic and political reasons for evaluating the outsourcing alternative.

7. Proposed Outsourcing Evaluation Process

4 *How should practitioners about to face outsourcing decisions conduct their evaluations?*

By combining the lessons learned from the participants' outsourcing successes and failures, an outsourcing evaluation process is proposed. Unlike other outsourcing decision methodologies, this process focuses on how a company should proceed if a vendor submits an attractive bid. While other methods assume a company should immediately engage in outsourcing, this process recommends that companies pause to address three important questions: Why is the vendor's bid more desirable than the internal IS bid? Could the internal IS department achieve similar savings without vendor assistance? If not, how does a company ensure that their outsourcing expectations are realized?

8.   Summary of Lessons Learnt and Recommendations

5   *What overall lessons can we learn from the successes and failures of practitioners who have already evaluated the outsourcing alternative?*

Seven lessons extracted from the research are summarized. These lessons would help an organization's understanding of the motivation, processes and consequences of IS outsourcing evaluations. The seven lessons are:

1   *Public information sources portray an overly optimistic view of IS outsourcing.*
2   *Outsourcing appears to be a symptom of the problem of demonstrating the value of IS.*
3   *Organizational members may initiate outsourcing for reasons other than cost efficiency.*
4   *An outsourcing vendor may not be inherently more efficient than an internal IS department.*
5   *The internal IS department may be able to achieve similar results without vendor assistance.*
6   *If a company decides to outsource, the contract is the only mechanism to ensure that expectations are realized.*
7   *The metaphor that IS is merely a utility is misguided.*

In summary, practitioners yet to face outsourcing decisions will find this book relevant and insightful. The concrete examples presented from participants' actual experiences should challenge conventional assumptions about IS outsourcing. Above all else, it is concluded that while an organization may decide to outsource some portion of its information processing activities, it should not outsource the management of IS.

Acknowledgements

Since the participants were guaranteed confidentiality, we cannot thank them by name, but nonetheless wish to express our gratitude to them for devoting their time and efforts to this project. The research could not have been done without their generous sacrificing of their time. They are, if you will, the unsung heroes of the research. In addition, we would like to thank Dennis McGuire, Warren Gallant, Peter Beeman and Dick Hansen for their assistance on the project, and Thomas Blitz for his invaluable comments on earlier drafts of our work. The financial backing of the Information Systems Research Center at the University of Houston is also gratefully acknowledged. Last but not least, we would like to thank Diane Taylor and the staff at John Wiley & Sons for their technical assistance and support in the production of this book. To all of you, our deepest thanks.

Houston, Texas   MARY CECELIA LACITY
November 1992   RUDY HIRSCHHEIM

1
Introduction

1.0 THE OUTSOURCING PHENOMENON

During the 1980s, executives were advised of the strategic role that information and information systems (IS) could provide to organizations. Through IS, companies could squelch competition, secure suppliers, obtain customer loyalty, and reduce the threat of new entrants. Executives were offered the IS victory stories of American Airlines, American Hospital Supply, and Merrill Lynch as evidence to the success of exploiting information systems. Many executives followed this advice by applying strategic IS models to their own organizations.

Entering the 1990s, one would assume the role of IS would escalate as we continue to grow from a domestic industrial society to a global information society. However, executives are now advised by many practitioners, academics and consultants to outsource their IS services along with their cafeteria, mail delivery, and custodial services. By acquiescing many or all of their information services, executives are promised savings of 10% to 50% off their IS expenditures. Prudent companies are advised to follow suit behind Eastman Kodak, American Bankshares, Enron, Continental, and others.

So what happened to the IS function in the past few years? Has IS suddenly become a commodity service that is best managed by a large supplier?

For one thing, executives could hardly attend to harnessing IS for competitive advantage while dealing with grim corporate realities: leveraged buyouts, corporate debts, hostile takeovers, acquisitions, increased competition from abroad, and a stagnant economy. In this environment, survival depends on downsizing and cost-cutting. Information systems, whose contribution is difficult to measure and demonstrate, become a likely target.

Many companies, in their exuberance to duplicate savings purported in outsourcing reports, jump on the IS outsourcing bandwagon without due consideration to the potential consequences. Sure, there are outsourcing successes, but there are also outsourcing failures. The ultimate goal is "smart-sourcing"—companies retain strategic applications while farming out only those services that vendors can provide more efficiently. Companies are warned, however, that even so-called "utility" services, such as data center operations, are often most efficiently managed internally. In this book, we explore the broad arena of outsourcing, noting when and where it appears appropriate. Under specific circumstances, such as when companies cannot control IS costs on their own or need to sell IS assets to generate cash, companies may wish to outsource. If so, to ensure that outsourcing expectations are realized it is prudent that organizations follow the stringent contract negotiation strategies presented in this book.

1.1 WHAT IS INFORMATION SYSTEMS OUTSOURCING?

The term "outsourcing," although not specific to IS in that it reflects the use of external agents to perform one or more organizational activities (e.g. purchasing of a good or service), is now in vogue in the IS domain and applies to everything from use of contract programmers to third party facilities management. The following taxonomy captures the range of outsourcing options:

> *Body Shop*—management uses outsourcing as a way to meet short term demand. The most common type of body shop outsourcing is the use of contract programmers/personnel that is managed by company employees.
> *Project Management*—management outsources for a specific project or portion of IS work. Examples of project management outsourcing include the use of vendors to develop a new system, support an existing application, handle disaster recovery, provide training, or manage a network. In these cases, the vendor is responsible for managing and completing the work.
> *Total Outsourcing*—the vendor is in total charge of a significant piece of IS work. The most common type is total outsourcing

of the hardware (e.g. data center and/or telecommunications) operations. The newest outsourcing strategy is to turn over the entire hardware and software support to an outside vendor. Some have gone so far as to euphemistically term this type of outsourcing, turning over the "keys to the kingdom."

Some may argue that information systems outsourcing does not warrant attention—after all, outsourcing options have existed since the dawn of data processing. As early as 1963, Perot's Electronic Data Systems (EDS) was handling data processing services for Frito-Lay and Blue Cross (Mason, 1990). Other outsourcing options, such as the use of contract programmers, timesharing, and purchase of packaged software, have been exercised for two decades (Hammersmith, 1989). What renews interest in IS outsourcing and demands our attention today is the dramatic change in scope. Early forms of IS outsourcing typically dealt with single-system contracts comprising a small portion of the IS budget (Gallant, 1991). "In the past, outsourcing was available in the form of such specialty applications as payroll, insurance processing, credit cards and mailing lists" (Hammersmith, 1989). Outsourcing has recently grown to span multiple-systems and represents a significant transfer of assets, leases and staff to a vendor that now assumes profit and loss responsibility (Eckerson, 1990a). Enron's $750 million, ten-year contract with EDS provides a typical example of the increased scope of IS outsourcing. The phrase "keys to the kingdom" can be applied to these new outsourcing arrangements where vendors actually operate, manage, and control information systems functions. It is this type of outsourcing arrangement that warrants attention and concern.

A "keys to the kingdom" outsourcing arrangement works as follows. The vendor typically charges a fixed fee for a pre-specified number of services, known as the "baseline." The customer is guaranteed that their IS costs for this baseline will be fixed over the contract duration, typically five to ten years. During the contract period, services not included in the baseline may be purchased from the vendor for an excess fee. Deals are often sweetened with financial incentives, such as stock purchases, loans at low interest rates, and postponed payments. At the outset, these deals are extremely attractive, especially to an organization that suffers financially. But the implications in the long term are unclear.

Nor is organizational interest in this new vogue of outsourcing likely to wane in the near future. In 1989, the outsourcing market was worth $12.8 billion and continues to grow at a 20% rate (Krass,

1990; Rothfeder & Coy, 1990; McCormick, 1991; McMullen, 1990). Daily reports document additional outsourcing arrangements: Eastman Kodak, First City, Freeport McMoRan, Hibernia, American Standard, Kendall, Kinney, Westwood Equities, Sun Co., Farm Credit Bank, Copperweld, Apache and Cypress Minerals to name a few (Gillin, 1990a; Huff, 1991; Radding, 1990). The Yankee Group estimates that every Fortune 500 Company will evaluate IS outsourcing and 20% will sign outsourcing deals by 1994 (Eckerson, 1990a). All indicants suggest that information systems outsourcing will touch many more lives during this decade. Outsourcing will affect senior managers as they are courted by outsourcing vendors, IS managers as they struggle to reduce costs on their own, IS personnel as they contemplate working for an outsourcing vendor, and users as they adjust to new faces and procedures.

As the outsourcing trend gains momentum, it is prudent to stop and reflect on several poignant questions:

1   *What do we understand about IS outsourcing so far?*
2   *What are the experiences (both good and bad) of those organizations who have made outsourcing decisions?*
3   *How is senior management's view of the IS function related to IS outsourcing evaluations?*
4   *What are organizational members' intentions for evaluating outsourcing decisions?*
5   *How should practitioners about to face outsourcing decisions conduct their evaluations?*
6   *What overall lessons can we learn from the successes and failures of practitioners who have already evaluated the outsourcing alternative?*

In this book, we attempt to provide this reflective stance by investigating the information systems outsourcing phenomenon from individuals who have already gone through the evaluation process. We report on the results of an 18-month research project undertaken between January 1991 and June 1992 whose purpose was the exploration of these six questions. The following section briefly describes the research method used to learn about the participants' outsourcing experiences.

1.2   RESEARCH METHODOLOGY

To investigate the outsourcing phenomenon, a series of in-depth interviews with 36 participants from thirteen companies were conducted. All but four of the 36 interviews were tape-recorded and transcribed into a 375-page, single-spaced document. (Note: four recordings were inaudible so in these cases it was necessary to rely on handwritten notes.) These transcribed interviews provided the basis of the findings presented in subsequent chapters.

The duration of the interviews, on average, lasted one and one half hours. Although some interviews were shorter or longer, all interviews followed the same protocol which proceeded from a very unstructured to a very structured format. During the unstructured portion, participants were merely asked to tell their outsourcing story. This allowed the participant free rein to convey his or her interpretation of events. After they completed their stories, participants were asked semi-structured questions designed to solicit information on specific outsourcing issues that may have been absent from their previous recollections. Finally, participants were asked to fill out a multiple-choice questionnaire that captured information about themselves, their companies and their IS departments. The questionnaires provided the demographic information described in the next two sections.

1.3 COMPANY CHARACTERISTICS

This section describes the participating companies' size, geographic location, outsourcing decision scopes and outcomes.

The thirteen case participants represent a wide variety of industries. Using *Fortune* magazine's industry classification taxonomy, nine companies are classified as members of the manufacturing sector and four companies are classified as members of the service sector (see Table 1.1).

Of the nine manufacturing companies, two belong to the chemical industry, three belong to the petroleum refining industry, and two belong to the mining industry. The two remaining companies, categorized as miscellaneous in Table 1.1, belong to large holding companies. However, most people associate one of these companies with petroleum and the other company with equipment manufacturing. All but two of the nine manufacturing companies appeared on *Fortune* magazine's 1990 *Fortune* 500 list, which ranks companies in terms of revenues. One of these exceptions expects to enter the *Fortune* 500 this year after a series of significant acquisitions. The other exception, although not in the *Fortune* 500 in terms of revenues, made *Fortune*'s top 50 list of the most profitable U.S. firms (McManus, 1991a).

Table 1.1   Case sites classified by Fortune magazine's industry taxonomy

Industry	# of sites	# in Fortune 500
Manufacturing Industries:	9	7
Chemicals	2	1
Petroleum Refining	3	2
Mining, Crude Oil Production	2	2
Miscellaneous (equipment/petroleum)	2	2
Service Industries:	4	4
Diversified service companies	2	2
Commercial Bank	1	1
Transportation Services	1	1
Total	13	11

The remaining four of the thirteen companies are classified by *Fortune* Magazine as members of service industries. *Fortune* compiles their Service 500 list differently than their manufacturing *Fortune* 500 list. Rather than compile one list ranked by revenues, *Fortune* maintains eight separate lists: the top 100 Diversified Services Companies, top 100 Commercial Banks, top 50 Diversified Financial Companies, top 50 Savings Institutions, top 50 Life Insurance Companies, top 50 Retail Companies, top 50 Transportation Companies and Top 50 Utilities (McManus, 1991b).

Two case participants appeared on *Fortune*'s 1990 list of top 100 Diversified Services Companies. Although most people consider the petroleum company to be part of the manufacturing sector, the company primarily generates revenue through the transportation and brokering of oil and natural gas, not through production.

The only financial company that participated in this study was listed in *Fortune*'s 1990 top 50 Commercial Bank list despite a $60 million loss. Since *Fortune* compiles this list based on assets, it is interesting to note that 18 of the top 50 Commercial Banks posted negative earnings that year.

The participant classified as a holding company was listed in the *Fortune*'s 1990 top 50 Transportation Companies despite a major loss. This case participant may be more appropriately classified as an information systems company since they serve as the IS department to their sister and parent companies.

Given that eleven of the thirteen companies appear somewhere in the *Fortune* 500 or *Fortune* Service 500, we can surmise that case

Table 1.2 *1990 revenue range of case participants*

Revenue	Number of sites
Over $10 billion	3
$1–10 billion	5
$500 million–$1 billion	4
Under $500 million	1
Total	13

participants were large in terms of revenues or assets. The specific range of revenues and net income for the case participants are found in Tables 1.2 and 1.3.

An interesting note that may attest to the dismal state of the economy, three of the thirteen sites suffered multi-million dollar loses in 1990—one of these three companies is currently protected by bankruptcy laws. Many of the other case participants, although they posted positive earnings, suffered slow growth in sales.

Attention now turns to the scope and outcome of the case participants' outsourcing decisions (see Table 1.4). Of the four companies that limited the scope of their outsourcing evaluations to data processing, all decided not to outsource this function. A variety of reasons were given: perceived lack of monetary savings, initiator of the decision used outsourcing to demonstrate to management the efficiency of the function, economies of scale could not be achieved unless the entire department was outsourced.

The two companies that limited the scope of their outsourcing decisions to data processing and telecommunications both decided

Table 1.3 *1990 net income ranges of case participants*

Net income	Number of sites
Over $200 million	5
$100–$200 million	1
$1–$100 million	4
Net income loss	3
Total	13

Table 1.4 *Scope of outsourcing decisions at case sites*

Decision domain	Number of sites	# that decided to outsource
Data center	4	0
Data center and telecommunications	2	2
All IS functions except planning and strategic applications	1	1
All IS functions	6	5
Total sites:	13	8

to outsource. One company seemed determined to outsource, despite the questionable financial justification for the decision. In the other company, data processing and telecommunications comprises 75% to 80% of the total IS costs, so this outsourcing decision is rather comprehensive. Both of these companies are currently transitioning data processing over to the vendor, so the long term consequences cannot be assessed.

One lone company decided to outsource everything except planning and strategic systems. The IS Manager of the company, who initiated the decision, justifies the retention of these functions by claiming they add value to the company. Others, however, counter that he kept these functions so he could keep his position.

Six of the thirteen companies considered outsourcing the entire information systems department. These decisions were all spear-headed by a senior manager, many of whom seemed to view the entire IS function as a utility. Of these six cases, five decided to outsource to third parties. Two of these companies, however, subsequently terminated their outsourcing arrangements due to poor service.

In sum, taken as a whole, the company participants represent a variety of industries, venues, and sizes. The outsourcing decisions at these companies span a variety of functions and decision outcomes. The next section describes the characteristics of the individual participants.

1.4 PARTICIPANT DEMOGRAPHICS

The characteristics of the participants discussed in this section are based on information gathered during the interviews and the questionnaires that 28 of the 36 participants completed.

Table 1.5   *Gender of participants*

Gender	Number of participants
Male	35
Female	1
Total	36

Perhaps the most notable demographic characteristic of this group is gender (see Table 1.5). Of the 36 people interviewed, 35 are men. The lone female participant is a Vice President of IS for a bank. She is also, coincidentally, the youngest person interviewed; at 32 years of age, she runs a $16 million budget. (Note: given the male dominance of the participant population, masculine pronouns are used during the remainder of this research, rather than the phrases "he or she" or "his or her". This convention facilitates readability— it is not meant to diminish the contribution of the female participant.)

The participants' job positions are categorized in Table 1.6. The term "senior manager" applies to any manager above the head of the information systems department. Titles of senior managers include Chief Financial Officer, Controller and Treasurer.

The IS Manager typically reports to one of these senior managers. IS Manager titles vary, including Manager of Information Systems, Director of IS, and Vice President of Information Services. Of the 13 cases, nine IS Managers were interviewed. Of the remaining 5 cases, one company no longer had an IS Manager since the

Table 1.6   *Job positions of participants*

Job positions	Number of sites
Senior Manager (CFO, Controller, Treasurer)	7
Manager, Director or Vice President of Information Systems	9
Information Systems Staff Manager (Reports to the head of IS)	14
Account Manager for the outsourcing vendor	4
Consultant	2
Total	36

Table 1.7 Years of company service (n = 28)

0 to 6 months	6 to 12 months	1 to 2 years	2 to 4 years	Over 4 years
0	0	0	9	19

outsourcing vendor reported to the Controller, one IS Manager was on vacation, one IS Manager had no information about the outsourcing decision, one IS Manager was in Los Angeles, and the last delegated his interview to his subordinate in charge of the outsourcing decision.

Fourteen information systems staff people were interviewed. These participants were usually responsible for gathering the technical and financial details for the request for proposals. In some cases, these participants were placed in awkward positions—they assisted the outsourcing effort even though outsourcing would eliminate their positions.

Only four outsourcing vendors were interviewed. After these initial interviews, it became apparent that the vendors were reticent because they felt the interviews breached their supplier–client confidentiality agreements. They advised us to direct all questions to the client.

Two consultants, both experts in outsourcing contracts, were interviewed. Rather than let their clients sign the vendor contracts, these consultants insisted that a custom contract be designed that included service level measures and penalties for non-performance. As will be discussed in subsequent chapters, every company that used a consultant considered the investment worthwhile.

Table 1.7 and Table 1.8 show the distribution of the participants' years of company service and years in their current positions. Together, they suggest a pattern that participants worked for a long period of time for the same company, but that their positions vary often. (This observation must be tempered with the fact that the

Table 1.8 Years in current position of participants (n = 28)

0 to 6 months	6 to 12 months	1 to 2 years	2 to 4 years	Over 4 years
2	1	8	11	6

Table 1.9 *Age range of participants (n = 28)*

Under 20 years	20 to 29 years	30 to 39 years	40 to 49 years	50 plus years
0	0	8	11	9

time frames in Table 1.7 need to be lengthened since the first three cells are empty.)

The last demographic issue addressed on the questionnaire is age (see Table 1.9). The majority of participants were in their late thirties, early forties.

The most important characteristic of this group was not captured in the questionnaires. All participants were privy to the details of the outsourcing decisions in their respective companies. Whether they initiated outsourcing, compiled information, or analyzed bids, they had strong opinions about the decisions their companies made about outsourcing. The disparity of views expressed by participants provided a rich picture of these outsourcing decisions.

1.5   CONCLUSION

In the past few years, information systems outsourcing has become a major concern to organizational members. All indicants suggest that the outsourcing trend will continue to gain momentum during this decade. To better understanding the outsourcing phenomenon, 36 individuals who have already gone through the process were interviewed. Their successes and failures provided significant insights that are of interest to practitioners yet to face outsourcing decisions. Whereas public information sources stress the economics of outsourcing evaluations, this research also attends to the internal politics associated with outsourcing, the threat of opportunistic behavior on the part of some vendors, and contract negotiation strategies.

2
Public Outsourcing Reports

2.0 INTRODUCTION

This chapter addresses the question: What do we understand about IS outsourcing prior to this research? This chapter summarizes the information contained in public outsourcing reports. The contents of this chapter were gathered through a literature search as well as through information sources identified by the research participants. Whereas the literature search was restricted to IS trade journals, participants identified two additional sources of information: outsourcing seminars and vendor solicitations. The overall lesson learned from scrutinizing public information sources is that these sources often portray an overly optimistic view of outsourcing because: (a) reports are made during the honeymoon period, (b) only projected savings are reported instead of actual savings, and (c) outsourcing failures are under-represented. Given the propensity of outsourcing accolades, there is little wonder why practitioners hold favorable outsourcing opinions.

2.1 LITERATURE OUTSOURCING REPORTS

The literature identifies a plethora of companies that decided to outsource all or part of their IS Departments (see Table 2.1). Table 2.2 presents the seven largest outsourcing arrangements. From the size of these contracts it can be understood why so many companies are considering becoming IS outsourcing vendors. In addition, the literature provides a Who's Who among various outsourcing vendors (See Table 2.3 and Table 2.4).

Table 2.1 *Outsourcing customers*

Customer	Vendor
American Bankshares	Perot Systems
American Ultramar	Power Computing
Apache	Power Computing
Bank South Corp	IBM
Columbia Pictures	EDS
Continental Airline Holdings	EDS
Copperweld	General Signal
Cypress Minerals	EDS
Dial Corp.	Andersen Consulting
Eastman Kodak	IBM, DEC, Businessland
Enron	EDS
Federal Home Loan Bank of Seattle	EDS
First City	EDS
First Tennessee National Corp	IBM
First USA	EDS
Hibernia	IBM
HUD	Martin Marietta
Kendall	Kentech
People's Heritage	Systematics
Permian Corp	EDS
Riggs National Bank	IBM
Security-Connecticut Life Insurance	EDS
Southeast Banking Corp	IBM
Southland	ACS
The City of Chicago	EDS
Wabco	Genix
Westar Transmission	EDS
Western Union	EDS
Westmoreland Coal	EDS

2.1.1 Why Organizations Outsource

The primary reason given to explain the outsourcing trend is simple: cost efficiency. Companies evaluate outsourcing to determine if current operating costs could be reduced as well as to efficiently access new resources such as technical expertise. Whether companies actually decide to outsource does not matter, costs are still reported as the only impetus for evaluating the outsourcing alternative:

> "The outsourcing evaluation is simply to see if there is a provider that can implement those plans in a more cost-effective, shorter time frame." (Floyd Griggs, Vice President of Information Systems at Signet; reported in Horwitt, 1990, p. 2)

Table 2.2   Top 7 outsourcing contracts

Company	Vendor	$ Amount in millions
System One	EDS	apprx. $2 billion
Enron	EDS	$750
First City	EDS	$600
Eastman Kodak	IBM	$500
National Car Rental	EDS	$500
First Fidelity	EDS	$450
American Bankshares	Perot Systems	$400

Source: Reported in Computerworld, April 8, 1991.

Table 2.3   Top 7 outsourcing vendors

Company	Revenues ($ millions)	Percent of market
EDS	5470	40.1%
IBM	3250	23.4%
Andersen Consulting	1440	10.5%
Computer Sciences Corp	1440	10.5%
DEC	1000	7.3%
KMPG Peat Marwick	600	4.4%
AT&T	500	3.7%

Source: Yankee Group as reported in CIO, June 1990, p. 34.

Table 2.4   Top 10 facilities management vendors

Company	Revenues ($ millions)	Percent of market
EDS	716	50%
Systematics	205	14%
Andersen Consulting	111	8%
IBM	81	6%
Affiliated Computer	30	2%
Hoskyns	28	2%
DEC	26	2%
Perot Systems	25	2%
McDonnell Douglas	24	2%
ADP	20	1%

Source: Gartner Group as reported in InformationWeek, May 20, 1991, p. 12.

According to the trade press, companies that decide to outsource report savings of millions of dollars that represent 10% to 50% reductions off IS budgets (Krass, 1990). Outlandish? Consider the following testimonies:

Gary Biddle, Vice President of Information Systems at American Standard, claims that outsourcing his data operations and nationwide network reduced costs by 40% (Rochester & Douglass, 1990).

Kenneth Sheridan, Executive Vice President of Systems and Operations at Southeast, expects to save 20% in IS costs over the 10-year outsourcing contract.

Richard Churchill, Senior Vice President of Data Processing for San Francisco Federal Savings, guesses that his five-year outsourcing contract with Dataline Inc. will save the thrift $2.3 million (Krass, 1990).

O.C. Russell, Vice Chairman of Hibernia National Bank, projects savings from the 10-year contract with IBM to range between $25 million to $100 million (Krass, 1990).

Gordon Kahn, Chief Financial Officer at Kendall, claims that his contract with Kentech will save $500 000 in annual salaries (Hamilton, 1989).

Paul Adams, Chairman of First American Bankshares's IS subsidiary, outsourced to Perot Systems to save the bank 15% per year (Anthes, 1991).

The list goes on—Heinz, Kinney Wall Coverings, Eastman Kodak, First City, Frito-Lay, Copperweld, Enron, and others all cite cost reductions as the major impetus behind IS outsourcing (Brown & Eckerson, 1990; Krass, 1990; Rochester & Douglass, 1990; Oltman, 1990).

For those companies that decided not to outsource, they claim that their IS organizations are more efficient than outsourcing vendors:

Entergy Corp., a utility company based in New Orleans, after soliciting several requests for proposals (RFPs) decided that the internal IS department could achieve many of the economies of scale offered by vendors (Rochester & Douglass, 1990).

Navistar solicited outsourcing bids after one vendor sent a letter claiming it could reduce costs by 50%. Bids from EDS and Perot Systems were promptly rejected. The savings simply were not evident: EDS's bid offered negligible savings and Perot Systems's bid proposed to increase Navistar's annual IS budget by $10 million (Wilder, 1990b, p. 112).

Avon Products Corp. also decided to maintain an internal IS department. "When the company decided its own IS organization was more efficient than the bidder, the employees were as proud as they were relieved" (O'Leary, 1990, p. 31).

Al Hyland, director of worldwide systems at Polaroid, consulted Arthur D. Little to "address the noise in the computer press about outsourcing" (Crane, 1990, p. 71). Arthur D. Little confirmed that Polaroid was "right on track", thus bringing an end to the consideration of outsourcing.

In addition to reducing current operating costs, the literature also reports that companies outsource to efficiently access new resources, such as additional technical expertise. Internal IS departments often claim that vendors nurture technical skills less expensively. Consider the following examples from Dial Corp, HUD and, surprisingly, American Airlines:

Dial Corp, a subsidiary of Greyhound, provides an example of a company that outsourced to access vendor expertise. Dial Corp hired Andersen Consulting to run their data center for five years. The impetus behind that deal was to borrow Andersen's expertise during a technology switch from IBM mainframes to local area networks (Krass, 1990; McMullen, 1990).

The U.S. Department of Housing and Urban Development (HUD) outsourced to Martin Marietta largely to access technical personnel. Before signing the $526 million deal, HUD had staffing difficulties: "Federal agencies often specify limits on employment, and contracting out is one way to save on body count" (Anthes, 1990, p. 119).

American Airlines has recently contracted with IBM, AT&T, HP and Novell to build InterAct, a new technology platform that converges data processing, office automation, personal computing and networking (Hopper, 1990).

American Airlines is a particularly interesting example of the growing acceptance of outsourcing. This company, the superlative example of information technology used for competitive advantage in the 1980s, is outsourcing its next large scale, integrated system. Straight from the pen of American Airline's Senior VP of IS, Max Hopper writes:

> "We look forward to the day when we can buy more and more of our hardware and software from third-party vendors capable of tailoring their systems to our needs. . .Our skills as electronic tool builders, honed over decades, will become less and less decisive to our information strategy. This may sound like bad news, but we welcome it. We're not in business to build computer systems." (Hopper, 1990, p. 120)

From the sample of articles presented above, the overwhelming message is this: outsourcing saves money on current and new resources. The question then becomes: "why can outsourcers reduce IS costs?" The argument given why outsourcing reduces IS costs is this: IS is a utility. As such, large outsourcing vendors can provide a cheaper service through economies of scale:

> Henry Pfendt, Director of Information Technology at Kodak, claims outsourcing comes down to one question: "Do you want to manage commodities?" (Kass & Caldwell, 1990, p. 14).

> "Like shoppers at a fruit stand, companies are picking an apple here or an orange there until they have selected a menu of outsourcing services" (Ward, 1991, p. 40).

> Elliot McNeil, Southland's IS Manager, signed a 10-year contract with ACS. He claims that IS is largely a utility—rather than pay for the entire plant, why not just pay for wattage used? "It's like the electric company; you use less, you pay less" (Ambrosio, 1991).

> "Outsourcing takes over all information systems functions, much the way an outside company would manage food service or laundry" (Gardner, 1991, p. 35).

IS being compared to electricity, fruit stands, and laundry services—are these reasonable metaphors? Proponents of outsourcing seem to view IS as a homogeneous product. As such, IS vendors should be able to reduce costs through economies of scale. In subsequent chapters, however, this assumption is challenged.

2.1.2 How Outsourcing Decisions are Made

Most of the practitioner literature implies that outsourcing decisions are rational decisions. The published impetus behind outsourcing includes legitimate goals such as cost efficiency, effectiveness, etc. Thus, the reports give the illusion that the process is essentially rational—senior management evaluate the alternatives, apply a low cost criterion, then select the most efficient option (Allison, 1971). Few report the politics, conflicts and compromises involved in outsourcing decisions. Some exceptions, which hint that outsourcing decisions may be viewed as political, are summarized below.

IS employees at Nashville Electric Services (NES) filed a lawsuit to prevent the company from outsourcing data center operations to Seltmann, Cobb and Bryant, Inc. IS employees claim the company (a) broke their charter that states job transfers are based on performance and seniority, (b) failed to hold a public bid, and (c) failed to hold a public meeting. Despite the lawsuit, management is forging ahead with the $40 million contract (Eckerson, 1990b).

Mason (1990) reports on several of Perot's attempts (and successes) at securing new clients such as Medicare, Blue Cross, Postal Service, General Motors, and others. The evidence portrays the outsourcing decision as very political—lawsuits, cover-ups, hostile memorandums, etc. These are common characteristics of many outsourcing coups.

Howard Anderson, managing director at Yankee Group, claims that many internal IS departments cannot achieve economies of scale because of organizational politics. The following is an excerpt from an interview with Anderson and Joanne Kelleher from *Computerworld* (Kelleher, 1990, p. 76):

"Kelleher: Aren't most companies aware of the need [to consolidate data centers]?

Anderson: Often they are, but frequently the problem is that the demands of the profit centers convolute the equation. Senior management sends mixed messages. They tell IS to economize, but they tell the profit centers that they have P&L responsibility. Essentially, they give IS a set of rubber teeth.

Kelleher: So if internal politics and power struggles are preventing effective utilization of information systems, outsourcing may be the answer?

Anderson: Yes. Sometimes the only solution is to go outside to solve internal problems."

Thus, the literature provides evidence for both possibilities: outsourcing decision-making processes may be viewed as rational or political.

2.1.3 Consequences of Outsourcing

Since the expanded scope of outsourcing—farming out multiple IS function—is relatively new, and the contract periods are long (most are 5- to 10-year contracts), the long term impacts of outsourcing are difficult to assess. In addition, since most outsourcing contracts are cloaked in secrecy, the short term impacts are also difficult to assess (Krass, 1990). As indicated in the previous section on why organizations outsource, most proponents forecast long term cost savings. Opponents, however, argue otherwise. These opposing views are introduced below.

Philip Dorn, president of Dorn Computer Consultants, predicts that outsourcing will cause a loss of competitive advantage because in-house IS expertise disappears. For this, he criticizes Kodak:

> "Obvious to any information technology practitioner—which, it must be added, the chief outsourcer and current Kodak IS boss is not—is what will happen 5 to 10 years from now. Long after the current outsourcing phenomenon has run its course and those who backed moving these functions outside have received their promotions and rewards, Kodak will find it has lost its ability to grasp the possibilities inherent in information technology. The bright people will be gone, and with them will have left Kodak's opportunities for taking advantage of the information technology development of the 90s." (Dorn, 1989, p. 52)

Another feared consequence of outsourcing is the threat of opportunism. As outsourcing vendors take control of the IS function, some fear vendors may take advantage of clients. In particular, companies that outsource may find themselves at a disadvantage during contract renewals. Ray Perry, vice president at Avon Products, recently notes: "It is difficult to disengage a contract. You've eliminated dedicated people. Three or four years later, you have to start at ground zero" (O'Leary, 1990, p. 35).

Others fear vendors may not maintain confidentiality. A vice president of a major oil company claims his company decided not to outsource for several reasons, among them was the fear of placing the control of confidential information in the hands of vendors. He argues that data about oil reserves, mixing formulas, etc., are best managed internally. Others, however, dismiss the threat of confidentiality. An Arthur Andersen spokesperson states that the concern over confidentiality is "a lot of smoke. If you're dealing with a reputable firm, it's handled by a confidentiality clause" (O'Leary, 1990, p. 34).

A third concern is that the outsourcing vendor may take advantage of the contract by charging excessive fees for services the company assumes the contract covers. Warren Gallant of Technology Partners, Inc., notes that many hidden costs are not specified in outsourcing contracts, such as the maintenance on personal computers, sales tax on equipment purchases, transfer of software license fees, etc. The latter cost can substantially reduce the cost savings achieved by outsourcing. John Brown, IS director at AM General, notes "If the fees [of license transferral] are sizable, that could sway a decision on whether to outsource" (Wilder & Margolis, 1990, p. 12). Outsourcing vendors often pass the cost of license transfers onto their clients. Joe Scott, director at Litton Computer Services, states, "We're not trying to gouge people, but if we're going to be charged more, we have to go to the customers" (Wilder & Margolis, 1990, p. 12).

Finally, many foresee that cost savings achieved by vendors could have been produced internally. Consultants at Real Decisions note that large companies operating at 150 million instructions per second should be able to achieve economies of scale on their own (Krass, 1990). Cy Hoormann, director of IS planning at Energy Services, agrees:

> "Fairly large data centers should be able to achieve many of the economies of scale enjoyed by outsource vendors. In-house data centers can automate and streamline operations and invest in new productivity-improving technologies just as outsource vendors do. Plus, in-house data centers have a big advantage over outside vendors that should give internal operations an advantage—they can underprice vendors' rates because they do not have to make a profit." (Rochester & Douglass, 1990, p. 4)

2.2 PARTICIPANTS' OUTSOURCING SOURCES

Participants in our study identified three sources of outsourcing information: trade journals, seminars, and vendor solicitations. The majority of these sources claim that outsourcing saves companies money and that outsourcing is the wave of the future.

Trade Journals: Participants agreed that trade journal reports on outsourcing are optimistic. Some participants theorized that the optimistic nature of the literature is based on the timing of press releases. They noted, for example, that outsourcing reports usually occur when the vendor and client have just signed a contract. During this honeymoon period, the client reports *anticipated* savings of 10% to 50%. To the participants' knowledge, the news never provides updates on whether savings were actually achieved. Thus, media reports reflect the client's most optimistic impression of outsourcing.

Outsourcing Seminars: Participants cited outsourcing seminars as another source of information. These seminars are typically conducted by outsourcing vendors in conjunction with a large consulting firm or research institution. Participants felt that the consulting firms give the audience the illusion of objectivity, but vendors actually seem to provide most of the information.

Vendor Solicitations: The other major source of information on outsourcing came from unsolicited discussions with outsourcing vendors. Participants claim that vendors flaunt long client lists in front of their CEOs. The list is particularly impressive when the prospective client's competitors appear in print. Once a vendor enters an industry, they call their client's competitors to offer them similar deals. The vendors claim to be experts in this industry and can therefore offer prospective clients big savings. Another client comes aboard, thus perpetuating the bandwagon effect.

Perhaps the best way to demonstrate that public reports are usually overly optimistic is to provide a specific example. The public accounts of Eastman Kodak's outsourcing arrangement serve this purpose. Every participant was aware of Kodak's outsourcing arrangements with IBM, Businessland and DEC. They were unfamiliar, however, with the fact that Kodak's successful arrangement may not be replicated in their own firms. In particular, two independent sources claim that Kodak's vendors used this site as a showcase for promoting the use of outsourcing in large companies.

First, let's examine what participants learned about Kodak's outsourcing arrangement from public sources. The literature states that Kodak outsourced non-essential tasks to concentrate on strategic issues (Oltman, 1990). Rather than managers worrying about pesky data center operations, they are free to concentrate on value-added application software. Kathy Hudson, Kodak's much acclaimed CIO, also claims that Kodak outsourced to offer better career opportunities for their IS employees:

"If you are a really good technical person—an expert in applications development, for instance, do you think you'll have a better career at a photography company or a computer company?" (Oltman, 1990, p. 78)

Vaugh Hovey, Kodak's Director of Data Center Services, noted that outsourcing is successful because Kodak entered into strategic "alliances" with their outsourcing vendors. Because Kodak sees its vendors as partners, they consummated these deals with gentlemen's agreements that are documented in contracts that are only a few pages long. News of Kodak's success story spread further when Kathy Hudson was identified as CIO of the year.

From the public's standpoint, Kodak's outsourcing success story is exciting. Outsourcing becomes associated with happy IS managers who now concentrate on more challenging issues, happy IS employees who are employed by companies that value their technical skills, and happy partnerships with vendors who reduce costs. In addition, IS managers may win awards and recognition for their outsourcing initiatives. Kodak's success story, however, is non-representative of most outsourcing situations since most companies cannot replicate Kodak's outsourcing arrangement. A consultant who worked at Kodak told us that Kodak and IBM have a unique business relationship because IBM planned to use Kodak as a loss leader to promote the acceptability of outsourcing in large companies. Participants did not understand that Kodak's relationship with IBM was a unique situation, and they will probably not be able to secure similar deals since vendors need only a few loss leaders to stimulate publicity.

2.3 CONCLUSION

Taken as a body of information, public sources on outsourcing send a powerful message to organizations: outsourcing will become the standard practice for managing information systems. These reports may become a self-fulfilling prophesy unless the overly optimistic reports are tempered with a more balanced view. The problem is that no company wants to report a failure. This simply may be a characteristic of human nature. After all, who wants to offer a personal failure for public scrutiny? When the rare failure is reported, company names are often disguised to protect organizational members. For example, one article titled, "I survived outsourcing" (Blair, 1990), described an outsourcing arrangement that was so horrendous that the company had to rebuild an internal IS department. The author only describes the company as a bank; nameless banks remain in our memories for a far shorter period of time than concrete examples like Kodak, Bank South, and American Standard.

In summary, public information sources about outsourcing are often optimistic because: (a) reports are made during the honeymoon period, (b) only projected savings are reported instead of actual savings, and (c) outsourcing failures are under-represented. The current study tempers the literature's claims by: (a) examining some outsourcing arrangements three to seven years into the contract, (b) exposing unanticipated excess charges that several vendors charged their customers, and (c) examining several outsourcing failures. Although the current research based on thirteen companies does not represent a random sample, it is we feel representative of the outsourcing population, and provides some alternative views which are absent from the literature.

3
Theoretical Foundation of Outsourcing Decisions

3.0 INTRODUCTION

The purpose of this chapter is to explain the theoretical foundation we used in our outsourcing study. Theories assisted us during two phases of research: the acquisition of knowledge, and the interpretation of this knowledge. For knowledge acquisition, theories prescribed which aspects of the outsourcing decision to attend to and which aspects to ignore. Interview questions derived from theory were designed to extract the participants' impressions of their motivations and behaviors about their outsourcing decisions. For knowledge interpretation, these theories provided a framework for analyzing participants' transcribed interviews.

Two alternative theories of organizational decision-making were adopted for this research: Oliver Williamson's transaction cost theory (TCT) and Jeffrey Pfeffer's political model. Williamson's theory was adopted because it represents the widely-accepted view that organizational members make outsourcing decisions based on an economic rationale. In addition, his theory specifically addresses outsourcing decisions, that is, the decision whether to produce a good or service internally or externally. Pfeffer's model was selected because it offers an alternative interpretation that focuses on power and politics. Together, these models were presumed to offer two alternative ways of interpreting the outsourcing phenomenon.

We adopt an "interpretivist's" view of the nature of theories; we presume that theories, such as transaction cost theory and the political model, are merely alternative ways for interpreting a phenomenon. They are not presumed to capture objective, deterministic "truths" about human motives and behavior. Rather, these two theories are seen as two useful interpretations for viewing human decision-making.

The wide acceptance of Williamson's and Pfeffer's theories stands testimony to the usefulness of their conceptualizations. Both models have a plethora of empirical and theoretical support. For example, Williamson's model has been supported by Malone (1987), Pisano (1990), Griesinger (1990), Hill (1990), Hesterly, Liebeskind, and Zenger (1990), Robins (1987), Bowen and Jones (1986), Lieberman (1991) and Hennart (1991a, 1991b). Pfeffer's ideas are grounded in the empirical works of Leavitt (1951), French and Raven (1959), Mechanic (1962), Emerson (1962), Stagner (1969), Perrow (1970), Bucher (1970), Hickson, Hinings, Lee, Schneck, and Pennings (1971), Allison (1971) and Tushman (1977). More recently, specific researchers have tested the political model of organizational decision-making: Hackman (1985), Lucas (1984), and Saunders and Scamell (1986). This body of evidence suggests that other researchers find these theories to provide useful interpretations of organizational reality.

For those readers interested in the details of transaction cost theory and the political model, a full discussion is presented in this chapter. This presentation is a summary of the author's descriptions of their theories found in Williamson (1975), Williamson (1979), Pfeffer and Salancik (1974), Pfeffer (1978), Pfeffer, Salancik, and Leblebici (1976) and Pfeffer (1981). For those readers interested only in the application of these theories to outsourcing decisions, the conclusion of this chapter may suffice.

3.1   TRANSACTION COST THEORY

Williamson developed transaction cost theory when he became troubled by a discrepancy between economic theory and organizational reality. Economic theory predicts that goods and services are most efficiently produced in specialized companies that are able to achieve economies of scale. Why then, Williamson questioned, has the twentieth century witnessed the growth of large bureaucracies that produce many functions internally? (Perrow, 1986).

Williamson proposes that costs are comprised not only of production costs, but transaction costs. Transaction costs, which are synonymous with coordination costs, consist of the costs of monitoring, controlling, and managing transactions. Thus, managers consider total costs (production costs plus transaction costs) when selecting between make-or-buy alternatives:

"The criterion for organizing transactions is assumed to be the strictly instrumental one of cost-economizing. Essentially this takes two parts: economizing on production expense and economizing on transaction costs." (Williamson, 1979, p. 245)

In many instances, Williamson theorizes, an internally produced transaction is more efficient because the transaction costs associated with monitoring an outside vendor outweigh the savings gained from the vendor's production efficiencies.

Williamson's work is largely influenced by Herb Simon's theories on organizations and decision-making. In particular, Williamson adopts Simon's concepts of bounded rationality, the assumption of shared organizational goals, and the three stage decision model. Williamson assumes that managers follow Simon's phases of decision-making where alternatives are generated, costs are assessed, then the least cost alternative is chosen. For a given transaction, managers generate two alternatives: produce the transaction internally (the hierarchy choice) or purchase the transaction from a vendor (the market choice). For each alternative, managers determine the production and transaction costs. Managers will then choose the least cost alternative (Williamson, 1975).

Thus, Williamson's primary theoretical construct is cost efficiency. He admits, however, that costs are often difficult to assess. He therefore attends to three additional constructs that managers can use as a heuristic for estimating costs: transaction types, the threat of opportunism, and uncertainty (see Table 3.1). These constructs all affect the underlying cost structure. That is to say that these constructs shift the relative advantage either towards or from the market choice. Each of Williamson's constructs is explained below.

Table 3.1   *Theoretical constructs of transaction cost theory*

Costs
  Transaction costs
  Production costs

Transaction Type
  Frequency — decreases production costs
  Asset specificity — increases production costs

Threat of Opportunism
  Small number of vendors — increases coordination costs
  Contracts — decreases coordination costs

Uncertainty — increases coordination costs

3.1.1   Costs

Williamson (1975) claims that costs come primarily from two sources, production and coordination. Production costs are the costs to produce the transaction, such as the costs of capital, labor, and materials. Coordination costs, i.e. transaction costs, are the costs to control and monitor workers (Malone, Yates, and Benjamin, 1987). Each organizational structure has its inherent cost advantages. Malone, Yates, and Benjamin (1987) summarize these advantages in Table 3.2.

Williamson assumes that markets provide cheaper production costs than hierarchies through economies of scale. In the outsourcing arena, outsourcing vendors are assumed to provide lower production costs than internal IS shops through economies of scale achieved by sharing computer hardware and software among multiple clients (Krass, 1990).

Williamson assumes that markets cause companies to incur higher coordination costs than if the transaction was handled internally. Companies must spend more money monitoring supplier behavior because they may behave opportunistically. Costs are also incurred while setting up contracts, paying bills, solving disputes, etc.

A hierarchical governance structure tends to have higher production costs than a market structure because an individual company cannot achieve economies of scale when the transaction is produced and used internally. For example, companies may purchase a mainframe computer from a computer manufacturer rather than incur the cost of building it themselves.

Williamson also proposes that a hierarchy would tend to have lower coordination costs than a market. The assumption is that employees are less likely to behave opportunistically compared with trading partners because mechanisms to monitor employees are already in place (Simon, 1976).

The most economically efficient choice is a trade-off between production costs and coordination costs. The question becomes,

Table 3.2 *Cost structures of markets and hierarchies*

Governance structure	Production costs	Coordination costs
Markets	Low	High
Hierarchies	High	Low

Source: Malone, Yates & Benjamin (1987).

under what circumstances is a hierarchy more efficient than a market? Williamson develops a framework, based on transaction types, which maps the most efficient alternative (make or buy) to transaction types. This framework is explained below.

3.1.2   Transaction Types

As the name of the theory implies, Williamson's unit of analysis for understanding how companies determine their governance structures (markets or hierarchies) is transactions. Despite the fact that transactions play the leading role in his theory, Williamson fails to ever define the term. Other researchers have defined transactions as "exchanges of economic or interpersonal resources" (Griesinger, 1990), or in more common terms, the exchange of goods or services.

Williamson proposes that some transaction types can be efficiently governed through markets, while others are more efficiently governed through hierarchies. In order to make this assessment, Williamson (1979) first categorizes transactions along two dimensions: frequency and asset specificity.

3.1.2.1   Frequency

Frequency refers to how often a transaction occurs, either occasionally or recurrently. Williamson never defines "occasional" or "recurrent", but definitions can be inferred from examples he provides in his writings. For example, the purchase of capital investments, such as machinery and buildings, is described as occurring only occasionally. The purchase of materials or supplies is characterized as occurring frequently. Note that the frequency dimension refers to buyer activity in the market, i.e. how many times a company seeks to initiate the transaction (Williamson, 1975).

3.1.2.2   Asset Specificity

Asset specificity refers to the degree of customization of the transaction. A transaction is highly asset specific if it cannot readily be used by other companies because of site specificity, physical asset specificity, or human asset specificity.

Site specificity.   Site specific transactions are transactions that are available at a certain location and can only be transported at a great cost. For example, buyers may favor hiring local workers rather than incurring the expense of moving workers from other areas.

Physical asset specificity. Physical asset specificity refers to how specialized the equipment must be to complete the transaction. Some transactions are homogeneous and do not require any special equipment or special production line configurations. Other transactions, however, must be custom-tailored to meet a company's particular needs.

Human asset specificity. Williamson pays particular attention to human asset specificity, which refers to how specialized the knowledge must be to complete a transaction:

> "Much of the knowledge required to make efficient economic decisions cannot be expressed as statistical aggregates but is highly idiosyncratic in nature: practically every individual has some advantage over all others in that he possesses unique information of which beneficial use might be made, but of which use can be made only if the decisions depending on it are left to him or are made with his active cooperation. We need to remember how valuable an asset in all walks of life is knowledge of people, local conditions, and of special circumstances." (Williamson, 1975, p. 5)

Specialized training, learning on the job and knowledge of a company's processes are examples of specific human assets required to complete a transaction. Williamson's recognition of the importance of human knowledge and expertise is noteworthy, since many economic theories treat labor as a homogeneous input (Thurow, 1983). Human asset specificity recognizes that people are not all equal in their abilities to create products or services—experience counts.

Although Williamson describes three types of asset specificity— site, physical, and human—he clumps them together under the general term "asset-specificity." Williamson classifies asset specificity into three categories—transactions may be either non-specific, idiosyncratic, or mixed.

Non-specific transactions. Non-specific transactions require standard equipment and non-specialized knowledge because transactions do not have to be tailored depending on the buyer. For example, a company purchase of standard office supplies does not require the manufacturer to alter his production setup, nor is specific knowledge about the customer required to complete the transaction.

Idiosyncratic transactions. Idiosyncratic transactions, on the other hand, require specialized equipment or knowledge. For example, custom-made software is idiosyncratic because specific knowledge about the company's unique business needs must be understood.

Mixed transactions. Mixed transactions have attributes of both; some aspects of the transaction are standard while other aspects require customization. For example, the purchase of company letterhead requires the print shop to customize stationery, but once the setup is complete, the printing process is routine.

3.1.2.3   Transaction Cost Framework

Using these two dimensions, frequency and asset specificity, Williamson creates a framework for categorizing transactions (see Table 3.3). Examples of each transaction type are also provided.

Williamson proposes that "the overall objective essentially comes down to this: for each abstract description of a transaction, identify the most economical governance structure" (Williamson, 1979, p. 234). Williamson matches the most efficient governance strategies for each portion of his framework in Table 3.4. Note that there is only one transaction type—recurrent-idiosyncratic—that naturally favors a hierarchical governance structure. Each of these governance

Table 3.3   *Williamson's transaction cost framework*

Frequency	Asset specificity		
	Non-specific	Mixed	Idiosyncratic
Occasional transaction	*Standard equipment purchase	*Custom equipment purchase	*Plant construction
Recurrent transaction	*Standard material purchase	*Customized material purchase	*Site-specific transfer of intermediate product across successive stages

Source: Williamson (1979, p. 247).

Table 3.4 *Efficient governance strategies*

Frequency	Asset specificity		
	Non-specific	Mixed	Idiosyncractic
Occasional transaction	Market governance with contract equivalent to a sale	Market governance with trilateral contract	
Recurrent transaction		Market governance with bilateral contract	Hierarchical governance

Source: Williamson (1979, p. 253).

structures is discussed to demonstrate the trade-offs between production and coordination costs.

Non-specific/occasional and non-specific recurrent transactions. In general, Williamson hypothesizes that a market provides the most efficient governing structure for non-specific investments that are either occasional or recurrent. Since non-specific transactions are homogeneous, a market structure provides cheaper production costs than a hierarchical structure. Suppliers in the marketplace are able to achieve economies of scale since the standard product or service may be sold to multiple customers. Coordination costs are minimal because the buyer does not need to monitor the vendor:

> "The traditional economic analysis of exchange in a market setting properly corresponds to the legal concept of sale, rather than contract, since sale presumes arrangements in a market context and requires legal support primarily in enforcing transfers of title." (Lowry, 1976, p. 10)

Since there is nothing peculiar about the transaction, the specific identity of each party is irrelevant. For example, when a buyer purchases a homogeneous product, such as an apple from the local grocer, neither the buyer nor the farmer need to know each other. Under these circumstances, transaction costs are minimal.

Thus, when the transaction is standard, i.e, non-specific, coordination costs are negligible. Therefore, the main criterion between selecting a market or hierarchy is production costs. Williamson argues that the market will always be able to provide cheaper production costs through economies of scale.

Occasional-mixed and occasional-idiosyncratic transactions. Williamson proposes that a market governance strategy is more efficient for occasional transactions. The production costs for an internal hierarchy are higher than for a market because the company must acquire capital and maintain a trained staff, even though these resources are only used periodically. Williamson (1979) notes, however, that the transaction costs of monitoring the vendor for these transaction types can be expensive. The company must guard itself against unforeseeable contingencies by providing for third-party arbitrators to resolve principal–agent disputes.

Mixed-recurrent transaction. Mixed-recurrent transactions are characterized as on-going and semi-idiosyncratic. Williamson is less bold in his assertions, but claims "outside procurement may be favored by scale-economy considerations" (Williamson, 1979, p. 250). The market may be able to provide economies of scale for those aspects of the transaction that are less asset-specific. Transaction costs of the market option should not be too expensive since both parties have incentive to sustain the relationship—the company gets a steady supply, the vendor gets a steady stream of revenue. The vendor is particularly interested in maintaining the relationship since the vendor invests time to learn the specifics of its client's business. Bilateral contracts, where mutual obligations of both parties are spelled out, are appropriate.

Recurrent-idiosyncratic transactions. Incentives for selecting a market structure weaken as transactions become recurrent and idiosyncratic:

> "The reason is that, as specialized human and physical assets become more specialized to a single use, and hence less transferable to other users, economies of scale can be as fully realized by the buyer as by an outside supplier." (Williamson, 1979, p. 252)

Since production costs of hierarchies and markets for recurrent-idiosyncratic transactions are approximately equal, the decision criterion for minimizing costs focuses on transaction costs.

Coordination costs will be cheaper with an internal hierarchy. Since the transaction occurs frequently, the cost of setting up an internal monitoring system is readily justified. Coordination costs for a market structure would be more expensive since the contractual agreement would need to be more complex.

Williamson notes, however, that a market governance strategy may be efficient if the buyer sacrifices relevant design features in favor of a more standardized good. For example, a company may wish to produce a recurrent-idiosyncratic transaction internally but may be short-staffed. This company may opt for a less idiosyncratic transaction and seek a supplier to provide the good or service.

Thus, Williamson proposes that when only the transaction type is considered, markets are more efficient for all transactions except recurrent-idiosyncratic transactions. We now turn to see how the threat of opportunism alters the underlying cost structures of certain transaction types.

3.1.3   Threat of Opportunism

Williamson notes that under certain conditions, the coordination costs of the market choice can be substantial if the vendor behaves opportunistically. Opportunism extends the notion that people act in their own self-interest to "self-interest seeking with *guile*" (Williamson, 1975). People may not always be trustworthy, honest, or purport fair representations. He suggests, however, that opportunism is only a threat when there are a small number of vendors available to provide the service. He maintains that markets with a large number of suppliers minimize opportunism because "rivalry among larger numbers of bidders will render opportunistic inclinations ineffectual" (Williamson, 1975, p. 27). Companies may still wish to buy transactions from a market with few suppliers, but they are admonished to reduce the threat of opportunism by signing appropriate contracts.

3.1.3.1   Small Number of Suppliers

Williamson believes that opportunistic behavior can occur when there are a small number of suppliers because the buyer has limited choices. With few alternatives, the company is in a poor position to bargain with the vendor. This is particularly true during contract renewal. Unlike most economic theories of market size that treat suppliers as substitutes, Williamson recognizes that conditions change during contract execution. Thus, when a buyer first enters a market, there may be a large number of suppliers to choose from. No one supplier may have a substantial advantage over the others, since each is assumed to have minimal knowledge about the idiosyncrasies of the buyer's business. The buyer may select a supplier based on who provides the required service for the lowest cost. During this initial selection stage, opportunism is not a serious threat. However, once a supplier is selected, it gains valuable knowledge about the customer's organization during the contract period. Thus, at the end of the first contractual period, the supplier has an advantage over the other vendors in the marketplace. When the buyer scans the marketplace, other suppliers will be at a competitive disadvantage. Renegotiation with the original supplier will be the most attractive alternative, but results in a situation called "small numbers bargaining," where the supplier may behave opportunistically (Williamson, 1975; Pisano, 1990).

The impact of small numbers on the bottom line: the company may not save as much money as they think by outsourcing. The vendor may squeeze excess charges from the company or may not perform as promised. To retaliate, the company expends even more money to reconcile contract disputes. Thus, the costs associated with the market choice may be greater than an internally produced transaction. Savvy managers, however, can avoid these post-contract pitfalls by signing better contracts. Contracts can be used to reduce the threat of opportunism (and thus coordination costs) before the deal is consummated.

3.1.3.2 Contracts

Williamson argues that companies can buy transactions from markets with few suppliers if they negotiate appropriate contracts. For each transaction type, Williamson (1979) describes the types of contracts that should be used to organize principal–agent relations: classical, neoclassical, and relational (see Table 3.5).

Classical contracts. Williamson claims classical contracts are used when buyer and seller exchange a discrete, homogeneous product or service. The term "sale" may even be more relevant than the term "contract." The identity of the parties is treated as irrelevant, since the vendor doesn't need to know anything specific about the customer's business in order to produce the transaction. Using Williamson's terminology, classical contracts are used for non-specific transactions that are purchased on the market. Examples include buying merchandise from a retailer, food from a grocery store, gasoline from a retail gas station, etc.

Table 3.5   *Appropriate contracts for transaction types*

Frequency	Asset specificity		
	Non-specific	Mixed Idiosyncratic	
Occasional transaction	Classical contracting	Neoclassical contracting	
Recurrent transaction		Relational contracting	

Source: Williamson (1979, p. 253).

Neoclassical contracts.   Williamson claims neoclassical contracts are used where transactions are occasional. Since these transactions are only created once (or a few times), all future contingencies cannot be predicted and spelled out in the contract. For example, no matter how well an aircraft is engineered on the draft table, no one knows whether the design will function until the test pilots take her for a spin. Williamson recommends that occasional transactions charac-terized by a great deal of asset specificity might be more efficiently governed by an internal hierarchy. However, a market governance may become the efficient alternative if a mechanism for solving disputes is established in the contract. For example, third party arbitration can be used to resolve arguments and evaluate perform-ance and thus diminish the transaction costs of litigation. Neoclassi-cal contracts recognize that the world is complex, agreements are incomplete, and some contracts will never be reached unless both parties have confidence in the settlement machinery.

Relational contracts.   Williamson proposes that relational contracts are used for recurrent transactions exchanged between buyer and seller. If a buyer and seller exchange a transaction on a regular basis, they tend to develop a relationship:

> "The fiction of discreetness is fully displaced as the relation takes on the properties of a mini-society with a vast array of norms beyond those centered on the exchange and its immediate process." (Williamson, 1979, p. 238)

By contrast with neoclassical contracts whose reference part is always the original agreement, relational contracts may be adapted as the relationship between buyer and seller changes over time.

In summary, Williamson believes that contracts can be used to reduce the threat of opportunism. In the next section, the condition of uncertainty is explored to determine its impact on the underlying cost structure of make-or-buy decisions.

3.1.4   Uncertainty

Williamson notes that transactions are conducted under uncertainty when it is very costly, perhaps even impossible, to describe the complete decision tree, i.e. gather all the information required to make an informed decision. Uncertainty, as used by Williamson, is synonymous with complexity:

> "Most decision problems, unlike board games, such as chess, are not deterministic but involve decision-making under uncertainty. For these, the comprehensive decision tree is not apt even to be feasible. As Simon indicates, however, and is maintained here, the distinction between deterministic complexity and uncertainty is inessential." (Williamson, 1975, p. 23)

Under conditions of uncertainty, the efficiency of one governance structure over another may change. In particular, uncertainty increases transaction costs for asset-specific investments. The parties must spend considerable time and money to develop "a machinery to work things out since contractual gaps will be larger and the occasions for sequential adaptations will increase in number and importance as the degree of uncertainty changes" (Williamson, 1975, p. 254). The company may opt for three alternatives: sacrifice design features to make the transaction more standardized, surround the transaction with an elaborate contract, or produce the transaction internally.

Williamson (1979) proposes that altering the degree of uncertainty for non-specific transactions will not alter the relative advantage of markets over hierarchies:

> "Recall that non-specific transactions are ones for which continuity has little value, since trading relations are easily arranged. Increasing the degree of uncertainty does not alter this. Accordingly, market exchange continues and holds across standardized transactions of all kinds, whatever the degree of uncertainty." (p. 254)

Thus uncertainty will alter the underlying cost structure of a governance mechanism depending on the asset specificity of the transaction.

3.1.5 Williamson's Propositions Summarized

Williamson's theory proposes that decision-makers choose the most cost-efficient governance mechanism. He further proposes that each governance mechanism has underlying cost advantages which are contingent upon transaction type, threat of opportunism, and the level of uncertainty. His propositions are summarized below:

1 When only production costs are considered, markets are more efficient than hierarchies due to economies of scale.
2 When only transaction costs are considered, hierarchies are more efficient than markets due to internal control mechanisms that prevent opportunism.
3 When production and transaction costs are considered, markets are more efficient than hierarchies for all transactions except:
   (a) recurrent-idiosyncratic transactions or
   (b) asset-specific transactions with a high degree of uncertainty or
   (c) transactions with a small number of suppliers.
4 Markets may be made more efficient than hierarchies for exception (a) by sacrificing custom design features.
5 Markets may be made more efficient than hierarchies for exceptions (a) through (c) by minimizing the transactions costs associated with opportunism via appropriate contracting.

This chapter now proceeds with the major suppositions of Pfeffer's political model of organizational decision-making.

3.2 THE POLITICAL MODEL

The political theory of organizational behavior has its roots in the works of Marx (1973, 1976) and Weber (1947, 1949). Salient concepts adopted from political philosophers include the relationship between power and structure, the recognition of opposing interests and the ubiquitous role of conflict (Burrell & Morgan, 1988). However, current political models found in the organizational literature temper the more radical ideas of Marx and Weber in favor of a more functionalist perspective, one which Burrell and Morgan (1988) title "conflict functionalism." Conflict functionalism rejects some of the assumptions of rational models, such as the notion of shared organizational goals, use of information solely to reduce uncertainty, and rational decision processes. However, conflict functionalism assumes that organizations are inherently stable and that conflicts are played within the legitimate domain of organizational norms. Through such legitimate behaviors as the use of information, use of outside experts, use of a particular decision criterion, etc., stakeholders are able to promote their position in an unobtrusive manner.

The political perspective attends to two main constructs—power and politics. Power can be defined as the *potential* of an actor to influence the behavior of another actor on a particular issue (Tushman, 1977). Politics can be defined as "the structure and process of the *use* of authority and power to effect definitions of goals, directions, and other major parameters of the organization" (Tushman, 1977, p. 207). Pfeffer (1981) offers a coherent delineate of power and politics:

> "If power is a force, a store of potential influence through which events can be affected, politics involves those activities or behaviors through which power is developed and used in organizational settings. Power is a property of a system at rest; politics is the study of power in action." (p. 7)

Pfeffer (1981) develops his entire theory around these concepts of power and politics. His basic assumptions are (a) power enables stakeholders to influence a decision, but (b) political strategies enacted during the decision-making process may alter power-balances. The bottom line: *a priori* predictions about decision outcomes cannot be made since the result emerges from dynamic political processes. Although one cannot predict outcomes, one can understand organizational decision-making processes by attending to power and politics. Power will help in understanding the stakeholder's ability to influence the decision prior to the decision process. Politics will help in understanding how stakeholders mobilized their resources to sway the decision.

Pfeffer's ideas on power and politics are discussed in the following sections. He identifies five main sources of power and the most commonly used political tactics (see Table 3.6).

3.2.1   Power

Pfeffer (1981) claims that power is not a fixed, immutable property—there are no general definitions of "powerful" or "powerless" actors. Instead, he proposes that power is a relative term. Pfeffer (1981) offers the following example:

Table 3.6   *Theoretical constructs of the political model*

Power
   Authority
   Resource acquisition
   Dependency & low substitutability
   Uncertainty absorption

Political Tactics
   Selective use of decision criteria
   Selective use of information
   Use of outside experts
   Building coalitions
   Cooptation

"To say, for example, that the legal department in a specific firm is powerful, implies power with respect to other departments within that firm during a specific period of time. That same legal department may not be at all powerful with respect to its interactions with the firm's outside counsel, various federal and state regulatory agencies, and so forth." (p. 3)

Thus, the concept of a sub-unit's power is only meaningful when compared to another sub-unit. To determine power, Pfeffer proposes that the sources of power for each stakeholder group involved in the decision should be assessed. In particular, he proposes that power is derived from authority, creating dependencies, providing resources, absorbing uncertainty and being irreplaceable (low substitutability).

3.2.1.1   Authority

Researchers who conduct organizational research from the political perspective seem to agree that power is primarily a structural phenomenon (Pfeffer, 1981; Tushman, 1977; Allison, 1971; Welsh & Slusher, 1986):

"Power is, first of all, a structural phenomenon, created by the division of labor and departmentation that characterizes organizations." (Pfeffer, 1981, p. 4)

The proposition that power is a function of position within the structure stems from the writings of people such as Marx and Weber. For Marx, power lies in economic structures which control factors of production; for Weber, power is located in bureaucracies which legitimize politics through administrative structures (Burrell

& Morgan, 1988). Pfeffer adopts Weber's notion that position within an organization is an important determinant of power. Pfeffer, unlike Weber, is not a critic of corporatism; he merely postulates that power and position are related rather than arguing for the emancipation from bureaucratic tyranny.

Pfeffer sees structure as a key source of power because it legitimatizes the exercise of power. "When power is so legitimized, it is denoted as authority" (Pfeffer, 1981). Authority is essentially an institutional code within which the use of power is organized and legitimized (Pettigrew, 1973). Pfeffer (1981) notes:

> "Weber emphasized the critical role of legitimacy in the exercise of power. By transforming power into authority, the exercise of influence is transformed in a subtle but important way. In social situations, the exercise of power typically has costs. Enforcing one's way over others requires the expenditure of resources, the making of commitments, and a level of effort which can be undertaken only when the issues at hand are relatively important. On the other hand, the exercise of authority, power which has become legitimated, is expected and desired in the social context. Thus, the exercise of authority, far from diminishing through use, may actually serve to enhance the amount of authority subsequently possessed." (p. 4)

Pfeffer offers empirical evidence from Leavitt (1951), Mechanic (1962), Stagner (1969), and Perrow (1970) to support his claim that power is related to authority. Mechanic, for example, studied superior–subordinate relationships and found that lower level employees rarely challenge their superiors. He reasoned that the superior's power derived from authority was greater than the subordinate's power derived from special skills, special knowledge, and access to information. Pfeffer concludes from this and other studies: "it seems apparent that power in the organization is determined by structural position" (p. 131).

3.2.1.2 Resource Acquisition

Pfeffer argues that resource acquisition is a critical source of power. Resources may be acquired from within the organization through budget allocations and through external sources such as the government or research institutions. Resource acquisition yields power because "he who has the gold makes the rules" (Pfeffer, 1981, p. 101).

Most of the empirical support that correlates resource acquisition and power comes from studies of university budget processes. Pfeffer and Salancik (1974), for example, studied budget allocations at the University of Illinois. They found that the acquisition of organizational resources and power are related:

"Measures of departmental power in a university are found to be significantly related to the proportion of the budget received, even after statistically controlling for such universalistic bases of allocation as work load, national rank, and the number of faculty." (p. 135)

The more resources a member brings into the organization, the more power he accumulates.

3.2.1.3 *Dependency and Low Substitutability*

Emerson (1962) was one of the first researchers to stress that power plays a considerable role in organizational decisions. From Emerson's perspective, power is defined in terms of dependence:

"Power resides implicitly in the other's dependency. . .The dependence of actor A upon actor B is (1) directly proportional to A's motivational investment in goals mediated by B, and (2) inversely proportional to the availability of those goals outside of the A-B relationship." (Emerson, 1962, p. 32)

Pfeffer (1981) adopts Emerson's idea that power comes from offering something of value that few other sources can provide. He used the following observation to support this idea.

Computer programmers can deliberately increase their power by making the organization more dependent on them and by perpetuating a belief that they are irreplaceable. Pfeffer accuses programmers of enacting several strategies which include refusing to document systems so that knowledge about the system is inaccessible, deliberate use of specialized language and symbols that "make the expertise look even more arcane and difficult to comprehend" (p. 114) and ensuring that individuals with similar knowledge are not brought into the firm.

3.2.1.4 *Absorbing Uncertainty*

Pfeffer (1978, 1981) proposes that the ability to absorb uncertainty contributes to power. The impetus for considering uncertainty coping as a source of power comes from the work of Cyert and March (1963) and March and Simon (1958). These researchers view task uncertainty as a major element in organizational decision-making. The sub-unit in the organization gains power by absorbing uncertainty on behalf of the organization. Note that uncertainty is defined as a lack of information (Hickson et al., 1971), therefore, the sub-unit that has assess to information absorbs uncertainty (Pfeffer, 1978).

Pfeffer offers two empirical studies from Hinings, Hickson,

Pennings, and Schneck (1974) and Salancik and Pfeffer (1978) to support the relationship between power and the ability to absorb uncertainty.

Hinings, Hickson, Pennings, and Schneck (1974) tested their strategic contingencies theory using data gained from seven manufacturing firms. The findings indicate that the ability to absorb uncertainty was the most important indicator of power: "Thus the correlations accord with an interpretation that coping is most important in power, supported by immediacy, non-substitutability, and pervasiveness, in that order" (p. 35).

Salancik and Pfeffer (1978) gathered data from 54 people in seventeen organizations that had recently faced equipment purchase decisions. They found that individuals who could absorb uncertainty by providing information about the proposed new equipment had the most influence on the decision.

In summary, Pfeffer believes that the sources of power include authority, resource acquisition, dependency, low substitutability and uncertainty absorption. These sources of power represent the stakeholders' potential to influence decisions. However, power is a dynamic concept, and during a decision-making process, different stakeholders may enact political tactics that change the balance of power. Such strategies are described in the next section.

3.2.2   Political Tactics

Pfeffer and others describe numerous political tactics which are employed to influence decisions. These tactics include the selective use of decision criteria, the selective use of information, use of outside experts, building coalitions, and cooptation. These tactics all fall within the domain of "legitimate" behavior. Pfeffer notes that these strategies are effective because stakeholders unobtrusively sway the decision in their favor.

It is interesting to note that Pfeffer ignores the possibility that actors may lie, steal, cheat, shirk, threaten, or blackmail to influence decision outcome. His reasoning:

> "Power is most effectively used when it is employed as unobtrusively as possible. The exercise of power and influence is facilitated by the legitimation of the decision process, decision outcomes, and the power and influence itself. Most strategies for the exercise of power involve attempts to make the use of power less obtrusive, and attempt to legitimate and rationalize the decision that is to be made as a result of the exercise of the social power of an actor in the organization." (p. 137)

Ignoring dirty politics facilitates the study of power in organizations. The political strategies discussed in this section are relatively easy to assess in a field study. Decision-makers are more likely to discuss legitimate behaviors, such as using outside experts, rather than illegitimate behaviors, such as insider trading.

3.2.2.1 Selective Use of Decision Criteria

A common tactic to legitimize a stakeholder's position is to select the decision criteria. Pfeffer notes:

> "Given the availability of multiple measures for assessing alternatives, one use of power involves advocating the use of criteria which favor one's position. In a decision situation, it is difficult and not very legitimate to argue for the validity and choice of a given course of action on the basis of power of the social actor favoring the particular choice. Rather, choices must be legitimized and power is better exercised unobtrusively. One strategy, then, involves the selective stressing of certain criteria that favor the position advocated by the particular social actor in question." (p. 138)

The following example corroborates the existence of this strategy. In a study of the budgetary process at the University of Illinois, Pfeffer and Salancik (1974) found that departments tend to suggest budget allocation criteria based on their relative positions. The department with the greatest number of students argued budgets should be appropriated based on student headcount; the department that was ranked high in a national survey suggested that ranking should be the primary criterion; the department that received the most grants argued that research funds should be the major criterion. Thus, department heads offer criteria which promote their relative advantage.

In this study, Pfeffer and Salancik show that when there is a lack of clearly defined decision criteria, actors attempt to influence the decision by appealing for criteria that promote their decision preferences.

3.2.2.2 Selective Use of Information

Political actors can sway decision outcome by presenting "objective" data to support their position. Pfeffer (1981) quotes from Peter Drucker: "Anyone over the age of twenty-one can find facts to support his or her position." Although Pfeffer (1981) believes actors selectively choose information, he does not accuse them of deception:

"Social actors may attend more to facts that support their position, and remember these facts or arguments better. Thus they may convince themselves of the correctness of their position, regardless of its impact for their immediate self-interest. In other words, rather than self-interest working directly to affect advocacy of certain criteria for choice, self-interest may also work through processes of selective perception and retention." (p. 140)

Ciborra (1987), on the other hand, paints a pejorative view of the motivation behind information selection:

"... there are other incentives to gather and use information, apart from task uncertainty; information can be misrepresented, promises and commitments can be false, data incomplete, tracks covered, etc., all in order to induce others to make decisions most benefiting us in the first place. Or another possibility is that information can be selectively disclosed to persuade or bias; what this in fact means is that it can be used as an instrument of power to win or gain a better position in the daily organizational games." (p. 257)

Another effective tactic to influence a decision outcome is to refute the opposition's data. In order to successfully refute someone's data, however, one must be granted an audience with the decision-maker. Pettigrew (1973) studied computer-related decisions and found that three IS managers each gathered information to justify their selection of a favored computer manufacturer. The person able to influence the final purchase refuted his opponent's data. This person was the only one of the three who had access to the board: he exerted "biases in favor of his own demands and at the same time [fed] the board negative information about the demands of his opponents" (p. 191). Pettigrew's study shows how control of information and access to communication channels influences decisions.

Another study by Allen, Madison, Porter, Renwick, and Mayes (1979) shows that managers perceive that information use is a common political tactic employed in organizational decision-making. Eighty-seven respondents indicated that information is withheld, distorted, or used to overwhelm. The objective of these information uses is to give "the impression of rationality and logic by use of quantitative data in the form of graphs, formulas, tables, and summation" (p. 79). One respondent of this study admitted his most effective strategy was arriving at a decision subjectively, then summoning his staff to gather "objective" data to support him.

Thus, information plays an important role in political decision-making. Since many view information as non-political, rational, and objective, information can be unobtrusively manipulated to influence decision outcomes.

3.2.2.3   Use of Outside Experts

Pfeffer (1981) argues that consultants are used to bolster one's position:

> "The use of outside expertise, particularly management consulting expertise, can be seen as serving a function similar to that of the selective use of objective criteria. First, the outside expert can permit power to be used to affect decisions in a somewhat less visible way. Second, outside expertise can serve to legitimate the decisions reached and to provide an aura of rationality to the decision process." (p. 142)

Pfeffer also notes that outside consultants rarely submit novel or unfamiliar recommendations to a company; they merely tend to develop systematic formalization of their clients' predetermined intentions. This is a potent criticism of the entire consulting profession, but Pfeffer argues that outside experts legitimize a stakeholder's position by offering "objective" verification. Outsiders are presumed to be reliable and knowledgeable, thus their recommendations are perceived as valid. Pfeffer notes that consultants can hardly be viewed as objective—sponsoring executives tend to execute control of access to the experts and experts may obtain future business from managers who are pleased with their recommendations. Pfeffer (1981) concludes his discussion on outside experts:

> "The use of outside experts provides legitimacy to changes that might otherwise be advocated. The expertise itself provides the assurance that decisions are being made using rational, organizationally relevant criteria." (p. 146)

3.2.2.4   Building Coalitions

Pfeffer argues that coalitions (i.e. temporary alliances) are an effective strategy for rallying support and legitimizing a stakeholder position. The theory behind coalitions is "strength in numbers." Coalitions can be formed with external or internal constituents.

Coalitions with external constituents are effective when the outside agency has some direct interest to the organization's decision outcome. For example, coalitions formed between grant agencies and grant applicants can lead to their mutual benefit when applicants promise to match funds in exchange for the grant.

Coalitions with internal alliances can also be affective. Political log-rolling, where two departments agree to provide mutual support, can lead to benefits for both. Coalitions can also be bought— support in exchange for resources. For example, IS managers can promise to allocate systems staff to users in exchange for user support against outsourcing.

Thus, the formation of temporary alliances may prove an effective strategy for influencing decision outcomes.

3.2.2.5 *Cooptation*

Cooptation is the last tactic that Pfeffer identifies. Cooptation is a strategy employed to sway the opposition to favor one's position. Pfeffer feels the most effective way to quiet the opposition is to give the opposition representation on a committee. The idea is to subject the opposition to group norms:

> "Cooptation is so often effective because it exposes the coopted representatives to informational social influence, and confronts them with conformity pressures and the necessity to justify their actions. Cooptation provides labels and expectations that increase identification and commitment to the organization, gives the representatives a stake and legitimate position in the organization, and motivates them to be interested in the organization's survival and success." (p. 167)

An example of effective cooptation is to place a person accusing a firm of unfair hiring practices on a selection committee. Exposure to the quality and quantity of applicants, in addition to the responsibility of hiring, can unite former opponents.

In summary, Pfeffer assumes that political strategies are activities organizational members engage in during decision-making processes. He attends to strategies that are unobtrusive and legitimate— selection of criteria, selection of information, consultation with outside experts, formulation of coalitions, and cooptation. Pfeffer thus chooses to ignore illegitimate behaviors (stealing, threatening, etc.) and preventative behaviors (building cabals, finding mentors, ingratiating, etc.).

Pfeffer's insights can be summarized with three points. First, power is important because it indicates the relative advantage of one stakeholder group over another. Second, the balance of power may be altered during the decision process as stakeholders enact political tactics to sway decisions. Third, the most successful organizational politicians rely on legitimate behaviors since they are unobtrusive.

As a final note on Pfeffer's political model of behavior, although the term "politics" is pejorative, Pfeffer never intends to disparage or belittle actors using political behavior—indeed it is a behavior widely observed and followed. He merely describes a decision process where actors first determine the outcome, then build an economic rational.

3.3 CONCLUSION

This chapter presented two theories of organizational decision-making—Williamson's transaction cost theory and Pfeffer's political model—that provide different interpretations of outsourcing decisions. The researchers brought these theories to the field of inquiry for two purposes. First, to generate interview questions to extract knowledge from participants. Second, to interpret the participants' perceptions of their outsourcing experiences as relayed in the transcribed interviews.

Williamson's transaction cost theory suggests that the only reason a company would consider outsourcing is to reduce costs. When approaching an outsourcing alternative, managers must consider two types of costs: production costs and coordination (i.e. transaction) costs.

Considering production costs, Williamson proposes that outsourcers often achieve economies of scale that elude smaller, internal IS shops. Williamson warns us, however, that outsourcers only have a production cost advantage over in-house production for products and services that are standard. When a high degree of customization is involved, in-house production costs may be lower. The question then becomes, how does the decision-maker view different IS functions? Which IS functions are standard? Which IS functions require high customization? As we traverse through the cases in the next chapter, we witness some managers who view the entire IS department as a utility service that can be more efficiently outsourced. Other managers restrict the utility view of IS to data center operations and telecommunications management.

Considering coordination costs, Williamson proposes that out-sourcing causes higher coordination costs because the customer must monitor a vendor's behavior. Coordination costs can be particularly high, Williamson cautions, when a customer has few alternatives other than one vendor. In order to reduce coordination costs, the customer should pay particular attention to contract details. The contract may be the only mechanism for preventing coordination costs from escalating to a point of negating the savings from the vendor's production efficiencies.

Pfeffer's political model offers a different interpretation of outsourcing decisions. He notes that objective cost figures, especially for long-term decisions like outsourcing decisions, are virtually impossible to predict. Instead, Pfeffer notes that power and political tactics play an important role in organizational decision-making—an idea that rational, economics models ignore.

To understand outsourcing decisions, the political model suggests that we focus on the power of the IS department, the vested interests of different stakeholder groups, and the political tactics they may enact to sway decisions in their favor. For example, Pfeffer's model causes us to ask questions such as: Can IS managers make objective outsourcing decisions? Can vendors submit realistic bids or will they plan to cushion profits by charging clients excess charges after the contract is signed? Did any stakeholder groups selectively choose decision criteria or information to sway the outsourcing decision? Did any senior executive possess so much power that a unilateral decision was made without consensus?

The differences in the theories are readily apparent, but there is also one very important similarity: both theories presume that people act in their own self-interest. Transaction cost theory merely assumes that people within companies band together to compete against other companies for resources such as market share. The political model merely assumes that people within companies band together to compete for the company's resources such as budgets, promotions, and rewards. Neither theory is meant as a pejorative criticism of people working in organizations, but merely as a neutral description. This should be particularly underscored for the political model since its very name often connotes negative images. Williamson and Pfeffer have the same goal in mind: an organizational theory that provides a way to describe and interpret decision-making.

4
Case Descriptions

4.0 INTRODUCTION

This chapter describes the outsourcing decision-making process at thirteen organizations. The material in this chapter provides the "raw data" for our analysis of outsourcing evaluations taken up in subsequent chapters of the book.

Our discussion involves two phases: the description of "facts" and the identification of the participants' intentions. The unit of analysis for our discussion is the company. By placing each outsourcing decision in the context of the company's history and culture, a better understanding of participants' intentions and behaviors arise.

Description of "Facts." "Facts" are the occurrences in which participants share a common view of the outsourcing phenomenon. These "facts" include the historical background of the company, the decision process, such as the timing of the evaluation, and the number of vendors solicited, and the outcome of the decision. By attending to a company's unique precipitating factors, a better understanding of participants' intentions and behaviors is possible.

Identification of Intentions and Interpretation of Behavior. Once the outsourcing evaluation has been placed in its appropriate context, the participants' intentions and behaviors can be analyzed. To assist in this analysis, two organizational theories of decision-making are used: Pfeffer's (1981) political model (which interprets managerial decision-making in its political context), and Williamson's (1975) transaction cost theory (which adopts a rational, economic perspective of organizational decision-making). (See the previous chapter for a detailed description of each.)

From Pfeffer's political perspective, actions are viewed in terms of power and political tactics. A common interpretation that arises from this venue is that many decision-makers initiate outsourcing decisions to protect their interests. Organizational members that have something to gain by outsourcing may initiate the decision and gather "objective" data to support their position. Opponents to outsourcing may also initiate outsourcing so that they can bias the evaluation process. Whether proponent or opponent, decision-makers often have something to gain by leading the evaluation process.

Using Williamson's transaction cost perspective, outsourcing decisions are interpreted in a different light. Since organizations only survive if they are profitable, each organizational member must contribute to profitability by increasing revenues or containing costs. Organizational members are assumed to attend to costs, transaction types, and the threat of opportunism from outsourcing vendors to make prudent outsourcing decisions. From this perspective, decision-makers evaluate outsourcing to reduce costs, receive a cash infusion, or improve cash flow by trading capital assets for fixed expenses.

In most cases, a political as well as an economic interpretation of a participant's behavior is plausible. Participants expressed the capability of operating on many levels. Neither the political nor the transaction cost model adequately explains the participants' behavior. In other words, our analysis does not unveil an ultimate, objective conclusion about decision-makers' intentions and behaviors but rather alternative ways to understand the outsourcing decision.

In some cases, however, one particular model dominates. For example, outsourcing decisions at FIRM2 and FIRM8 make much more sense from a political perspective—one is hard pressed to find a transaction cost rationale at these sites. In these situations, one particular model may dominate because it truly provides a perceptual filter that corresponds better to the participant's view of the phenomenon. Of course another possibility is that we as researchers failed to investigate the situation thoroughly, thus ignoring evidence that supports the alternative perspective. In these situations, an attempt was made to explain the dominance of one theory over another.

Case Format. The case analyses are presented in a similar format (see Table 4.1). Each case has an introduction, historical background, description of the decision process, and an analysis of the case from the political and transaction cost perspectives.

Table 4.1   *Format of the case analysis*

I.	Case Introduction
II.	Historical Background
III.	Outsourcing Decision
	A. Decision-Making Process
	B. Outcomes and Consequences of the Decision
IV.	Analysis from the Political Perspective
V.	Analysis from the Transaction Cost Perspective
VI.	Case Study Conclusion

Case Introduction. The purpose of the introduction is to present the evidence gathered for this particular case. This allows the reader to judge the strength and validity of the following case discussion. The reader is introduced to the individuals who participated in our study. Although individuals have been assigned pseudonyms, the reader will understand their involvement in outsourcing and the titles they hold within their companies.

Historical Background. The historical background provides a brief description of the company, its major strategies, financial stability, and the traditional role of the IS department within the company. The purpose of this section is to explain the precipitating factors that led an organizational member to initiate an outsourcing decision.

Decision Process. The outsourcing decision processes are presented in chronological order, beginning with the initiation of the evaluation following through to the decision outcome. The outsourcing stories are reconstructed from the transcribed interview notes and documents, such as requests for proposals, vendor bids, and management recommendations.

Analysis of the Cases. Once the historical background and the outsourcing decision have been described, the cases are interpreted to shed meaning into the behaviors of organizational members. As noted above, the political and transaction cost models are used to guide the interpretation.

Case Conclusion. The purpose of the case conclusion is to integrate the interpretations developed in the political and transaction cost analyses. This section also discusses whether one particular model sheds more insights on the case than the other.

Protecting Case Participants. Anonymity was deemed necessary to protect the identities of the participants as well as to make participants more likely to discuss sensitive issues. What is lost by not knowing company names is gained by the richness of what the participants shared.

The cases are presented in order of their decision outcomes (see Table 4.2). The outsourcing decisions in the first five cases resulted in companies maintaining their functions internally. In the next six cases, companies decided to outsource to third party vendors. FIRM6 and FIRM8 only outsourced their data center operations and telecommunications functions. FIRM11 outsourced the majority of its functions, but retained the planning functions along with the development and support of its strategic mining systems. FIRM7, FIRM9, and FIRM10 outsourced their entire information systems departments including applications development, support, data processing, and telecommunications. At the time of this writing, all but FIRM7 were pleased with the service they receive from their vendors.

The companies in the last two cases, FIRM12 and FIRM13, were engaged in long term outsourcing contracts that they later rescinded. These companies were dissatisfied with the level of service they

Table 4.2   *Outcome and scope of the outsourcing decisions*

Case code name	Decision outcome(s)*	Functions considered for outsourcing	Initiator of the decision
FIRM1	No/No	Data center	IS Manager (both decisions)
FIRM2	No	Data center	IS Manager
FIRM3	No	All	Vendor sent letter to CEO
FIRM4	No	Data center	Senior Manager
FIRM5	No	Data center	IS Manager
FIRM6	Yes	Data center, Telecommunications	Senior Manager
FIRM7	No/Yes	All	IS Manager (1st decision) Senior Manager (2nd decision)
FIRM8	Yes	Data center, Telecommunications	IS Manager
FIRM9	Yes	All functions except strategic systems	IS Manager
FIRM10	Yes	All	Senior Manager
FIRM11	Yes	All	Senior Manager
FIRM12	Yes/No	All	Senior Manager (1st decision) IS Manager (2nd decision)
FIRM13	Yes/No	All	Senior Manager (1st decision) IS Manager (2nd decision)

*Four companies evaluated outsourcing on two occasions, yielding a total of 17 outsourcing decisions.

received from their vendors. They also provide evidence that outsourcing does not necessarily represent a permanent decision— a company can rebuild an entire IS department.

4.1   FIRM1

FIRM1 is among four of the thirteen cases that evaluated outsourcing twice. FIRM1 is unique, however, because it was the only company which decided to maintain the function internally on both occasions. FIRM1's first evaluation occurred immediately after the company was created in 1985 when the IS manager was hired to provide computing resources for this new organization. The second evaluation occurred in the later part of 1990 when the IS manager initiated several projects to respond to user dissatisfaction.

Three individuals at FIRM1 were interviewed: Gordon, the Manager of Information Systems; Stanley, the Manager of Data Processing; and Miles, the Network Services Manager (see Table 4.3).

In order to understand the two outsourcing decisions at FIRM1, the history of the company is briefly explained to place these outsourcing decisions in their proper context.

4.1.1   Historical Background of FIRM1

In 1985, senior management at a large petroleum company which we will call ENERGY decided to bundle two loss-making refineries

Table 4.3   *FIRM1 participants*

Name used in this case	Job title	Involvement in outsourcing
Gordon	Manager of Information Systems	Gordon claims he sponsored both outsourcing decisions.
Stanley	Manager of Data Processing	Stanley was involved in the second outsourcing evaluation. He provided the financial analysis, interacted with the vendors, and recommended not to outsource.
Miles	Network Services Supervisor	Miles was aware of the outsourcing decision and its impact on morale.

along with a non-profitable chemicals facility, to create a new wholly owned subsidiary, called FIRM1. ENERGY's senior management hoped that FIRM1 would become profitable if it was freed from bureaucratic restraints. FIRM1's new management team took advantage of this additional latitude. Rather than pursuing the prior management's strategy of operating at full capacity, they altered production to reflect changes in market demand.

Along with this new autonomy, FIRM1 also became responsible for its own line and staff functions—including information systems. FIRM1's new management team hurriedly structured a new organization to support its new refining and chemical company. The newly appointed CFO at FIRM1 recruited Gordon away from his IS technology and planning job within another ENERGY subsidiary. Excited about the possibility of running his own IS department, Gordon accepted the position of FIRM1's Manager of Information Systems.

4.1.2   FIRM1's First Outsourcing Decision

Gordon's first challenge was to determine how he was going to provide information services for FIRM1. He decided to adopt ENERGY's manufacturing systems and to buy new financial software packages. The question was, where would he run these systems? Gordon could build a data center of his own or he could outsource data processing to a third party vendor. He decided to get estimates for both alternatives. Gordon requested a bid from an outsourcing vendor and he hired a consultant to help him with his internal bid. Gordon planned to compare the bids and select the low cost alternative.

4.1.2.1   FIRM1's First Outsourcing Decision Process

Gordon, the consultant, and the outsourcing vendor visited two ENERGY data centers that were currently running FIRM1's systems. They calculated FIRM1's requirements for machine cycles, storage, and personnel. The vendor submitted a bid that was 25% more costly than Gordon's internal bid. When Gordon was asked why the vendor's bid was so high, he replied:

> "The fat was in the fact that they had to make an enormous number of changes and modifications to the types of processing to conform to [the vendor's] standards and requirements. And the other thing—they would only provide interface to their computer center with their own analysts

and programmers. So they put in the contract administrators that you had to interface with. Anything above and beyond that, any work above and beyond that, they would only allow their folks to do the work. They weren't in the time-sharing business. They didn't want your programmers sitting down at a data station developing programs on their computers."

4.1.2.2 Outcome and Consequences of FIRM1's First Decision

The result of the first outsourcing decision was to provide data processing services within FIRM1's newly organized internal IS department. Gordon was hoping that his department would report directly to the CFO, but he reports to the controller. Gordon and the controller decided to structure the IS department along functional lines.

Gordon hired over 60 information systems professionals. Within the first year, this staff successfully built a data center, migrated the manufacturing systems from ENERGY to FIRM1, and installed new financial systems. When asked how he was able to accomplish this, Gordon provided two reasons. First, the data center was rather easy to erect since he inherited ENERGY's hardware. Second, he was able to quickly implement the financial systems because he didn't alter the code. He explains:

"Because we were a start-up operation, there was enough flexibility— there wasn't an ingrained attitude about how to run each function that you had to adapt the system to the function. The function still had enough flexibility that you could adapt your accounting group to the accounting system rather than getting the accounting system to meet the whims and idiosyncrasies of everyone in the accounting group."

4.1.3 FIRM1's Second Outsourcing Decision

From 1985 to 1989, Gordon feels he provided cost-efficient information services to his FIRM1 users. In 1990, however, he realized that his users were looking elsewhere to satisfy their information needs. Gordon frets, "People that we had serviced and supported in the past weren't coming back to us for return business." Instead, his users were buying PC-based solutions without consulting him. Gordon grew concerned. Although his superiors were not cognizant of the situation, he felt his contribution to the company would inevitably come into question. Gordon claims he pursued two courses of action to rectify the situation. First, he initiated another outsourcing study to determine if he could provide a more efficient data processing service. Second, he hired a consultant to determine if he could organize his information systems department more effectively. His outsourcing decision is examined below.

Gordon decided to limit the outsourcing evaluation to data center operations. He explains, "If you looked at where my costs were, my operation was hardware and software dollar intensive." Gordon claims he appointed Stanley, his manager of data processing operations, to create an RPF and solicit vendor bids. Stanley, however, contends that he initiated the outsourcing decision:

> "I said I wanted to personally evaluate outsourcing, evaluate the project to move the data center, which subsequently, I don't think Gordon was—he said, 'yeah sounds good.' I don't think there was any executive pressure from anybody to do this."

Stanley claims he wanted to evaluate outsourcing because he read in the trade literature that data centers reach economies of scale at 200 MIPS. Since he was only running a 28 MIP shop, he thought outsourcing could save FIRM1 money.

4.1.3.1   FIRM1's Second Outsourcing Decision Process

Regardless of who initiated the decision, Stanley was indisputably in charge of the investigation. He created an RPF that described, in detail, FIRM1's requirements for software, hardware, and data center personnel over the next five years. He solicited five companies to put in proposals, three of which eventually submitted bids. One of these three companies was ENERGY, the other two were outsourcing vendors. Stanley says he requested a bid from ENERGY because he was familiar with its operation and felt he could use its bid to gauge the validity of the other bids. He explains:

> "I spent thirteen years working at ENERGY myself so I knew the people. I worked on the chargeback system, Gordon and I worked on the chargeback system years ago. So we had a lot of knowledge of it. So I used them as an outsourcing vendor knowing full well that the politics probably would never allow that to happen."

Stanley explained that FIRM1 and ENERGY were competing in the same market, so their information systems had to be run at separate data centers.

The results of the bidding showed that FIRM1's projected costs were less than ENERGY's bid and one of the two vendor bids, but slightly higher than one of the vendor bids. Although this latter bid was 7% less than FIRM1's bid, Stanley did not recommend outsourcing:

> "I would call this only a first cut evaluation. If these numbers had been 50% savings, that would have been cause to assign some people to make sure these numbers are accurate and that we can really do outsourcing for this."

4.1.3.2 *Outcome and Consequences of FIRM1's Second Decision*

Stanley formally presented his recommendation to the controller in the first quarter of 1991. Stanley claims the controller was rather indifferent to the entire outsourcing project:

> "His only questions were 'Do the people know I am doing it?' He was concerned about the people side of it. He didn't ask any questions."

Gordon feels the primary consequence of the outsourcing decision is that he can prove he is efficient. Although he has mixed emotions about this result:

> "The conclusion that came out of this particular thing was that we could not replace what we were doing at the price we were doing it. Now that's been good news and bad news. The good news is that I really am comfortable that we have a very effective and very efficient mainframe computer operation. The bad news is that now having communicated that well to management, is making any kind of change an astronomical task to overcome their biases. So the fact that we are very efficient is the good news because you can't replace it for that cost. But getting the ability to invest is going to be a very difficult job...if it isn't broke don't fix it."

Now that the background and a description of both outsourcing decisions have been presented, these decisions can be interpreted from the political and transaction cost perspectives.

4.1.4 FIRM1's Decisions from a Political Perspective

One interpretation of Gordon's actions is that his outsourcing decisions were politically motivated. By examining his lack of power with FIRM1, we see that Gordon must constantly justify his contribution to upper management. One strategy he employed is to consider outsourcing. What better way to prove that you provide a cost-efficient service? Upon closer examination, Gordon employed several political tactics during both outsourcing decisions to ensure that the internal management of the function appeared as the most efficient alternative. This discussion proceeds with an assessment of Gordon's power within FIRM1.

4.1.5.1   Power of FIRM1's IS Department

There are three indicants from Pfeffer's (1981) political model that suggest that the IS department is not a very powerful entity within FIRM1: authority, resource acquisition, and substitutability.

Authority: placement of the IS department within FIRM1. According to the political model, power is first and foremost a structural phenomenon. Thus, placement of the IS department within the corporate structure is a major indicant of power. From the birth of FIRM1, we see that senior management has not placed much importance on its information services department. Although Gordon hoped he would report directly to the CFO, he reports to the controller, placing him three reporting levels away from his CEO.

Resource acquisition: senior management's view of information systems. Reporting to the controller burdens Gordon since his boss is notoriously cost conscious. Thus, technology investments must be economically justified—a difficult task in the world of information systems. Since senior management views IS as merely a necessary overhead, Gordon claims he has trouble acquiring additional resources from his management:

> "Recognize that in their mind, computers are not strategic. So making investments in large computers or computer systems are not what they are comfortable with doing. They are comfortable with making investments in large manufacturing plants, but not into computers and computer systems."

As an overhead function, senior management has tightly controlled Gordon's budget. He says his budget has remained essentially flat over the years. He has such trouble acquiring additional resources from senior management that he decided to outsource PC support rather than ask his management to hire more staff:

"The reason for making the decision [to outsource PC support] is not economics because I couldn't make a good honest business decision when we initially got into this. My concern was we were growing so quickly, so rapidly in terms of the absorption of personal computers that to try and internalize that—to do it with my regular staff— would have sent me back to the management team every other month asking for a person to do that."

Stanley corroborates that senior management views IS as non-strategic. He says senior management wants the IS department to function like a non-obtrusive phone system. This makes Stanley's job difficult, since he is only set up to fail:

"I am the data processing manager of a fairly classical mainframe operation. If it breaks, it's my fault. If it's late, my fault. If response time is lousy, it's my fault. And we do something good every now and then but nobody notices that. So it is really my function in the company that gets the headlines. We're the ones that spend all the obscene dollars to buy all this equipment. It is also my function that is not ever the hero in the company. I can make Gordon fail, but there is nothing I can do to make him a hero."

From these comments, we see that Gordon and Stanley have trouble acquiring resources since management views IS as an overhead cost.

Substitutability: user's external procurement of information resources.
The political model suggests that power arises when there are no readily available substitutes for a department's products or services. Since Gordon's users substituted his services for those of outside companies, yet another piece of evidence suggests his lack of power. In particular, Gordon's users were buying their own PC-LAN based systems. Although he tried to control the use of outside resources, he says, "I couldn't really get a handle on it."

Given these three indicants of power—Gordon's lack of authority suggested by his reporting level, his inability to acquire resources because senior management views IS as non-strategic, and high substitutability evidenced by the users' acquisition of external computer solutions—we can surmise that FIRM1's IS department is not very powerful. Given this lack of power, Gordon may have initiated the two outsourcing decisions to bolster his own credibility within the company. Since outsourcers could not apparently manage the IS function for less money, Gordon "proves" to his senior management that he is cost-efficient. Indeed, Gordon employed several political tactics to suggest that his outsourcing decisions were politically motivated. These tactics are examined below.

4.1.4.2   *Political Tactics*

Subscribers to the political model of organizational decision-making describe a variety of political tactics, including the selective use of information, selective use of decision criteria, use of outside experts, building coalitions, and cooptation. From the study of Gordon's and Stanley's actions, two more political tactics are identified, namely, the selective use of decision alternatives and delegation to a biased party. These two additional tactics are described in the context of FIRM1's decision.

Selective use of decision alternatives. Selective use of decision alternatives is a tactic that decision-makers can use to sway the decision in their favor. Decision-makers pick superfluous alternatives to camouflage their preferred outcome. They ignore other viable alternatives to prevent these options from competing with their hidden agenda. The selection of at least some alternatives gives the illusion of a rational decision, but actually decision-makers pick additional options that they know will be rendered undesirable compared to their preferred solution.

In the case of FIRM1, Gordon limited his outsourcing decision alternatives by evaluating only one outsourcing vendor and by restricting the scope of the decision to time-sharing. The vendor that Gordon selected to submit a bid was a well-known facilities management company. Since this company is not in the time-sharing business, it submitted a bid to manage the entire data processing function. If Gordon had really wanted a time-sharing bid, one might question why he didn't solicit bids from specific time-sharing vendors. Gordon contends that few viable and trustworthy vendors existed at the time.

Another issue is that Gordon's internal bid may be incommensurable with the vendor's bid. The vendor's bid included the price of contract administrators, analysts, and programmers. Gordon claims the vendor's bid was 25% higher because of the personnel and conversion costs. Gordon's internal bid just considered the costs of the hardware and software—not personnel or conversion costs. This may explain why the internal bid was 25% less expensive than the vendor's bid.

Delegation to a biased party. When decision-makers want to influence the outcome of a decision, one successful political tactic is to delegate the decision-making task to a biased subordinate. The manager sends an equivocal message to the subordinate that he wants an "objective" evaluation, but at the same time the manager realizes that the subordinate has a vested interest, and therefore can hardly be expected to make a totally impartial judgment. This tactic is successful because the manager divorces himself from the actual process so it appears that the decision is unbiased. The manager relies on the subordinate to gather the justification for his preferred solution.

In the case of FIRM1, Stanley admitted that (a) he was biased against outsourcing, and (b) he conducted the evaluation to increase his credibility:

> "Okay, I have a bias to do it myself, this is what I enjoy doing. This is a fun job. I've made a career in this business."

> "While it was an outsourcing study, it was also designed to enhance my personal credibility when it came time to ask for some more bucks."

From these quotes, Stanley appears to want the study to prove that his operation is cost-efficient so he could substantiate additional funding to upper management. In particular, Stanley wanted to upgrade to a more sophisticated operating system on his system and move to relational databases.

Although Stanley contacted the vendors and made the final recommendation, he delegated the compilation of the technical specifications to two systems programmers. These programmers knew that they would probably be unemployed if the decision resulted in outsourcing. When asked about the fate of these professionals if FIRM1 outsourced, Stanley responded:

> "I told them their job would be lost and we didn't go that far. But what I told them is if we can't do it better, we need to go out of business, we should go out of business. Aren't we better than anybody else? You know, who's going to argue with that?"

As an interesting aside, these two systems programmers have a surprising history: both previously worked for companies that outsourced. One transferred to the outsourcing vendor, then quit. The other refused to transfer.

The validity of the outsourcing assessment did come under question from two sources. First, in his memo to senior management,

Stanley warned management that the figures were only rough estimates:

> "Each of these companies are most anxious to explore a marketing opportunity with FIRM1. However, they are generally geared to market to the financial executive of the company as opposed to the data processing manager. As in other marketing arenas, each of these vendors promises tremendous results and dramatic savings. However, they are difficult to pin down to a reliable dollar quote without extensive time and research. A comprehensive review of the alternatives to a FIRM1 data processing operation would need to spend several man-months to ensure fully accurate results."

Second, the question of the validity of the assessment was also raised by Stanley's superiors during his management presentation:

> "I honestly attempted to be as objective as possible, but I admit that even when I presented to Tom—he's vice president and controller—I probably would not ever be perceived as completely unbiased and non-prejudiced."

In conclusion, the interpretation of actors' behaviors from the political perspective is that both used outsourcing to promote the interests of the IS department rather than for the interests of FIRM1. Since three indicants of power suggest that the IS department possesses little power, both Gordon and Stanley needed to bolster their own as well as their department's credibility. In the first decision, Gordon used outsourcing to convince his management that he was not building an empire. In the second decision, Stanley used the outsourcing evaluation as a way to justify future hardware investments.

4.1.5   FIRM1's Decision from a Transaction Cost Perspective

In the previous section, much evidence suggests that both decisions were politically motivated. Evidence presented in this section suggests that Gordon and Stanley evaluated outsourcing to try to improve FIRM1's financial position. The transaction cost view of their actions, however, is limited to the second outsourcing decision as a confidentiality agreement precluded any detailed financial data for the first decision to be made available.

Transaction cost theory assumes that decision-makers share the common goal of cost efficiency. Decision-makers are assumed to select the most economical alternative by attending to costs, transaction types, and the threat of opportunism (Williamson, 1975). By analyzing Gordon's and Stanley's actions from this perspective, a different interpretation arises. Rather than meeting self-serving ends, they may have considered outsourcing as a sincere attempt to provide low cost data processing services for their users.

4.1.5.1 Costs

When Gordon discovered that his users were buying computer solutions from outside vendors, he suspected that vendors could provide computing resources for less money than his own DP shop. If this proved true, Gordon claims that he was willing to outsource. He seemed very concerned that users bypassed his authority, since he viewed his function as the technology gatekeeper. Users may buy incompatible systems or ignore security and controls if his department did not coordinate technology purchases. If outsourcing was more efficient, Gordon wanted to manage the interface between users and vendors to ensure proper service. Therefore, from the transaction cost view, Gordon's decision to evaluate outsourcing can be interpreted as an act to pursue corporate objectives.

Stanley's actions may also be interpreted in this light. He claims his decision to outsource was motivated by the trade literature. He read that outsourcing could save money, and wanted to determine if he could reduce costs at FIRM1:

> "I have read and have no reason to dispute that probably the most efficient, cost-effective mainframe shop is somewhere in the 200 MIP range. And a 28 MIP shop is darn small, so if I had a 100 MIP shop or a 200 MIP shop, I would only have one copy of the operating system and so forth. So it was efficiencies of scale. So I probably had a bias that possibly outsourcing would save FIRM1 a lot of money because we were so small."

Stanley claims he pursued two actions to ensure that his evaluation was unbiased. First, he would keep his job even if outsourcing was pursued:

> "The one mechanical thing I did to attempt to be as unbiased as possible, is that in every one of them [the scenarios], I still had a job. I just defined it a little differently."

Second, Stanley also claims he solicited a bid from ENERGY even though he knew that this option was politically infeasible. Since he knows ENERGY's data processing system, he was confident he could use its bid to assess the validity of his internal bid and the vendor bids. This benchmark provides some evidence that Stanley really was trying to save FIRM1 money.

4.1.5.2   Transaction Type

Because costs are often difficult to determine, Williamson claims that decision-makers use a heuristic to determine which transactions are most efficiently governed through the market. In particular, he suggests that non-specific, recurrent transactions can be more efficiently acquired from a vendor. Following this line of reasoning, Gordon may have limited the scope of his evaluation to the data processing function because he felt that this was the only opportunity where a vendor could improve his efficiency:

> "If you looked at where my costs were, this area [Data Center Operations] was hardware and software dollar intensive and not much with people. The clerical level people, computer operators—not a high expense. The real issue here is how much you have tied up in the hardware and software...The intent was to concentrate on getting most effective— what we asked the folks to do was to take a look at each one of these things and try to present a bid that was cafeteria style."

The term "cafeteria style" is worth noting since it corresponds with Williamson's notion that commodity services are more efficiently outsourced.

Gordon also claims it is difficult to maintain a qualified staff in a small shop and felt a vendor may be able to provide a better service:

> "We had a lot of money tied up in this large computing environment, and it seemed obvious to me that the entire world would not necessarily be growing big computers anymore. It's becoming difficult to find people to do MVS, and if we were going to move to relational, it's been difficult to find database administrators, hard to find DB2 people. And at the same time it took you so long to build and put anything into that type of environment that your clients get really restless and frustrated."

This quote provides some evidence that Gordon was willing to outsource if dollar savings were evident. Since this function is costly and qualified personnel are difficult to obtain, he thought outsourcing might provide a viable alternative.

4.1.5.2   Threat of Opportunism

Williamson speculates that the threat of opportunism increases the cost of outsourcing. Since companies must spend time monitoring the contract, coordination costs may cancel out savings. Gordon and Stanley felt that opportunism was only a threat from certain vendors. For example, Stanley said he read in the trade literature that certain vendors take advantage of their clients:

> "At the same time I was nervous because I read in the rags about how he is [Stanley identifies a famous outsourcer] and how his style is once he gets his little toe in the door. He swarms you with thousands of his eagles, and at the executive level, he takes over."

Stanley and Gordon's strategy to reduce the threat of opportunism was to limit bid solicitations to reputable firms.

In summary, the transaction cost perspective provides one interpretation of Gordon and Stanley's behavior. By attending to costs, transaction type, and the threat of opportunism, they determined that maintaining the function internally was more economical than outsourcing to a third party.

4.1.6   FIRM1—Conclusion

This section integrates the different interpretations that arise from examining the outsourcing decisions from two alternative theoretical lenses. From the political model, we see two individuals trying to increase their personal and departmental credibility. From the transaction cost perspective, we see their actions as a sincere attempt to reduce data processing costs for the overall benefit of FIRM1. Which view is right? A reasonable argument could be made for either interpretation.

For the first decision, the political model sheds more insight into Gordon's behavior. This conclusion, however, must be tempered with the fact that evidence for the transaction cost model was not made available to us. In 1985, when Gordon was first appointed as IS director of the newly formed FIRM1, this was his first opportunity to manage an entire department of his own. This was a magnificent career opportunity for Gordon. Realizing that the financial situation at FIRM1 was tenuous, however, he had to assure his management that he was providing an efficient service. Gordon stated that the primary impetus behind the outsourcing evaluation was to convince his management that he would provide the least expensive data processing alternative:

"I did this because I was scared to death that if I didn't take the initiative that it was going to be there. In a start-up operation I had to satisfy my management that I was not building an empire."

By evaluating outsourcing, Gordon demonstrated his commitment to higher corporate goals. By looking at the actual decision process, however, one suspects that Gordon may have stacked the deck against outsourcing. He only contacted one vendor and since the vendor's bid contained personnel and conversion costs, Gordon was able to provide a lower data processing operation than the vendor. Since management only views the decision outcome, Gordon was able to justify the expenditures required to create his IS department.

For the second outsourcing decision, evidence can be found for both a political and economic interpretation of behavior. Evidence that supports the political model included the IS department's lack of power and the use of two political tactics, namely, the selective use of decision alternatives and delegation to a biased party. Stanley admitted that outsourcing numbers were rough estimates and failed to pursue the vendor's bid which indicated a 7% savings. In addition, the controller viewed the entire outsourcing evaluation with skepticism. Evidence that supports the transaction cost view can be seen in the comments of Gordon and Stanley to sincerely wish to reduce IS costs.

If one was forced to rectify these seemingly disparate views of behavior, one could simply appeal to pluralism. Gordon and Stanley may have simultaneously pursued both selfish and corporate motives. If outsourcing was more efficient, they could save their company money and still preserve their positions by coordinating the outsourcing arrangement. If outsourcing was not more efficient, as their analysis concluded, they presumably gain credibility by demonstrating to management that their function is already efficient.

4.2   FIRM2

FIRM2 is one of the five organizations in this research who decided against outsourcing. The outsourcing decision at FIRM2 is unusual in that Anthony—the Director of Advanced Technology who investigated outsourcing—admits he performed the exercise largely as a defensive maneuver. Anthony was asked by his IS manager to write a report on outsourcing to present to senior management. The gist of this report was to enlighten management on the risks of outsourcing information systems.

Anthony was the only individual at FIRM2 interviewed for this research (see Table 4.4). At the time of this writing, Anthony had completed the rough draft of his report, but had not submitted his findings to senior management. Anthony's report as well as a consulting firm's evaluation of FIRM2's application development and support functions are used to demonstrate to senior management the efficiency of FIRM2's computing operations.

4.2.1 Historical Background of FIRM2

FIRM2 is less than twenty years old, yet it is one of the largest publicly-held companies in the United States. The company has grown rapidly during the last two decades through an aggressive acquisition strategy. FIRM2 currently operates 300 companies worldwide and annually generates over $1 billion in sales. These 300 companies operate rather autonomously—the corporate office merely sets some financial guidelines and provides administrative services. These operating companies are very powerful because FIRM2 does not replace the management staff of its acquired companies. Anthony explained the situation:

> "FIRM2 has always tried to acquire profitable companies. If a company is profitable, then it does not make a whole deal of sense to change the management if they are willing to stay on. That, combined with an intentional decentralized philosophy, makes it more challenging to implement corporate-sponsored programs."

A main objective of corporate headquarters is to provide cost-effective support to its operating companies. There are only 700 people in the central office—a rather lean number for a company with over 20 000 employees.

The IS department is headed by Anthony's boss, Jay, Vice President of Administrative Services and IS. Jay operates with a

Table 4.4 *FIRM2 participants*

Name used in this case	Job title	Involvement in outsourcing
Anthony	Director of Advanced Technology	Anthony was asked by his boss, the VP of Administrative Services and IS, to write a report on outsourcing.

relatively small budget—$30 million—which represents about 0.05% of revenues. Jay has trouble delivering an effective service with such a small budget. Anthony notes, for example, that when he was hired in 1985, there were no on-line systems. People in the decentralized offices filled out forms and mailed them to the central office for processing. Since then, several on-line financial systems have been implemented, but the majority of the application portfolio can hardly be considered current. Senior management is unwilling to invest significant dollars for a staff function.

Given this environment, Jay is aware that he is vulnerable to outsourcing unless he can demonstrate his efficiency to senior management. With the stage set, we now embark on Anthony's quest to evaluate outsourcing.

4.2.2   FIRM2's Outsourcing Decision

In 1991, Jay assigned Anthony to write a report on the current trend in outsourcing and the potential implications for FIRM2. The report is to be presented to senior management to educate them on the pros and cons of outsourcing. Anthony begins his story by explaining why his boss wanted to explore the current vogue in information systems management:

> "A lot of the industry is nervous. Industry observers for the last couple of years have been saying, 'If you don't look at outsourcing, somebody will do it for you.' So we have undertaken a review of what the outsourcing market looks like."

Anthony feared that senior management had already considered outsourcing to some extent: "In fact there has been a rumor that [outsourcing vendor] has tried to come in. Whether or not that is entirely true, I don't know." Anthony also said that a former officer of FIRM2 now works as a partner in an outsourcing vendor. He notes, "So we are not unknown to the outsourcing people."

4.2.2.1   FIRM2's Outsourcing Decision Process

Anthony's investigation began by referencing current periodicals, CD-ROM on-line databases, and Gartner Group reports on outsourcing. He found most of the literature to be overly optimistic. He then consulted an expert in information systems outsourcing who warned Anthony about the vendors' present cost structures and savings which may never be realized in the long run. Anthony included several of the consultant's admonishments in his report. Anthony decided not to consult any outsourcing vendors because, "I didn't want to get involved in that", he explains. So, he wrote a draft of his report based on his literature search and conversations with the outsourcing consultant.

4.2.2.2   *Outcome and Consequences of FIRM2's Decision*

Anthony said the main purpose of his report is to enlighten his senior management. In his report, Anthony noted several facts about outsourcing that are often neglected in the trade literature. First, many companies that have outsourced were either in or headed for serious financial trouble. In these circumstances, outsourcing was used to refinance the company. Second, many internal DP shops possess economies of scale comparable to a vendor, so vendors do not possess an inherent cost advantage. Third, Anthony pointed to the risk that outsourcing eliminates all your data processing options. He notes that prohibitive start-up costs make it infeasible to return to in-house processing if outsourcing fails.

Anthony's report focuses on outsourcing negatives. He feels that companies outsource out of desperation and that they rarely realize projected savings. Since the report has not been distributed, the consequences of this outsourcing evaluation can not be assessed. The question remains whether Anthony's defensive stance on outsourcing will be successful enough to prevent outsourcing.

Jay and Anthony's behavior is now analyzed from the political and transaction cost perspectives.

4.2.3   FIRM2's Decision from the Political Perspective

By Anthony's own admission, his task was one of creating a report to fend off rumors of a suspected outsourcing bid. Jay was prudent to initiate the study since an assessment of the power of the IS department reveals several vulnerabilities of the IS organization to outsourcing.

4.2.3.1   *Power of FIRM2's IS Department*

The first issue to explore is the current power of FIRM2's IS organization. Three indicants of power—the position of the IS department within FIRM2, senior management's view of information systems, and the IS budget—suggest that the IS department is not very influential. The IS budget has been discussed in the previous section. The other two indicants of power are discussed below.

Authority: position of the IS department within FIRM2. FIRM2's organizational chart indicates that IS sits two levels below the CEO. Anthony commented that the IS department should have a higher reporting level, yet "the IS group here, as with many companies that haven't seen the light yet, reports to finance." Jay reports to the CFO whose main agenda is keeping IS costs low.

Resource acquisition: senior management's view of information systems. Jay finds it difficult to acquire resources for investment in new technology. Although he would like to develop strategic systems to support corporate objectives, Anthony sighs, "As a result of the light budget growth, we can't support our CEO as much as we would like to." Anthony feels the reason is because IS services are not valued:

> "It was not in the eyes of executive management—and I think in the eyes of a lot of IS folks as well—we are not in an information intensive business."

In summary, FIRM2's decentralized philosophy and senior management's view of information technology indicates that the IS department is not very powerful. However, this lack of power does not necessarily mean that the IS department is vulnerable to a potential outsourcing bid. Nevertheless, Jay has initiated several tactics to bolster the image of his department.

4.2.3.2   Political Tactics

Jay initiated political tactics that may have successfully fended off an outsourcing attempt. Besides asking Anthony to write a report on information systems outsourcing, he hired an outside consultant to demonstrate his department's efficiency.

Use of outside experts to assess efficiency. Pfeffer believes that managers often hire consultants to corroborate their hidden agendas. Since consultants are viewed as outside experts, they presumably make unbiased assessments of an organization. Pfeffer notes, however, that consultants can hardly be viewed as unbiased since they are paid to perform. In addition, he notes that consultants rarely generate original recommendations, rather, they are paid to confirm the internal management's preferences.

At FIRM2, Jay hired an outside consulting firm to compare FIRM2's cost effectiveness with other IS shops of a similar size. The results were extremely favorable in the data center operations and telecommunications functions. However, the applications development and support functions did not fare as well. The consulting firm found that costs were high due to (a) the large number of languages supported at FIRM2, (b) the high turnover of analysts, (c) the shortcuts taken in the early phases of development, and (d) the development of custom software rather than buying packaged solutions. Anthony did not comment whether recommendations from this study had been implemented. In any case, Anthony claims Jay was pleased with the outcome:

> "Once we had those numbers in hand, we were pretty comfortable with where we were. We were comfortable that a third party coming in with an outsourcing pitch would have a tough sell."

Thus, Anthony and Jay are confident that their efforts adequately protect the IS department from outsourcing. Equipped with Anthony's and the consultant's reports, they feel they have demonstrated to management that their function is effective.

In summary, the outsourcing evaluation at FIRM2 can be construed as a political maneuver against outsourcing. Given the IS department's lack of power and whispers that outsourcing vendors were wooing senior management, Jay and Anthony tried to counter the optimism about outsourcing by writing an outsourcing report.

4.2.4 FIRM2's Decision from the Transaction Cost Perspective

Jay and Anthony's behavior is difficult to assess from a transaction cost perspective, since they did not solicit vendor bids. One could argue, perhaps, that the data center efficiency audit was proof enough that vendors could not provide a less expensive service.

One piece of evidence, however, suggests that Jay's behavior, at least in other areas, subscribes to Williamson's assumption that managers pursue corporate objectives. Anthony claims that Jay looked at the CEO's objectives and asked, "How can information systems support him?" Jay has made a sincere attempt to directly contribute to the CEO's main objectives:

> "The CEO's two biggest hot spots: one is get us re-positioned as a services company that works in [omitted for confidentiality purposes].

The other major thrust that [the CEO] has is quality. We have embarked on a total quality management (TQM) process."

According to Anthony, Jay was the first FIRM2 manager to implement TQM. He tells the story:

"IS was in fact the first group involved in a total quality management process. We did it before it became a hot button for everybody else. Jay has been an instrumental player in that for the process in both IS and corporate. We went first of all through—we are much further ahead in the metrics. We pulled ahead to determine and understand what our contribution is and how we control that in light of quality. There are opportunities for IS to provide information system support to other parts of the organization in conjunction with quality."

In particular, Jay wants to train the entire organization in TQM. Anthony says, however, "We may not be funded to the point where we can operate those kind of services." Jay encounters mixed messages from his senior management. According to Anthony, the CEO says "quality" but the CFO's main agenda is "keeping cost under control in a period of slow growth, which makes it difficult to justify IS growth." However, Jay's initiative in TQM has helped bolster his reputation as a company man.

Jay's attempt to pursue corporate objectives provides some evidence that, at least in the TQM area, his behavior can be interpreted from a transaction cost perspective. Extrapolating his behavior to the outsourcing arena—Jay may know in his heart that outsourcing is a poor alternative for FIRM2. Rather than waste the time to gather and evaluate bids, he may have used the outsourcing report as an economical way to convince management that outsourcing is not a viable alternative for FIRM2.

4.2.5   FIRM2—Conclusion

In the introduction to this chapter, it was noted that in some cases one theoretical lens sheds considerably more understanding than the other. In the case of FIRM2, the political model appears to provide a more coherent interpretation of Jay and Anthony's behavior than the transaction cost model. The IS department is not very powerful when one considers reporting level, company philosophy, and the meager IS budget. Given this lack of power and the rumors that outsourcing vendors were courting senior management, Jay may have initiated the outsourcing evaluation as a defensive maneuver. Equipped with Anthony's outsourcing report and the consultant's favorable report on data processing, Jay and Anthony feel they can fend off an outsourcing attempt. The case of the outsourcing decision at FIRM2 may provide a valuable lesson to IS directors in similar positions: the best defense is a good offense.

4.3 FIRM3

FIRM3 provides an excellent example of how to successfully market the IS organization to top management. The Vice President of Information Systems spent years selling the value of information systems to his CEO. When financial troubles plagued FIRM3, an outsourcing vendor reportedly offered to buy FIRM3's information systems assets. The CEO promptly rejected the proposal without so much as a financial analysis. This case concentrates on the strategies the VP of Information Systems implemented prior to the outsourcing decision. By examining these strategies, it will become clear why outsourcing was abruptly dismissed.

The participants interviewed for this case are found in Table 4.5. Of the four interviewed, Ronald, the VP of Information Systems, was the only one who had direct and intimate knowledge of FIRM3's outsourcing decision. The others provided additional insights of FIRM3's IS operation.

Table 4.5 *FIRM3 participants*

Name used in this case	Job title	Involvement in outsourcing
Ronald	Vice President of Information Systems	Ronald, along with the CEO, decided not to outsource.
William	Director of Systems Coordination	William considered outsourcing several functions within his department.
Scott	Director of Technical Support	Scott studied the efficiency of data center operations.
Gary	Director of Worldwide Telecommunications	Gary possessed little knowledge of the outsourcing decision.

4.3.1 Historical Background of FIRM3

FIRM3 is an international company that explores, produces, refines and markets oil and natural gas. During the early 1980s, FIRM3 was profitable and sustained a healthy net income. In the mid 1980s, the company fell on hard times and went through a major restructuring plan. By 1988, earnings were positive again and they have continued to remain strong, despite the economic recession.

During the financial difficulties, FIRM3's CEO was searching for ways to generate cash which set the stage for the outsourcing decision.

4.3.2 FIRM3's Outsourcing Decision

Compared to the trauma of dealing with its severe financial difficulties, FIRM3's outsourcing decision was rather inconsequential. In a two-hour interview with Ronald, less than fifteen minutes were spent discussing the actual outsourcing decision.

4.3.2.1 *FIRM3's Outsourcing Decision Process*

FIRM3's outsourcing decision process took less than two weeks. In 1988, the president of a large outsourcing company wrote a letter to FIRM3's CEO. According to Ronald:

> "There was a letter, the chairman of the board of [the outsourcing vendor] wrote a letter to our chief executive officer saying that they would be most interested in paying substantial cash for our whole IS organization. That includes all the people and they would be very happy to meet with him, and discuss that with him."

The CEO then called Ronald and asked him the amount of money this vendor would likely pay for FIRM3's information systems assets and people. Ronald responded, "I said, based on what they had done elsewhere, I'd say about $250 to $400 million." The CEO was not interested and told Ronald to decline the vendor's offer.

> "He says, 'I'm not interested in letting other people,'—that's the CEO talking—'have access to our data. I don't have to go outside for use of our data, so prepare a letter back to the chairman of [the outsourcing vendor] and say we appreciate your offer but at this time we consider our information technology as part of the strategic work that we have, and we're just not interested in pursuing that at this time.' And so that put that on one side of the ledger—he washed his hands of it and he was through with it."

The CEO may have been through with the outsourcing decision, but Ronald was not. As a result of this interaction, Ronald initiated his own contact with the vendor.

Because of FIRM3's poor financial situation, Ronald knew that all departments were expected to cut costs or increase revenues. Even though the CEO rejected the outsourcing proposal this time, there may be a next time. Therefore, Ronald decided to initiate conversations with the vendor about the possibility of a joint partnership between FIRM3's information systems department and the vendor. Ronald wanted to create a separate company, naming himself as president or vice president. According to Ronald's proposal, FIRM3's systems would be modified to perform generic oil industry functions so that they could be sold to other oil companies. Ronald estimated that his plan could have generated about $250 million in cash for FIRM3.

4.3.2.2 Outcome and Consequences of FIRM3's Decision

The outsourcing company was interested in Ronald's proposal because it wanted an entrée into the oil industry. However, FIRM3's CEO and chairman rejected the idea. Ronald claims they rejected his proposal because (a) they did not trust outsiders and (b) they use the IS organization as a training ground for top executives. Ronald explains the issue of trust:

> "I don't think you are comfortable—if you are a CEO—sitting down talking about your long-term strategy with an outsourcer by you instead of an IS man that works directly for you. Our management is not ready to accept the third party—an outsider as it were—in that position."

Ronald also explained that FIRM3 uses the information systems department as a corporate training ground. Over the course of his career, Ronald had reported to all of FIRM3's senior vice presidents. Ronald notes they rejected outsourcing partly because "they felt like if it was kept as a separate company out there, that would disappear from them." The final outcome of the outsourcing investigations thus resulted in maintaining the status quo.

In the analysis section of this case, Ronald's management style and political tactics are examined. By successfully selling his department to top management for over 35 years, he built up a substantial defense against outsourcing.

4.3.3   FIRM3's Decision from a Political Perspective

During the interview, Ronald summarized the role of the CIO and discussed the importance of organizational politics. Although "politics" has a pejorative connotation, Ronald stressed that "politics" really means networking with executives and industry leaders to accomplish objectives and is thus positive rather than negative.

To Ronald, good politics means good business. Politics means marketing the function to senior management and establishing personal credibility. Once this is accomplished, the IS manager is in a position to contribute to corporate strategies, command more resources, and influence corporate decisions. In simpler terms, Value + Credibility = Power. FIRM3's IS department's power is assessed in the following section.

4.3.3.1   Power of FIRM3's IS Department

Indicants of Ronald's departmental power include authority, resource acquisition, and low substitutability.

Authority: reporting levels from CEO and committee representation. Reporting level from the CEO is presumed to be an indicant of departmental power. At one time, Ronald reported directly to the chairman, but in 1972, a senior vice president level was added to the hierarchy. For the remainder of his career, Ronald reported to one of the senior VPs. Although two reporting levels from the CEO and chairman, he interacted with them about once a month.

Another indicant of Ronald's power was his representation on two important committees, the Corporate Research Committee and the Operating Committee. The former committee decides how to allocate large sums of research dollars. The latter committee sets strategies and allocates resources. Ronald notes his contribution to these committees:

> "The Operating Committee. . .these are the top executives in the area. And you're making decisions outside of the IS world. And they look to your expertise, your *management* expertise and your knowledge of technology to help them make those right decisions."

Ronald's exposure on these committees increased his power because senior managers came to know and trust his opinions.

Resource acquisition: internal and external.   The ability to acquire resources has been deemed an indicant of power because "those who have the gold make the rules" (Pfeffer, 1981). If this adage is true then Ronald possesses a significant amount of power. At his disposal are a huge amount of IS resources, a large IS organization, and a massive IS budget. His budget, one may note, is larger than the revenues of many Fortune 1000 companies.

In addition to these company granted resources, Ronald generates about $17 million a year through selling his data center services to clients outside of FIRM3. He successfully competed against some of the top outsourcing vendors to win these clients. He confines the outsourcing business to 5% of his processing capability, however, to prevent losing focus. This amount is enough to foster a marketing mentality and demonstrate value without sacrificing service to his FIRM3 users.

Low substitutability. Low substitutability is another indicant of power. The theory is that if the organization has few alternatives to accepting a department's services, this department becomes powerful. Although FIRM3 users rarely by-passed the IS department, Ronald was aware that users could buy information systems solutions on the market. To prevent this, he guaranteed competitive prices so that the users would not be tempted to go elsewhere. According to Ronald, his IS operation had an inherent competitive advantage over outside vendors since he did not have to make a profit. If he could not produce a less expensive solution, then his IS function did not deserve to exist. In addition to competitive prices, Ronald offered excellent service because his staff was trained to look at IT as a solution to business problems, not technical problems.

In summary, from three indicants of power—authority, resource acquisition, and low substitutability—FIRM3's IS department seems to possess significant power within the organization. Since FIRM3 was one of two of the cases where IS was deemed powerful (the other case is FIRM10), the issue warrants further exploration. In particular, one nagging question that surfaces: How does an IS department become powerful? How does it acquire resources, gain credibility, and influence corporate strategies? FIRM3 provides a unique opportunity to explore some tactics for gaining departmental power. Ronald explained his tactics for selling the concept of IT over his 35-year tenure at FIRM3.

4.3.3.2   Political Tactics

The political model stresses that stakeholders initiate political tactics to influence the decision outcome in their favor. Pfeffer implies a chronology—the initiation of a decision triggers the mobility of power and political tactics. Throughout Ronald's interview, his philosophy seemed to reverse the chronology: *use political tactics to gain a general credibility, not to influence specific decisions.* Once a manager gains credibility, he does not have to expend as much energy influencing specific decisions. Thus, use political tactics in a proactive manner to market the department, not to react to problems as they arise. This philosophy certainly seems effective— how many other CEOs would dismiss outsourcing during times of financial mayhem without as much as an economic justification?

In this section, we see how Ronald has spent his entire career building coalitions and demonstrating the value of his department. His story begins over 35 years ago.

Building coalitions: winning top management support. Ronald says that FIRM3 bought its first computer in the 1950s. By 1967, the computing function had become important enough to warrant its own department. The first IS department head was previously a refining manager. At this time, he told his subordinate, Ronald, "we have all the computing power we ever need." Although Ronald did not agree with this technical recommendation, he thought his manager was effective because he established a good rapport with FIRM3's senior executives. In particular, Ronald learned the importance of managing expectations and selling the value of information systems. In 1972, when Ronald's boss was moved to another division, Ronald was appointed Vice President of Information Systems.

As vice president, Ronald went to the corporate headquarters at least once a month to visit with the executive team:

> "I went to the city, I usually had one or two things to do, I made it a point when I went in, I went up to the chairman's office and many times his secretary was there when I'd get there and I'd say, 'tell the chairman and CEO, tell Harry I'm in the building. Could I talk to him? I'm available.' I went right down the hall to the president, who at the time was Michael, and said, 'I'm in town for a week if you have any questions about computing, I'd be glad to talk to you about it.' I would also visit every senior vice president on the executive floor. I would stick my head in the door and say, 'Hey, I'm in town, what can I do to help?'"

Ronald felt that he established a good rapport with the executive team by being visible, available, and helpful. He also wanted to train the executive team on the value of information technology.

Selling IS: the executive computer class.   In 1967, Ronald established an executive computer concepts class. All managers over a certain level were required to attend. Ronald explains that the CEO supported this training effort:

> "We'd make it a point that every one of our executives attended that four day class. Every time we got as many as ten or fifteen people at the general manager level who had not taken the course, I'd call [to schedule the course]. And we'd schedule it and we'd get the CEO's signature saying, 'You've been selected to attend a computer concepts class. Please be at the homestead on four o'clock on Sunday, signed Harry Thompson, CEO.' Very few people found excuses."

Ronald says the purpose of the class was to "get people understanding that IT has more to contribute than just writing payroll checks."

Market IS: become a profit center/use of outside experts.   Ronald's biggest challenge was trying to change the accounting of the IS department from an overhead account to a profit center. Ronald felt a profit center was the only way to unequivocally demonstrate the value of IS. Whereas the rest of his tactics might be considered political, this agenda would parade his costs in black and white.

Opposition from users, however, initially halted this project. They feared that their costs would increase if they were charged for information services. Ronald was determined and spent almost three years laying the groundwork for an accounting change. In 1983, he started to send his users mock bills:

> "I started sending out memos, if I were billing you this is what your bill would be. So I started into a form of billing even though it wasn't on the books anywhere."

Ronald sent out the bills to gradually acquaint his users with the cost of information services. During this time, Ronald also had to ensure that his services were cheaper than outsourcers. If the department ever became a profit center, users might substitute his services for vendor services if FIRM3's prices were not competitive. Ronald hired a consultant to compare his costs with those of other similar-sized shops. The consultant took a series of FIRM3's applications, normalized them, and compared FIRM3's costs with those of four large service bureaus. FIRM3's costs were competitive. Ronald claims he hired the consultant to provide ammunition against user inquiries:

> "If when you start billing your customers as a controlled expense is it not anticipated that the users will say, 'Hey, could I get this done cheaper elsewhere?' Wouldn't it be nice to be able to answer that question before it was asked?"

Although Ronald instigated these efforts in 1983, it was not until 1986 that he succeeded in convincing his management to change the function. At that time, other department heads bragged to management that they were reducing costs but that "this damn computer overhead is eating us up alive." The chairman of the board and the CFO called a meeting with Ronald to review his budget. Ronald describes the chairman's aggressive behavior during this meeting:

> "He would sit there and pistol whip me to death about my expenses and I had to answer to everyone of them. I wasn't making him happy because he wasn't getting me to agree to reduce my costs. I said I'd be glad to cut expenses. . .anything that my user organization doesn't need, just let me know. If the Marketing guy doesn't want me to do invoicing, we'll shut her down tomorrow."

Ronald was well prepared for the confrontation. He showed the chairman that the other departments were only able to reduce their costs because Ronald's department had automated their functions. For example, the transportation department reduced its costs because Ronald automated sixteen terminals. The computers now handled dispatching, security, and invoicing. Through Ronald's efforts, the transportation manager reduced headcount by 40 people. Ronald proved to the chairman that he was contributing to FIRM3's bottom line but that the accounting mechanism camouflaged his profitability. After that meeting, the chairman turned to Ronald and said, "You are not part of the problem, you are part of the solution." This was a great victory for the IS department—it was finally made a profit center.

Ronald continued to provide excellent service. His prices were so competitive that he acquired a surplus. Rather than keep these profits, he reimbursed his users. Ronald explains the affect of his department's image:

> "When I started doing it, my billing system started generating a profit for me. That really looked good because the service departments can't

generate—the service organizations should not have a profit. So I'd have a profit all year long and in December I'd send the bills and say, 'Because you increased your usage, I'm giving you a rebate.' This made my users happy."

Demonstrate efficiency: become an outsourcer.   As a corporate citizen, he wanted zero profit, but as a business man, he wanted to continue to demonstrate his department's worth. As noted earlier, he started to offer data processing services to outside customers. Outsourcing is a powerful way to demonstrate efficiency since prices are obviously low enough to compete with outsourcing vendors.

In summary, we see some of the strategies that Ronald employed to market his department to senior management. By understanding the history of Ronald's reign as IS director, we gain more understanding of FIRM3's abrupt outsourcing decision. Since Ronald had spent years demonstrating his contribution to profitability, he was able to dismiss the outsourcing option rather swiftly. Ronald concludes with this thought:

"Now how you do that today [sell IS], I really don't know. How a company that hasn't done it. . .they are vulnerable to outsourcing."

Again, Ronald's philosophy is to use political tactics to act, not react. One of Ronald's last statements captures his view of the relationship between action and outsourcing:

"So I think the concept of your IS person being part of the management of the company—not just a technician sitting on the sidelines—is something that keeps you from outsourcing."

Since political tactics require time and planning, IS managers do not have the luxury of pursuing these options during an outsourcing evaluation. By then, it is too late.

4.3.4   FIRM3's Decision from a Transaction Cost Perspective

Transaction cost theory assumes that decision-makers perceive a problem, generate alternatives, then pick a low-cost solution. Again, a chronology is implied: the initiation of the decision precedes a cost analysis.

As a consummate professional, Ronald never waited for the outsourcing decision to evaluate his costs. Rather, he spent his entire career measuring, assessing, and controlling costs. Perhaps the outsourcing decision was so abrupt because Ronald had consistently proved his costs were low by (a) hiring experts to measure efficiency, (b) charging users for services so they knew their exact computing costs, and (c) successfully competing with outside vendors.

One might question how the same actions (use of experts, overhead accounts, becoming an outsourcer) can be used as evidence in both the political and transaction cost analyses. Granted, Ronald emerged as an eminent politician in the previous analysis, but all his actions could be construed as rational since he was trying to tie his contribution to profitability. He argues that good politics precedes good business. That is, if a department manager fails to sell his department or himself, he will be unable to contribute to the organization. By establishing credibility, senior executives learn to trust a manager's recommendations. Ronald feels that he was trusted because he always put the needs of the business before the needs of IS. He notes:

> "I feel like I was an oil man. I was an oil man first and a computer person second. And I think that has to be that if the person wants to have credibility."

In summary, Ronald feels that his actions were motivated by the desire to see FIRM3 succeed. His view of corporate reality is that organizational members must prove themselves before others will believe the validity of their recommendations.

4.3.5   FIRM3—Conclusion

FIRM3's outsourcing decision can only be understood when placed in its rich historical context. At first, one may question why the CEO dismissed the outsourcing offer when his company was in financial trouble. However, when one attends to the strategies that the IS director had implemented over the years, we understand that the CEO truly believed that IS was a value-added service, not just a cost-burden. As such, he was unwilling to farm this function to an outsider.

In the case of FIRM3, we also see a different application of the transaction cost and the political models. These models were not useful in evaluating the intentions and behaviors of members *during* the outsourcing decision, primarily because the decision process involved almost no activity. Rather, these models were more useful in analyzing behaviors *prior* to the decision. Both filters provide an explanation of the decision brevity.

From the political perspective, we see a savvy manager that understands corporate games: establish personal credibility, demonstrate the value of your function, and build coalitions with senior executives. This way, potential attacks (such as outsourcing) are less threatening. Most of all, cover your bases. This philosophy was particularly evident in Ronald's actions *after* the CEO dismissed outsourcing as a viable alternative. He approached the vendor and offered them a partnership in a new company with him as president or vice president. This way, Ronald preserved a position for himself and his staff in the case that outsourcing was re-examined.

From a transaction cost perspective, we see an oil man trying to improve profitability through automation and cost consciousness. After all, taking on outside clients increased profits, chargeback illustrated where he increased profits through automation, efficiency audits were used to assess costs; all of Ronald's tactics could be construed as economically-motivated. Since he can prove efficiency and allegiance to corporate goals, outsourcing was not a serious alternative. Why should the CEO waste his time conducting a financial analysis of outsourcing when he knew the outcome?

4.4   FIRM4

FIRM4, a huge conglomerate of petroleum, natural gas, and chemical companies, investigated outsourcing its data center operations to determine whether IS costs could be reduced. Management began the evaluation process by hiring a consultant to create a request for proposal (RFP). Next, they generated three alternatives: keep in-house, hire Vendor A, or hire Vendor B. For each alternative, they calculated quantitative, as well as qualitative, data. They finally selected the low cost solution: keep data processing in-house. According to the participants, FIRM4's outsourcing decision process epitomizes the tenets of Williamson's transaction cost theory. There is some indication, however, that politics played some role in the decision. Both interpretations of FIRM4's decision are discussed.

Two people were interviewed for this case (see Table 4.6). James, manager of planning, was intimately involved in FIRM4's outsourcing decision. Matthew was not involved in the decision, but he wrote a report on FIRM4's outsourcing decision. Matthew's report was based on interviews with James, the director of FIRM4's corporate data center, the manager of telecommunications, the manager of data center operations, and the data center manager.

Table 4.6   *FIRM4 participants*

Name used in this case	Job title	Involvement in outsourcing
James	Corporate Manager of Planning & Administration	James was a member of the Steering Committee in Charge of the Outsourcing Evaluation.
Matthew	Manager of a Divisional Subsidiary of FIRM4	Matthew wrote a very thorough report on FIRM4's outsourcing decision.

4.4.1   Historical Background of FIRM4

FIRM4 is a Fortune 100 company that employs over 50 000 people in 60 countries. It is comprised of several operating divisions and produces oil, natural gas, and industrial chemicals. These operating divisions operate rather autonomously with minimal direction from FIRM4's corporate headquarters.

Financially, FIRM4 flourished during the 1960s, 1970s and much of the 1980s but ran into financial difficulties near the end of the 1980s. In 1990, senior management decided to cut their costs through the sale of assets, reduced headcount, and budget cuts. This set the stage for the information outsourcing decision.

4.4.2   FIRM4's Outsourcing Decision

Matthew, a divisional manager, claims that FIRM4 considered outsourcing as a way to reduce IS costs for three reasons. First, his management believed the propaganda that outsourcing could reduce IS costs by 25 to 50%. Second, he suspected that vendors had contacted the CEO and were offering him tremendous savings. Third, he states that management perceived that IS was costing them too much money, over $130 million per year.

4.4.2.1   FIRM4's Outsourcing Decision Process

The first step in the process was the creation of an outsourcing steering committee, comprised of the CFOs from the major divisions. The committee was chaired by the Director of IS, although he was forbidden to vote. James describes the committee's function:

> "The steering committee was assigned the responsibility for doing all of the analysis, review, whatever needed to be done, and then to

make a proposal to [FIRM4] senior management saying this is our recommendation: we should outsource and we should outsource using vendor X, or we should retain it in-house and here is why."

The steering committee decided to hire an outside consulting firm to help them develop a request for proposal (RFP). Committee members felt that the in-house IS group should not create the RFP since they were going to be asked to submit a bid. After the RFP was complete, the committee solicited bids from the internal IS department and three outsourcing vendors. James notes that the committee displayed no favoritism towards the internal IS bid:

"The internal bid committee was treated exactly like the outside vendors. They didn't have any information given to them that the others weren't given. They were to respond in the same length of time that the outside vendors were."

One vendor refused to bid because the scope of the outsourcing evaluation excluded applications support and development. One vendor, who will be referred to as Vendor A, submitted a bid that indicated a 32% saving in data processing costs. The other vendor's bid—Vendor B—submitted a bid that was actually 9% higher than current IS costs. The internal bid committee submitted a bid that reduced IS costs by 43%.

James explained the discrepancy in bid amounts. The internal bid committee was able to reduce costs by proposing to consolidate the three data centers into one. Vendor A proposed the same action, which is why its bid is commensurable with the internal bid. Vendor B proposed that FIRM4 dismantle all its data centers and run its systems through the vendor's data center. The cost to convert systems to Vendor B's center increased the price.

In addition to comparing costs, the steering committee also made a qualitative assessment of the bids based on nine factors, including the quality of service, contract flexibility, and control over technical decisions. For each factor, the bids were rated on a Likert scale with three choices: advantage over current operations, no advantage (i.e. equal to current operations), or disadvantage over current operations. FIRM4 emerged as the preferred candidate because it had the greatest cost advantage and no noted disadvantages. Vendor A and Vendor B were both deemed as disadvantages on the contract flexibility factor—the steering committee feared that all outsourcing contracts are too binding. In addition, Vendor A's culture clashed with FIRM4's culture, while Vendor B's costs were too high.

4.4.2.2   *Outcome and Consequences of FIRM4's Decision*

In the summer of 1990, the steering committee presented its recommendation to senior management: accept the internal bid. Senior management agreed, provided that the IS department consolidate the data centers within six months. The IS department actually managed to complete the task in four months.

One year after the outsourcing decision, James claims that the decision successfully met the objective to reduce costs. In 1990, the IS budget was $130 million. Since then, the budget was reduced to $108 million, representing a 17% saving. The savings were achieved by (a) the data center consolidation, (b) negotiating better hardware leases, and (c) a reduction in staff. One must note, however, that this 17% saving falls short of the bid amount that indicated over a 40% saving.

FIRM4's case is now analyzed from the political and transaction cost perspectives.

4.4.3   FIRM4's Decision from a Political Perspective

From a political perspective, one interpretation of FIRM4's outsourcing decision is this: FIRM4 evaluated outsourcing to empower the IS organization so that they could consolidate the data centers. Prior to the evaluation process, the IS department tried several times to consolidate the data centers. Its efforts failed, however, because the operating divisions refused to allow it. The outsourcing evaluation, spearheaded by the upper echelons of management, provided IS with the power and authority to collapse two of the data centers. James explains in the following excerpt:

> "The divisions didn't want to give up their own data centers. They weren't happy about it at the time either, but it was explained to them by [FIRM4] management that we were going to reduce costs, there was going to be one data center."

James, however, contends that the decision was not political. He claims that there was no hidden bias in favor of the internal bid committee:

> "If the Internal Bid Committee had come out higher than the outsourcer, we would be paying somebody to process data today."

Perhaps James' assessment is correct. However, the political indicants are worth exploring. When one considers IS's lack of power, it becomes evident that it could not reduce costs without threatening the divisions with outsourcing.

4.4.3.1 *Power*

As noted in the other cases, indicants of the IS department's power include authority and substitutability.

Authority: reporting level and senior management's view. As noted throughout the cases, the number of reporting levels the IS manager sits from the CEO is presumed to be an indicant of power. At FIRM4, the IS manager is three reporting levels from the CEO: the IS manager reports to the controller, the controller reports to the CFO, and the CFO reports to the CEO. Buried three levels from the CEO, the IS manager rarely interacts with him.

Perhaps a better indicant of power comes from James' description of the CEO's view of systems:

> "All they [senior management] see is this amount of money that they have to write a check for every year. Year after year after year. Where is the benefit? IS says, 'Well, we process data faster than we did last year.' They say, 'So what?' IS says, 'Well, we can close the ledger faster.' And they say, 'So what? Where have you increased revenue? All you do is increase costs, year after year after year and I am sick of it. All I get are these esoteric benefits and a bunch of baloney on how much technology has advanced. Show me where you put one more dollar on the income statement.'"

From this quotation, we see that FIRM4's IS does not appear to be strategically recognized by senior management—they view the entire department as a cost burden. James, however, feels IS does not deserve this reputation:

> "The IS organization have a tremendous amount to contribute if they ever get out of the back room and be perceived as having an opportunity to participate in the resolution of problems rather than being one of those problems."

Low substitutability. The political model assumes that low substitutability creates power because the organization has no other viable alternatives. In the case of FIRM4, since senior management seemed willing to outsource, they viewed the IS department as dispensable.

In summary, three indicants of power suggest the IS department is not powerful: reporting level, senior management's view of the

IS department, and its willingness to outsource. Given this lack of power, the IS department was unable to implement cost-saving measures because there was too much resistance from the operating divisions. Perhaps senior management used the threat of outsourcing to empower the IS department to implement changes. Although the steering committee's decision process seems to be unbiased and based primarily on an economic rationale, several tactics may have been enacted to sway the decision in the IS department's favor.

4.4.3.2   Political Tactics

James claims that the outsourcing evaluation was void of politics. He claims that the internal bid committee was treated the same as the external bids. However, there is one difference, the internal bid committee was familiar with FIRM4's costs while the external vendors were not privy to cost detail.

Selective use of information.   Selective use of information, in this case—selective dissemination of information—is a tactic for influencing the decision outcome. Cost data is extremely useful when establishing a bid price. Any bid-maker can find ways to chop a budget if he knows the budget amount. Since vendors were only given volume figures (i.e—we need X number of MIPs, DASD), they were at a disadvantage.

Use of outside experts.   Another interesting aside that James shared during the interview was that the consulting firm hired by the steering committee was biased against outsourcing. The consultants may have influenced some of the committee members' views on outsourcing:

> "If there was any group that was biased or prejudiced against outsourcing it was [the consultants], which was a bit unusual because they didn't have any vested interest one way or another. But they were very concerned based on what they had seen happen to other companies who outsourced...they had seen some people who had outsourced and were very, very disappointed."

Thus, there is at least the possibility that politics played some role in the outsourcing decision. In particular, the selective use of information and the use of "objective" outside experts may have slightly tempered the decision in favor of the internal bid. James, however, disagrees with this assessment:

"As far as anybody playing any games internally so that we could win, so that we could protect the turf, that did not happen. . .it was very objective and above board."

4.4.4   FIRM4's Decision from a Transaction Cost Perspective

Both James and Matthew feel that FIRM4's outsourcing decision was a rational, economically-motivated decision. Each claims that the financial improvement of the overall organization was the sole objective. Much evidence supports their decision, especially when one considers costs, transaction type, and the threat of opportunism.

4.4.4.1   Costs

The evidence to suggest that the transaction cost interpretation is valid includes (a) management's view that outsourcing reduces costs, (b) selection of the low cost alternative, and (c) actual cost reduction.

Because of the slump in profits, senior management needed to reduce costs throughout the organization. After reading about outsourcing in the trade literature and talking to a few vendors, it decided to investigate outsourcing. Since these preliminary sources indicated up to 40% savings, the investigation seemed well worth it.

Another indicant that suggests that the outsourcing decision was economically-motivated was that the low bid was accepted. (In other cases in our study, the low bid was not always selected.) If the steering committee wanted to minimize costs, then the bid data certainly points to the internal bid committee.

Perhaps the greatest indicant that the decision was economically motivated is the fact that IS costs were actually reduced. The outsourcing evaluation was more than just an exercise—real cost-saving measures were implemented. Besides consolidating the data center, James says savings were achieved through headcount reduction and cheaper hardware agreements:

"There were definite reductions in the number of people, obviously it doesn't take as many people to run one data center as to run three individual data centers. So there were people savings. We also negotiated a hardware lease on a five year basis."

4.4.4.2   *Transaction Type*

According to Williamson's theory, recurrent, non-specific transactions are more economically acquired through the market. Some
indicants suggest that FIRM4 viewed data processing in this light.
James, for example, describes processing needs as a homogeneous
product:

> "We projected what we felt our hardware processing needs would be,
> and we told the vendor that we don't care what color this equipment
> is, we don't care if it is new or old, this level of processing, we want
> these many MIPs and we want this much DASD."

FIRM4 seemed to want to retain applications because of the labor
asset specificity required of those functions. Since specific business
knowledge is required, a vendor may not provide equivalent
expertise. That is why, James claims, the scope of the decision was
limited to data processing:

> "We limited the proposal to only data center operations. One of the
> major reasons for that was that FIRM4's IS organization is firmly mature.
> In the [corporate office], their average number of years with FIRM4 is
> in excess of ten...[With outsourcing], the expertise is gone. On day
> one, they may still continue to serve our needs, but those folks are
> going to be placed where the vendor thinks is the best return. And I
> am not being critical—if I was doing it, I'd do the exact same thing."

From these quotes, we see that FIRM4 seemed to attend to
transaction type when determining decision scope. James sums up
the situation as such:

> "Well, the hardware and software was not that big a deal. It was more,
> you know, where do we get the people? You just can't go out and hire
> them off the street and hit the ground running."

4.4.4.3   *Threat of Opportunism*

According to Williamson, the threat of opportunism raises the costs
of buying transactions from the market. FIRM4 appears to concur.
Another reason that the internal bid was preferred over Vendor
A's bid was the potential cost of attempting to terminate the
contract. James notes:

> "Another concern we had was that if we did a five year deal say, what
> happens at the end of the five years? If we don't get along well, or we
> want it back and we had transferred the people, then we are in a real

bad situation. . .One of the things that made the dollars greater for that bid [Vendor A] was for what they were going to charge for termination of the contract before the end."

In summary, the transaction cost perspective corresponds well with James' and Matthew's view on the subject. Participants initiated the decision to reduce costs. They attended to transaction type to determine decision scope. They measured costs and considered the impact of the threat of opportunism on those costs. Finally, they selected the low cost solution and successfully reduced the budget by $22 million. The textbook case—or is it?

4.4.5   FIRM4—Conclusion

The analysis of FIRM4's outsourcing decision from a political and economic viewpoint yields two interpretations.

The political lens offers the story of a powerless, ineffectual IS department that failed to collapse data centers because the opposition from the operating divisions was too great. Once senior management supported the idea and legitimated it through the outsourcing evaluation, IS succeeded in consolidating the data centers and reducing costs. Furthermore, the internal IS department was bound to submit the lowest bid since it had access to cost data that the others did not.

From a transaction cost perspective, we see the epitome of an economically-motivated, rational decision. They hired an outside consultant to develop the RFP. They generated two alternatives: make or buy. They calculated quantitative and qualitative data for each alternative. They selected the low cost solution: keep data processing in-house. Furthermore, they succeeded in actually reducing costs. Perhaps the most poignant evidence is James' testimony that the decision was unbiased and that no game-playing took place.

Both case participants would highly object to the political analysis of their company's decision. Recall when James was asked about the political interpretation, he adamantly denied it: "It absolutely was not [political]. It was real. It was very real. If the Internal Bid Committee had come out higher than the outsourcer, we would be paying somebody to process data today."

Yet James seemed pressured to tell the corporate version of the evaluation, rather than sharing his own impressions. Over an hour into the interview, James finally articulated his personal feelings about outsourcing, noting that these feelings did not temper his investigation:

"From a purely historical, personal, un-objective viewpoint, say hey, finally we have an opportunity to show these guys that we haven't done such a bad job after all. Give it to the outsourcing company. Let them escalate costs—which is what they are going to do...And it would have been easy for us to say, 'Hey you think you are paying too much now, let them save you 25% because in three years I guarantee you, you are going to be bleeding bad.'"

James offers one final thought on FIRM4's decision process:

"I think that given the situation that we were in at FIRM4, that we did the right thing. I don't say that from any kind of personal or career benefit. I truly believe it was the right decision. I worked myself out of a job by restructuring the organization to meet the dollar amount that we had to meet."

4.5   FIRM5

Before getting in to the outsourcing decision at FIRM5, it is appropriate for us to mention a discussion we had with a former outsourcing vendor who shared her views on bid solicitations. She stated that her company did not seriously consider bid requests initiated by IS managers, claiming that IS managers requested bids for two reasons: to get a free efficiency assessment, or to protect their senior managers from outsourcing vendors. When the vendor did indicate savings, the IS manager often implemented cost reductions himself without the assistance of the vendor. The practice was so common that the vendor started charging IS managers $20 000 to submit a bid.

At FIRM5, the former director of information systems claimed he initiated the outsourcing evaluation to see if he could reduce costs. There is, indeed, evidence to support his claim. Upon closer scrutiny, however, a second interpretation arises—the outsourcing evaluation may subscribe to the "free corroboration" strategy discussed above. Each interpretation is discussed in the forthcoming analysis.

Three people were interviewed at FIRM5 Headquarters (see Table 4.7): Thomas, the Assistant Treasurer; Adam, the Director of IS; and Peter, the Manager of Technical Support. The current Assistant Treasurer, who previously held the title of Director of Information Services, initiated FIRM5's outsourcing evaluation.

The case begins with a brief background of FIRM5's operations and the changing role of the IS department over the past five years.

Table 4.7 FIRM5 participants

Name used in this case	Job title	Involvement in outsourcing
Thomas	Assistant Treasurer	Thomas was formerly the Director of Information Systems. When he held that position, he initiated the outsourcing evaluation.
Adam	Director of Information Systems	Adam was formerly Assistant Treasurer. When he held that position, he provided the financial analysis for the outsourcing evaluation.
Peter	Manager of Technical Support	Peter provided the technical data to the outsourcing vendors.

4.5.1 Historical Background of FIRM5

In 1985, FIRM5 operated four, semi-autonomous companies. Each operating company had its own IS group that ran its own data centers and developed its own applications. These decentralized IS groups had a dotted line relationship to the corporate director of information services. The corporate IS director tried—unsuccessfully—to enforce standards on these IS groups. Since these operating groups were powerful, they ignored his commands. As a result, the corporate IS director could not easily consolidate information to satisfy corporate reporting needs.

In order to gain some control over the decentralized IS groups, the corporate IS director convinced senior management that FIRM5 could save money by consolidating the data centers. In 1986, the operating companies reluctantly packed their equipment and shipped it to their new corporate data center. The results of this data center consolidation were disastrous. Thomas explains the plummet in system availability:

"Now that was horrible because the service levels were absolutely terrible. We were down everyday. The solution to the problem was to IPL the system up there, so they go through the process of bringing the machine up. So we were down for hours each day, and we never could get a better level of service than that."

The corporate IS director lost all credibility and was promptly removed from that position.

Senior management's attention to Information Systems was quickly diverted in 1987 when a corporate raider attempted to take over the company. After a tumultuous process, the investment bankers agreed to strip FIRM5 of two of its profitable companies, leaving FIRM5 with the remaining two operating companies.

The impact of the break-up on Information Systems provided an opportunity for FIRM5 to start fresh. Since the newly formed company acquired the old data center, FIRM5 was free to build a data center at its new company headquarters. FIRM5's senior management hired Thomas as director of information services. In the course of six months, Thomas bought a mainframe, hired technical support and computer operations personnel, and moved analysts to headquarters. By the end of 1987, Thomas managed twenty-five IS professionals.

From the years 1987 through 1990, FIRM5 prospered as a company. Sales grew steadily primarily accomplished through acquisitions. Despite the financial success of the company, Thomas had trouble acquiring IS resources to meet increasing user demand. He said senior management viewed information systems as a cost burden and was therefore reluctant to invest in information technology. Thomas explains:

> "We have a philosophy at FIRM5 that information systems is here just to do data processing. So, needless to say, whenever I would go in and say, 'I need to upgrade the mainframe, we need to add staff, DASD,' it went over like a lead balloon. I experienced that in 1987, 1988, and 1989."

Thomas grew increasingly frustrated. In particular, he was having tremendous difficulties trying to meet the enormous demand for applications with his limited staff:

> "On the application side, we just couldn't get the job done. The backlog was growing and growing. We were looking at automation tools, CASE tools and such, but we didn't have the people to put on projects. We didn't even have dollars in the budget to have consultants come in and do it. So we were getting in a real crack. It started to build and build. Pretty soon we were at a pretty high level of frustration. I was struggling with the fact that I was in a position of allocating resources to all the different groups and I didn't have enough to go around."

In 1990, Thomas's frustration culminated in an executive meeting. At this meeting, Thomas proposed two things: (1) evaluate outsourcing the data center, and (2) reorganize the IS department so that users have control over their own IS resources. This meeting commenced FIRM5's outsourcing decision.

4.5.2 FIRM5's Outsourcing Decision

Thomas explains the two proposals he submitted to senior management:

> "I recommended that we evaluate outsourcing. The next recommendation I made was that we split applications development up, throw away the central information groups, and we left each of the five group executives who are responsible for the functional units, like we have marketing, manufacturing, supply, and distribution. Let each of those managers take the applications people that were currently working for them. Each gets their own resources."

Thomas claims that his proposal "got everybody's attention real quick." The executives were surprised that Thomas wanted to dismantle his kingdom. They asked him, "Why are you doing this?" Thomas explained:

> "I said, 'I cannot get any support from you all in how to allocate these resources. And we cannot be the traffic cop in this whole process because it is not right.' I said, 'I'm trying to satisfy everybody and it's not working.' So did that help? Since then, I've been to two officer meetings, so I guess it did."

Senior executives worried that outsourcing would result in the same service horrors they experienced when they shared their former data center, but they agreed to let Thomas evaluate the option. The executives did not, however, accept Thomas's second recommendation. They feared that a decentralized IS department would increase their IS expenditures. They agreed, instead, to support Thomas's allocation decisions. Thomas notes:

> "I had their attention now. And so some of the people who were bashing us backed off. Their group executives now tell their users, 'Back off, they are doing what they can.' So we got some relief there."

4.5.2.1 FIRM5's Outsourcing Decision Process

At first, Thomas attempted a unique outsourcing option that he thought would make his company famous. He called the IS director of another local company and suggested that they share a data center. Since FIRM5 and this company both needed to upgrade, Thomas thought they could split the costs of buying a larger machine. Thomas describes the futility of his efforts:

> "Those discussions never went very far because we always got into a big control issue. It was more of an ego issue that prevented us from doing something that could have gotten us a lot of press."

Discouraged by his entrepreneurial failure, Thomas turned to a more traditional outsourcing process. First, he contracted two vendors with whom he was familiar and requested bids for operating FIRM5's data center. Second, he delegated the task of gathering technical data for the bids to his Manager of Technical Support, Peter. Third, he asked Adam, then Assistant Treasurer, to run the financial analysis. After steps one through three, Thomas stepped out of the process. He explains why:

> "I tried to stay out of those meetings [with the vendors] as much as possible. I let Peter and the manager of computer operations meet with the vendor because I wanted it to be their project. I had initiated it and set it up, but I didn't want it to be my project. I wanted it to be their project."

Peter says he gave the two vendors all the technical data about hardware and software requirements. He also gave them SMF reports which measure the amount of resources each job execution requires. Peter says the vendors also asked for cost data. He gave them the 1990 first quarter budget, but decided not to provide them with additional financial data:

> "They were asking for data that had to do with our bottom line. And we didn't give them that data because we saw the situation as if we really wanted to get this bid of what it would take to get this job. We felt that they were in a position that if we gave them our total budget, they would back into a number."

Based on the 1990 first quarter budget, one outsourcing vendor submitted a bid that claimed to save FIRM5 over $3 million over the duration of the proposed five-year contract. Peter, however, claims that this bid was not valid because the vendor assumed the quarterly budget was indicative of the annual budget. Thus, the outsourcing vendor multiplied the quarterly budget by a factor of four to determine an annual budget. Peter claims that this was not a valid assumption since, "the numbers fluctuated significantly." He stated that his five-year budget projections showed that outsourcing would not save FIRM5 money. The second vendor declined to submit a bid. Thomas says:

> "They looked at our budget figures and came back and said, 'we cannot save you money. Now if your service levels were terrible and your operations were in a shambles, we'd bring something to the table. We know your operations and you are okay, so we don't even want to propose.'"

After analyzing the one bid, Peter terminated the outsourcing evaluation in the summer of 1990. Thomas promptly accepted Peter's recommendation to maintain the function internally.

4.5.2.2   *Outcome and Consequences of FIRM5's Decision*

Two consequences of the decision are noteworthy. First, Thomas acquired funds for his hardware upgrade. Second, Thomas gained recognition from the chairman that increased his credibility as a corporate player. Thomas explained that he wrote a memo to the chairman of the board to inform him of the decision. Thomas says his memo basically said:

> "We've evaluated this now, there is no economic benefit to the company for doing outsourcing right now. Similar levels of service would cost us more money. I recommend we conclude the evaluation."

Thomas says the chairman wrote a reply that said, "I agree, thanks for your efforts." Surprisingly, no changes in data processing occurred as a result of the outsourcing study. Given that the outsourcing evaluation was conducted to save money, it is rather curious that no cost-reduction measures were identified. Peter made the following comment:

> "As a result of having done this study, there is no difference now than if we had not done the study."

4.5.3   FIRM5's Decision from a Political Perspective

From the political perspective, one can interpret Thomas's decision as a defensive maneuver. Although Thomas claims that his senior management was not considering outsourcing, several vendors were already courting FIRM5's chairman. Since Thomas has little political clout within FIRM5, he may have initiated the outsourcing decision to eliminate the outsourcing option from senior management's agenda. The issue of power is addressed first.

4.5.3.1 Power of FIRM5's IS Department

FIRM5's IS department possesses very little power since senior management views information systems as an overhead cost. They do not willingly invest in new technology nor do they inform IS about their business strategies.

Senior management's view of information systems. All three participants expressed the view that senior management do not value information systems. Thomas, for example, explains:

> "FIRM5 does not have a desire to be a leader from a technological standpoint. We merely see systems as a way to process data. Competitive advantage and things like that did not enter into the reason for data processing, people don't see it as a tool for that."

Thomas tried to improve senior management's view of information systems. When he was in charge of the IS department, he was able to generate revenue by selling a credit card system to other competitors. Adam notes, however, that this initiative was not enough to sway management opinion:

> "Strategically though, as far as that goes, we are still considered a support function, a cost center. We are not considered a profit center even though we have the [credit card system] operation. It's not significant enough, say, as compared to refining and marketing operations."

On a brighter note, FIRM5's CEO did attend a CEO forum on information systems for competitive advantage sponsored by IBM. Both Thomas and Adam consider this a significant symbol that senior management may rethink their position on information systems.

Resource acquisition: failure to invest in new technology. Thomas expressed that he had difficulty acquiring funds to invest in new technology. In early 1990, for example, he was having difficulty in convincing management to upgrade the mainframe. Thomas claims one reason he initiated an outsourcing evaluation was to find a way to upgrade the mainframe:

"The next required upgrade takes you into a new series of processors and you increase your expenses significantly when you do that. So, what I was looking for, I was looking for a way to avoid that next huge increase in expense."

Because Thomas has little power, he has to lobby for every additional dollar.

Information systems lack of involvement in planning. Another indicant of the IS department's lack of power is that Thomas is not involved in corporate planning. In most cases, he is not even informed of strategies until they are already implemented. This makes his job difficult to effectively execute since he is constantly reacting rather than proacting. He describes one example that illustrates the problem:

"You know these acquisitions I told you we were doing? You know, they would tell us the day before the contract was signed and say, 'You need to do these people's data processing starting Monday.' I'd say, 'Give me a break. Where am I going to get people to do this?'"

Thus, it is evident that FIRM5's IS department possess little power. Given this absence of power, Thomas may have initiated the outsourcing evaluation as a tactic to prevent outsourcing.

4.5.3.2 Political Tactics

At the beginning of the interview, Thomas was asked whether his senior management had ever considered outsourcing. He responded: "No." Yet, later in the interview, Thomas was asked whether his chairman of the board would listen to a plea from an outsourcing vendor. He listed three vendors that had already approached the chairman. Thomas went on to explain the CEO's reaction to the vendors' sales calls:

"I'll tell you what he would do. He'd say, 'go talk to Thomas.' He did it many times. He'd say, 'Go talk to Thomas, he's our IS guy.'"

Peter notes that Thomas was prudent to look at outsourcing because it is inevitable that all organizations will evaluate IS outsourcing:

"I really got the impression that the impetus to evaluate outsourcing came from Thomas. His comments were that this was something that was going on in the industry. So, I really felt that we did that mainly because we felt that we would be in a position where the question would be raised about doing that. I felt that Thomas wanted to be in a position where he could say, 'We've already done that.' He wanted to be proactive rather than reactive."

From a political perspective, Thomas's actions can be viewed as a defensive maneuver. Thomas employed the tactic of selective use of decision alternatives by limiting the scope of the decision to a function he knows is already efficient. In addition, he delegated the task to an individual who would lose his job if FIRM5 outsourced. His laissez-faire attitude during the decision process may be indicative that he was really not interested in outsourcing.

Selective use of decision alternatives. Thomas limited the scope of the outsourcing decision to mainframe data processing—a function that is already cost-efficient. By his own admission, the service was great, the costs were low, and senior management was prejudiced against remote data centers ever since their earlier experience. Thomas explains the data processing service during the time of the outsourcing study:

"We were running the CPU with 99% availability, less than two second response time all the time, less than 1% response time 90% of the time. We were providing a great level of computing service."

In addition to excellent service, Thomas explains that data center costs were very low:

"We knew that we were running efficiently. We had low lease rents on our processors. We don't have a large staff. There are four people on our tech support group. We weren't spending an incredible amount."

Indeed, the data processing budget was only one fourteenth of Thomas's IS operating budget. Given these figures, it seems unlikely that a vendor could provide less expensive services.

Peter claims that Thomas also stacked the deck against outsourcing by making the decision to keep a particular computer system which is used to operate the laser printer. Peter explains the ramifications of this decision:

"Because Thomas made the statement that the system was going to stay. We weren't going to outsource that. Well, if you do that, you need to have operators. If you run three shifts a day, then you have three shifts of operators. So all of a sudden, we weren't eliminating operations staff."

Thus, Thomas selectively decided to limit the scope of outsourcing to a very narrow portion of his department—the portion that he knew was already efficient. Thomas did not consider outsourcing applications support or development, the two functions that were most ineffective. When Thomas was asked, "Why did you want to outsource what you were doing well and keeping what you were having trouble with?", he replied:

> "I feel that the service level has to be provided internally from an applications standpoint."

Delegation to a biased party. During the discussion of the FIRM1 case, delegation to a biased party was identified as another political tactic. At FIRM5, we saw that Thomas delegated the entire data gathering task to Peter and Peter's subordinate because he claimed he wanted it to be their project. When Thomas was asked how Peter could be objective, given he might lose his job, Thomas responded:

> "They didn't want it to happen, but if they were going to save us a bundle of money, they would let it happen."

Peter was asked, "Were you under the impression that if you outsourced you would leave FIRM5 or help manage the contract?" Peter responded: "I didn't know what my fate was going to be." He admitted that he was in an awkward position but explained that he had worked on many projects that could have potentially eliminated his job. This seasoned employee had the following philosophy towards the outsourcing evaluation:

> "So yeah, it's awkward in that respect, the other respect is that having gone through that experience, I was not about to relinquish control of my life. I was going to see where things led, where the opportunities were."

The situation remains rather curious, however, that Thomas delegated the task to Peter when outsourcing would eliminate his position.

To summarize, the political perspective offers a lens for interpreting Thomas's actions. Consider that Thomas knew (a) outsourcers were knocking at the door, (b) he needed money for a hardware upgrade, and (c) his data processing function was already providing an excellent, low cost service. Given the circumstances, one interpretation of Thomas's behaviour is that he subscribed to the "free corroboration" strategy discussed in the introduction. By soliciting bids for a function he already knows is efficient, he gathers documented proof that he is doing a good job. He is thus better able to justify additional funding when he needs to upgrade technology. From this perspective, Thomas's political savvy paid off—his management gave him the dollars to upgrade the mainframe.

4.5.4 FIRM5's Decision from a Transaction Cost Perspective

The transaction cost perspective assumes that managers are motivated to select the most cost-efficient alternatives by attending to transaction types, costs, and the threat of opportunism.

4.5.4.1 *Transaction Type*

From the political perspective, Thomas was accused of limiting the scope of the outsourcing evaluation to a function that was already efficient. From a transaction cost perspective, Thomas's decision can be viewed as prudent, since non-specific, recurrent transactions are often more efficiently produced by a vendor. Thomas stated that he viewed data processing as a utility:

> "I needed to determine what was the most cost-effective way to deliver computer resources to the company. Our outsourcing evaluation was limited to evaluation of the processor. And receiving the service much like when you flip on a light switch and get electricity."

Thus, Thomas may have chosen to limit the scope of the decision to data processing since he views it as a utility. As such, third parties theoretically can provide a lower cost service due to economies of scale.

4.5.4.2 *Costs*

If Thomas was following the tenets of transaction cost theory, his motivation for evaluating outsourcing would have been to provide the most cost-efficient service for his company. He notes:

> "As good corporate citizens, we were trying to do what was right. If the economics made it a good decision and we could ensure an equivalent level of service, we would have done it."

Adam corroborates that Thomas's only motive was to reduce costs. He was rather impressed with Thomas's actions:

> "It was interesting to me that an IS department was investigating this kind of process. I thought that was foresighted on his part. From what I heard, a person in his position typically would not have done that. That is really a threat to job security. And Thomas knew that to be the case. He said, 'Hey, this is my job but I need to take a look at this.'"

4.5.4.3 *Threat of Opportunism*

Transaction cost theory stipulates that outsourcing could increase costs if the vendor takes advantage of the client. This, however, did not seem to concern Thomas. He felt that the two vendors he solicited bids from were reputable. Therefore, he did not fear that either vendor would opportunistically take advantage of FIRM5 if a contract was signed.

Adam and Peter, however, were more reluctant about trusting the vendors. Adam expressed doubts about the believability of vendor bids:

> "If you are 100% confident in what they tell is true, great. But if you have any doubts about that, then you take a leap of faith."

Peter was more concerned about outsourcing after a contract was signed. He felt that an outsourcing vendor would not be motivated to contain growth. Since the vendor would generate extra revenue by selling additional MIPS and DASD, Peter felt that the vendor might encourage uncontrollable growth. Other than that, the managers at FIRM5 did not believe that vendor opportunism was a significant threat.

In summary, the transaction cost perspective offers a different interpretation of Thomas's actions. As a good corporate citizen, he was trying to reduce costs for his company. He was confident that he would not be punished for such noble efforts:

> "You know I didn't feel any risk that I personally would be out on the streets. Okay? That probably has something to do with it. I mean, I'd be lying to you if I thought I would be unemployed. But it was a great job. Lord knows what the next job would be. But, if you can go in and show something that is clearly right for the company, I don't see that anyone is going to punish you for that. So that was in the back of my mind. But first and foremost was, 'Hey we are spending a lot of money

on this, and we still continue to spend a lot of money on this in years to come.'"

4.5.5 FIRM5—Conclusion

In the case of FIRM5, we see that Thomas himself cites multiple motivations for initiating the outsourcing decision. During the course of the interview, he stated three reasons for initiating the outsourcing decision. First, he says he did it because he was frustrated over the lack of support he was receiving about allocating his limited staff to competing systems projects:

"Why did we do it? I mean that is the issue. There was a level of frustration that we were all feeling—that had something to do with it. . .The frustration came out in the meeting because we came down nose-to-nose. They said, 'Why are you doing this?' I said, 'I cannot get any support from you all in how to allocate these resources. And we cannot be the traffic cop in this whole process because it is not right.' I said, 'I'm trying to satisfy everybody and it's not working.'"

Second, he states he was sincerely trying to make an economical decision:

"As good corporate citizens, we were trying to do what was right. If the economics made it a good decision and we could ensure an equivalent level of service, we would have done it."

Third, he was trying to figure out how to upgrade the hardware and thought outsourcing might be an alternative:

"So what I was looking for, I was looking for a way to avoid that next huge increase in expense."

In Thomas's mind, there is no doubt that his intentions were both politically and economically motivated. It is also interesting to note how others perceive Thomas's behavior.

Adam perceives a rational decision process, motivated by the need to reduce costs. He was so impressed with Thomas's outsourcing decision that he plans to initiate his own outsourcing investigation in the future:

"The repercussions of this exercise are that I suspect we will go through this exercise in another year or two, just to make sure that we are cost competitive. Maybe to highlight again that the area may not be as efficient as it could be. If we find out that we can do it cheaper outside, we have to seriously consider that option."

Peter, on the other hand, viewed the entire outsourcing evaluation as a political exercise:

"It really came down to an exercise. We did not try to make outsourcing work. What we were really trying to do was to come up with the justification for why we shouldn't outsource. That's what it boiled down to."

In the case of FIRM5, no one interpretation of the outsourcing evaluation stands out. Thomas may have initiated a political decision or he may have sincerely been trying to reduce costs. In his mind, the decision possessed elements of both. Of course one might question how both theories can generate useful interpretations. The response is this: human motivations and behaviors appear to be complex—even paradoxical. Thus, a single theory cannot provide enough richness to capture the entire picture.

4.6 FIRM6

FIRM6 is the first case presented in this report where the company decided to outsource. In early 1991, FIRM6 signed a ten-year contract that encompasses data processing and telecommunications. Thus far, FIRM6 is pleased with its decision. Managers involved in the decision stress the importance of negotiating an airtight contract. They admonish that the vendor should not necessarily be trusted to perform. Therefore, all pertinent obligations must be specified prior to signing the contract. By agreeing to services, service levels, performance measures, and penalties for non-performance in the contract, companies can protect themselves from the threat of opportunism on the part of the outsourcing vendor. The lesson learned from this case is that companies who want to outsource better play hardball if they want to win in the outsourcing game.

Three of FIRM6's managers involved in the decision were interviewed for this case (see Table 4.8). The outsourcing consultant that FIRM6 hired to negotiate the contract was also interviewed.

4.6.1 Historical Background of FIRM6

The crisis in the banking industry during the past decade is well documented. Many banks became insolvent when third world

Table 4.8 FIRM6 participants

Name used in this case	Job title	Involvement in outsourcing
Janet	VP and Director of IS	In charge of the outsourcing decision.
Chuck	Financial Manager	Provided the financial analysis.
Frank	Manager of IS Group	Monitors the outsourcing contract.
Stephen	Consultant	Helped negotiate the contract.

countries' debts went unrequited. When the recession halted housing starts and closed businesses, even more financial institutions closed their doors. FIRM6 survived the turbulence in national and international economies, although it suffered several years of meager earnings. Although FIRM6 managed to do reasonably well in 1989, earnings once again plummeted in 1990. The CEO's annual letter to the stockholders pledged to implement a "Corporation-wide cost reduction program which includes staff and expense cutbacks in virtually every department." Chuck, the IS department's Financial Manager, confirms that the squeeze is evident to all FIRM6 employees:

> "The bank has had a tough couple of years here. There are no pay increases, health insurance went up 50%, education reimbursement was cut in half, people are going out the door left and right. We've had 30% turnover this year so far."

For the past several years, FIRM6's senior management has gone into survival mode. Budgets were slashed in each department. Jack, the Senior Vice President of Operations, was among the department heads who needed to decide where costs could be reduced. He turned to his IS organization to determine if outsourcing could provide some relief. This is where Janet, the VP and Director of IS, enters the story.

4.6.2 FIRM6's Outsourcing Decision

Janet has been with the bank since 1987. She moved into operations as the Director of IS in 1990. According to Janet, her boss, Jack, began to investigate outsourcing earlier that same year. She feels that Jack was looking at outsourcing because as a practice, it was becoming quite popular in the banking industry. Janet notes:

"So he really felt, and I think quite correctly, that outsourcing was something people were talking about. Other organizations had done it, especially in banks, that were the same size as us, and he felt that this was a question that he was going to be asked. That says, 'you better tell me why or why not to outsource.' And that was what really stimulated his curiosity."

Janet claims that Jack was not predisposed for or against outsourcing. She says, "He didn't know, he really didn't know, and he wasn't on any particular timetable." He was willing to outsource if savings were realized.

4.6.2.1 *FIRM6's Outsourcing Decision Process*

Janet describes the steps Jack took before she was transferred to the IS department. The first thing Jack did was to hire an outside consulting company to come into FIRM6 to determine the efficiency of its computer operations. The results of this study were (a) there was no money to be saved on the applications side and (b) the data center shop was outdated and needed to be upgraded. Janet comments on the consultant's findings:

"They basically said that you run a great shop if this was fifteen years earlier. There are a tremendous amount of things that you don't take advantage of, including automation in the data center, balancing your hardware so that your processor and your storage are the same technology. And really exploit the stuff you have on the floor and use it. And they said that they felt that we could have done it all ourselves, here are the things you need to do to do that."

After that study, Jack began to have some conversations with a major outsourcing vendor. He was only interested in outsourcing the data center, which was 80% of its operating budget. He felt that his applications staff was extremely effective. In fact, FIRM6's staff is often contracted to develop systems for the Treasury Department of the United States. This particular vendor, however, was only interested in the deal if the entire IS department was outsourced.

Jack also contacted another outsourcing vendor, but this vendor only supports companies that use its software. Finally, he turned to the consulting company that performed the efficiency study. This company is very large and has recently entered into the outsourcing market. Janet and Jack did not prepare a formal request for proposal (RFP). Janet notes:

> "His intuition was—unlike most of those [companies that outsource]— he didn't want to go into a big RFP, getting all the vendors to come in. It sort of clashes with our corporate culture."

Negotiations began in mid 1990 but were halted when FIRM6 assumed a failed savings and loan. The entire IS staff was devoted to integrating the savings and loan into their current systems. Later in 1990, negotiations resumed. This is when Janet took over the major responsibility for the outsourcing project. Janet and the vendor spent one entire month defining the scope of the contract. She felt that the vendor only wanted to assume the most lucrative pieces of the business. She describes the situation: "In their initial proposal, they did what I call 'pear-picking' which is going after the things they liked." She finally put together "sort of an RFP" which states what services the vendor was required to resume in order for the deal to materialize.

After the vendor and Janet agreed on the services, she hired a lawyer and a consultant, both experts in outsourcing, to help her negotiate the contract. Chuck, the Financial Manager, was also very involved in negotiations. Chuck notes:

> "And that's when Janet and I and the attorneys sat down every day for three solid months of drafting up the agreement, negotiating the terms, conditions, and services."

They used October, November, and December of 1990 as the baseline period. During this time, FIRM6's current service levels were assessed to establish a base for evaluating the vendor's service level. Statistics were gathered for such services as batch turnaround, system availability, system response time, network performance, and number of print lines. These baseline measures were included in the contract. The vendor is obligated to meet or exceed the current level of service.

An unexpected problem loomed over contract negotiations in early 1991. A major software vendor sent FIRM6 a bill for $500 000 to transfer its software licenses over to the outsourcing vendor. Chuck ignored the bill because "we never had a contract with them." The software vendor then threatened to shut down the bank. Chuck tells the story this way:

> "We called our attorneys. Our attorneys called their attorneys. Ours said, 'How dare you threaten to shut down a national bank. You think

you can shut down a national bank?! I think you better call a bunch more attorneys if you are going to do that stuff.' But that was a very difficult ten day period for me—after they sent us that shut down letter. Our attorneys sent a real tough letter back. Finally, [the software vendor] said, 'I think we better go over and see these people.' Thursday morning they came in and it was a shouting match back and forth. And they said, 'We don't have to put up with this.' And they got up and left. Their attorney called me the next day and apologized for their marketers. 'Sensitivity to customer needs' and all that stuff. The next week we negotiated from $500 000 down to $110 000."

That was in March 1991. FIRM6 sent the bill to its outsourcing vendor. (Janet had a clause in the contract making the outsourcing vendor liable for any transfer fees.) Two weeks later, the software vendor announced its new policy: customers that outsource will not be charged transfer fees. However, the software vendor still expected its $110 000. The outsourcing vendor and the software vendor are still battling that issue.

4.6.2.2 Outcome and Consequences of FIRM6's Decision

In the midst of that crisis, FIRM6 and the outsourcing vendor signed a ten-year contract. The vendor purchased FIRM6's information assets for several million dollars. The entire deal was worth between one and two hundred million dollars. Chuck estimates that the bank will save 15 to 18%, depending on the calculations. Janet is confident FIRM6 will realize the savings because of the tight contract she negotiated.

Her outsourcing contract is unique in two ways. First, she pays for one thing: CPU minutes. Most outsourcing vendors charge for every processing component such as CPU minutes, tape mounts, DASD storage, etc. She did not want all these separate items because:

> "You've got to have a lot of people to manage that [if you get charged for every resource] to make sure that they are counting all of that stuff right."

Second, she was also this vendor's first client who succeeded in getting a cash penalty clause in the contract for non-performance. Cash penalties are defined for failure to meet the performance standards for response time, batch delivery deadlines, and availability. These cash penalties give Janet confidence that the vendor will meet its performance standards.

The long term consequences of this decision are difficult to assess.

When asked if there had been any major problems with the vendor, Janet indicates, no:

> "Not really. Just because I was intimately involved in the process. And we have been able to use the contract as a vehicle to resolve disputes. So far we haven't had to pop anything up to these so called committees that were created."

The only point of contention thus far has been the issue of reporting on computer utilization. Currently, the vendor is using IBM's RMF data, but these reports fail to separate system-oriented computer use from application-oriented computer use. Janet used the contract to show that the vendor must use SMF data, which separates system and application numbers.

Janet does admit that she may be overly optimistic about the deal. Thus far, the transition has been smooth, but the vendor is still processing FIRM6's data from its old data center. Janet anticipates the level of service will not be degraded when the vendor relocates the data center elsewhere which they will do at some point in time. However, she did express some trepidation:

> "This is also the honeymoon year. You interview me in a year and I probably will feel different. I don't think I'll be negative, but you got to give the deal a go, and we are only six months into it."

Frank, the manager in charge of monitoring the contract, warns that "just because you outsource, doesn't mean you are let off the hook from managing the service." He is determined to make the deal work and to realize the savings. He will manage a team of "performance system tuners" who determine run time improvements. This function is crucial since outsourcing vendors are "not rewarded for saving you money."

Janet offers a final comment on the risk of outsourcing: "I'm not worried about the operational risk. . .the biggest risk is that something is going to happen in technology that we did not adequately describe. And we'll wake up in four or five years and want something different."

The outsourcing decision is now evaluated from the political and transaction cost perspectives. In this case, the transaction cost theory offers a better description of the process than the political model. In particular, Jack and Janet's attention to savings and opportunism fit rather well into Williamson's theory of organizational decision-making.

4.6.3   FIRM6's Decision from a Political Perspective

Although the evidence overwhelmingly suggests that Janet's out-sourcing decision was economically motivated, there are several political issues that may have influenced the decision. In particular, her lack of power prevented her from implementing cost-saving measures on her own. Thus, her only feasible alternative was outsourcing. But here too, she used at least one political tactic to convince her management that outsourcing was the best alternative for FIRM6. The analysis begins with the issue of power.

4.6.3.1   Power of FIRM6's IS Department

The core concept of power is the ability to influence decisions. When a decision requires changes to corporate culture, significant power is required to successfully implement the decision. In the case of FIRM6, Janet lacked the power to initiate changes on her own that would save her company money. Stephen, the outsourcing consultant, was the only person interviewed who discussed the issue of power in relation to Janet's decision.

Stephen had no doubt that FIRM6's superordinate goal was to reduce costs since "there isn't a bank in the United States that isn't in trouble." When Stephen was asked if the outsourcing vendor could really provide services cheaper than FIRM6, he replied:

> "If you are saying, what can they do—and one of the conclusions that we come to is that there is very little that an outsourcer is going to do that you couldn't do yourself. The question is: Can you do it? And it's not physically can you do it, it's politically can you do it?"

From Janet's prior quotation on the consultant's assessment of the data center, we learn that the consulting firm believed that FIRM6 had the ability to upgrade the data center and to implement cost-saving measures on its own. In other words, FIRM6 did not need an outsourcer to instigate change. This then raises the question: "Why did FIRM6 not consider doing it themselves?" Stephen, again, feels that the political climate prevented Janet from successfully changing the data processing procedures to be more efficient. In particular, he felt that significant dollar savings could be achieved if Janet had implemented a chargeback system.

Stephen claims it is difficult to contain costs without a chargeback system because users view the services as free. For example, every time a user calls a FIRM6 analyst to change a program, the request is granted. Stephen notes that this is extremely expensive, but the concept of "monthly releases" could not be implemented at FIRM6 without opposition. He does not fault Janet for using the outsourcing option to achieve cost savings. From his experiences, IS directors do not have enough power to implement changes without senior management support:

> "I don't want to shoot the IS directors—they may very well want to do it [implement cost saving measures], but they are not in authority to do so. The philosophy of the company doesn't dictate that the shops be run that way."

Thus, Stephen's opinion of Janet's outsourcing decision is that she could not overcome the corporate culture to implement cost cuts on her own. Janet counters that in order to save money in the long run, she would have had to invest money up front. Given the financial situation, she had little hope for acquiring these funds.

Even though she felt that outsourcing was the best alternative for FIRM6, she was not totally politically naive. She realized that she had to sell the idea of outsourcing to her senior management. Early on, she built coalitions—an effective tactic for influencing a decision outcome.

4.6.3.2 *Political Tactics*

Building coalitions. Janet and her boss had to sell the idea of outsourcing to her senior management. Very early on, she started building coalitions to support the outsourcing decision. She describes her strategy as follows:

> "One of the things we did very early on, including last summer and spring, is that the key executives got involved in this. That was the president of the bank, the vice chairman, the treasurer of the bank—which is like a CFO type position—and the manager of retail who is an enormous user of our services such as ATMs and branch automation. Early on there was some opposition in those areas."

When asked who opposed outsourcing, Janet replied:

> "Interestingly, the CFO. He was very skeptic. He and the retail people, their biggest issue was control. Everything they knew about these deals was that you lose control."

Janet tried to persuade them early on that FIRM6 would not lose control because she would negotiate a tight contract. This did ease their concerns somewhat. Janet says, "And they were not satisfied, so we worked with them over the summer to go through it, then the economics became extremely desirable." Thus, Janet did successfully employ the tactic of building coalitions to rally support for outsourcing.

In summary, the political perspective offers one interpretation of Janet's behavior. Although there is no evidence that she instigated the outsourcing decision to meet self-serving needs, political aspects influenced her decision. In particular, her lack of power prevented her from implementing cost-saving measures on her own. Therefore, she turned to outsourcing as a viable solution. Given the risks of outsourcing, Janet initiated the tactic of coalition building to sway the decision to her preferred outcome.

4.6.4 FIRM6's Decision from a Transaction Cost Perspective

Most participants indicate that this outsourcing decision was economically motivated. After all, 1990 was a troubled year for FIRM6. Given this economic climate, Janet's boss investigated outsourcing as a way to reduce costs. FIRM6's decision-making process corresponds well to Williamson's transaction cost theory. In particular, Janet attended to transaction type, costs, and the threat of opportunism.

4.6.4.1 *Transaction Type*

Transaction cost theory stipulates that utility services are best provided by an external provider. This assertion is based on the assumption that a vendor, who specializes in a good or service, achieves economies of scale. The theory also stipulates that idiosyncratic transactions (i.e. specialized goods or services) can be provided cheaper internally. When Janet was asked why she considered outsourcing for only the data processing part of her operations, she gave a response that is in accordance with transaction cost theory:

> "We did look at applications because we felt we needed to do that, the conclusion to the study, not unlike our gut feeling, is that we are best to manage that ourselves."

Her applications developers are often hired by government agencies to develop systems, so Janet felt that this was a value-added service that should not be outsourced. She did, however, feel that she could save money by outsourcing data processing because the vendor was able to achieve economies of scale.

Economies of scale. Janet is confident that this contract will save her money over the next ten years because she feels that the outsourcing vendor has inherent natural advantages that allow it to provide data processing services at a cheaper cost. When asked why she thought the vendor could provide the services cheaper, she responds:

> "Number one, they have the automation tools, their equipment is less expensive, over time they don't pay the same price to run systems software and hardware. And they get the benefit of running multiple companies out of one data center."

4.6.4.2 Costs

Probably the best indicant that Janet's decision was economically motivated was that she was concerned with saving money. None of the people interviewed felt that the numbers were rigged in favor of outsourcing, but rather, they felt that every effort was made to make an unbiased, cost-based decision. Janet's boss, in particular, wanted complete objectivity in the estimates, since he will be held accountable for the contract over the next ten years. Janet tells a story of her boss calling her in the middle of the night about the accuracy of the numbers:

> "He called me in the middle of the night. He's embarrassed to remember this—right before we went to the board with the final numbers. And he said he had a bad dream and could not sleep. 2:30 in the morning he wakes up and calls me. He said, 'Are you sure about these numbers?' And I told him yes and asked, 'Are you okay now?' My husband asked who it was, and I told him my boss had a bad dream."

When Janet was asked whether her decision was truly economically motivated, she responded affirmatively. She said the numbers overwhelmingly favored outsourcing:

> "The numbers were too compelling in one direction. I mean we had run enough of the numbers to know that on the financial side we were getting squeezed from the capital acquisition side. Whether we were leasing things, buying things, it didn't matter. Either way, we were entering into some very expensive financial commitments [if she tried to upgrade without outsourcing]."

In order for Janet to realize cost savings, she knew she had to negotiate a tough contract to prevent the threat of opportunism.

4.6.4.3 *Threat of Opportunism*

According to transaction cost theory, cost savings may not be realized if the vendor behaves opportunistically. The vendor might take advantage of its client if it knows its client is totally dependent on it. Outsourcing fits these circumstances because once a client signs up with the vendor, there is no choice in the short run but to use the vendor's services. Williamson theorizes that the contract is the best mechanism for preventing vendors from taking advantage of their client. Janet concurs. She spent months negotiating the terms of the contract. Whenever the vendor pressed her to sign early and work out details later, she declined. Because of her negotiating skills, she is confident that she will realize the 15 to 18% savings.

To summarize, Janet's outsourcing decision process corresponds well with Williamson's transaction cost theory. Because the bank was in financial trouble, she tried to negotiate a deal that would guarantee savings for FIRM6.

4.6.5 FIRM6—Conclusion

By analyzing Janet's intentions from the political and transaction cost perspectives, a rich explanation of FIRM6's outsourcing decision emerges. Although Janet's decision process fits well with Williamson's theory, we see that political aspects influenced the decision. If Janet had the power to acquire resources for the upgrade and the power to initiate the cultural changes to realize savings on her own, she might never have outsourced her data processing operations. Thus, the political climate may have precipitated this seemingly rational outsourcing decision. Perhaps this case underscores the need to study decision-making in context. By attending to the historical and political factors that precipitated this rational decision, we see that constructs from both theories shed meaning into the intentional actions of decision-makers.

4.7 FIRM7

FIRM7 evaluated outsourcing on two occasions. The first decision, spearheaded by IS personnel in early 1988, resulted in keeping the IS function in-house. The IS personnel conducted this first investigation primarily as a defensive maneuver against outsourcing. They hoped that their outsourcing evaluation would prevent their senior management from turning over their department to an outsider. Their efforts, however, did not eliminate the option from senior management's mind. The second outsourcing evaluation, championed by the CEO, resulted in a ten-year contract with an outsourcing vendor which went into effect in early 1989. Three years later, the operating divisions in FIRM7 are extremely dissatisfied with the vendor's service. Because the CEO signed the contract with minimal input from his information systems staff, he left FIRM7 in a weak position. Users accuse the vendor of total non-performance, yet the CEO still claims he made a prudent decision.

Five individuals involved with FIRM7's outsourcing decisions were interviewed (see Table 4.9). The case begins with an explanation of FIRM7's growth strategy and how the IS function fits into the overall organizational structure.

Table 4.9 *FIRM7 participants*

Name used in this case	Job title	Involvement in outsourcing
Trevor	Manager of Information Systems (Prior VP of IS in one of the operating divisions)	Trevor manages the remaining IS team who monitor the contract and provide an interface between the users and the vendor.
Gary	Vice President of an operating division	Gary is a major user of information services.
Dennis	Account Manager (Prior VP of the Computer Utility)	Dennis was formerly the VP of the Computer Utility at FIRM7. He played a major role in the first outsourcing decision. After the contract was signed, he became an account manager for the vendor.
David	Account Manager	David is Dennis's current boss. He is the number one man in charge of the account.
Walter	Outsourcing Consultant	Walter is an ex-employee of the outsourcing vendor who worked on this account during the transition.

4.7.1 Historical Background of FIRM7

During the 1980s, FIRM7 pursued the vision to become one of the world's largest providers of energy. Through an aggressive acquisition program, FIRM7's revenues doubled between 1983 and 1988. At this time, the company had four operating divisions, each with its own Vice President of Information Systems. These VPs of IS managed applications development and maintenance for their operating companies. All remaining functions were managed by the CIO in the centralized corporate offices. The CIO reported to the Senior Vice President in charge of the corporate staff.

Early in 1988, after the series of mergers and acquisitions, the corporate IS staff consolidated the IS budgets for these entities. Gary, VP of one of the operating divisions, says, "And when top management saw those dollars it was extremely stressful." The information systems budget was growing because the demand for services was growing—the data center needed to be expanded from 60 MIPS to 150 MIPS to accommodate the new acquisitions. During this period of rapid expansion, however, senior management was sending the message to the CIO: contain your costs. Dennis, VP of the Computer Utility, says, "That was one of the hardest things for senior management to understand, that you can't shut the budget and control this." The conflict between two incompatible organizational goals—IS growth and cost containment—motivated the CIO, VP of the Computer Utility and the VPs of IS from the operating divisions to consider outsourcing.

4.7.2 FIRM7's First Outsourcing Decision

Dennis claims the first decision to evaluate outsourcing was economically motivated:

> "In 1988, we were forced to look at the economics: product prices were low, we were experiencing a lot of growth within data processing. Since I was vice president of the utility, I had the responsibility of staying on top of what size computers to use. That was growing. We were at the point where we were going to have to make decisions about bigger machines, more technology, and large capital outlays. We thought that would be a good time to look at ways to be smarter and save money— to deliver the growth so that it doesn't cost us as much money."

4.7.2.1 FIRM7's First Outsourcing Decision Process

Dennis suggests that the outsourcing evaluation was rather superficial—informal discussions were conducted with one outsourcing vendor. After these discussions, the IS managers involved in the decision decided that outsourcing would not fit into FIRM7's culture. Dennis notes:

> "It was more of a business decision. There were still dollar savings—that's what you get when you outsource— major, major dollar savings. But then it was the culture. If you have all these groups being FIRM7, the data center being the [vendor], that would not be as effective. You don't have control over the whole piece of it."

Considering that Dennis claims that the motivation behind the outsourcing investigation was economics—it is interesting to note that outsourcing was dismissed without any economic evaluation.

Another strategy that Dennis and his colleagues pursued during this time period was to create a document which listed all the functions that the IS department provided to their users. This document was used to demonstrate that the IS department did a lot more for its users than merely run their programs. For example, it provided consultation, trained users to be computer literate, and scanned the environment for new technology. Several FIRM7 employees called this document a "wish list"—that is, they claimed the document actually stated what the IS department *could* provide, rather than what it actually provided.

Thus, the decision process was cursory. The IS professionals held some informal meetings with an outsourcer and created a document to show their management the variety of services they received from their IS department.

4.7.2.2 Outcome and Consequences of FIRM7's First Decision

The output from the outsourcing evaluation was a management report created by Trevor, then the VP of one of the operating divisions. Trevor likes to refer to this document because it foreshadows many of the problems with the subsequent outsourcing arrangement. The following quote from this report warns that outsourcing will be costly unless data processing needs can be predicted with certainty:

> "[The vendor] makes sense in a very stable environment where resource requirements and growth can be realistically predicted and the company can provide [the vendor] with a complete and detailed forecast of services. Deviations are costly and if they do not fit [the vendor's] operating standards, extremely costly to obtain."

Trevor felt that since FIRM7 could not predict growth, that outsourcing would be a risky proposition. This report, however, did not eliminate the outsourcing alternative in the mind of the CEO. He was still searching for ways to make his entire company more effective.

4.7.3 FIRM7's Second Outsourcing Decision

In 1988, the CEO hired a major consulting firm to evaluate the effectiveness of FIRM7's organizational structure. The consulting firm recommended that FIRM7 outsource its entire information systems function. Thus, FIRM7 once again evaluated the outsourcing option.

4.7.3.1 *FIRM7's Second Outsourcing Decision Process*

Later that year, the same outsourcing vendor was contacted again. According to Dennis, after a few high level meetings, the senior management of FIRM7 and the vendor decided, "Let's make a marriage." After those initial meetings, the CIO asked Dennis to provide data to the vendor so it could prepare a bid.

The major issue during this data gathering phase was to determine the current level of information services at FIRM7. This "bundle of services" would provide the baseline measure so that the vendor could determine the costs, growth, and savings for its bid. The baseline time frame was a six-month period spanning the end of 1988 through early 1989. The outsourcing vendor would be contractually bound to deliver the average service level measured during this period.

Contract negotiations were brief. FIRM7's CEO and the outsourcing vendor decided to go ahead with the contract with the understanding that details would be worked out in the future. As will be shown, this move proved detrimental for FIRM7.

David explains that the contract covers three types of services: (1) data center operations, (2) application development and maintenance, and (3) utility services such as security, database administration, training, and PC support. Since the contract was signed before the baseline period was finished, the services defined in the contract are incomplete. These three areas of the contract are described below.

Data center operations. FIRM7 would be sharing a data center with several of the vendor's other clients. FIRM7 is charged for computer resource units, known as CRUs, which include CPU minutes, DASD storage, tape mounts, print lines, and other data center resources. The contract specifies that FIRM7 receives a fixed number of these resources (determined by the baseline) for a fixed price.

Applications development and maintenance. For applications development and maintenance, FIRM7 receives a fixed number of man-hours of service known as full-time equivalents (FTEs). Since FIRM7 had X (figure omitted for confidentiality purposes) people devoted to applications in 1988, it is entitled to X full-time equivalents. FIRM7 may use these man-hours in any way it wishes.

Utility services. The third group of services are called "utility services." Utility services capture any service that falls outside of data center operations, applications development, and applications support. Examples of utility services include database administration, report distribution, office moves, training, workbench support, and report distribution. Services, service levels, and measures were not defined for this portion of the contract. The contract, according to David, merely says that the vendor provides "whatever FIRM7 was doing in 1988." The utility services is considered the weakest part of the contract.

Gary perhaps best captures FIRM7's opinion of the contract when he states, "It's a flawed document at best." The contract does not define service levels, performance measures, service reports, penalties for non-performance, or credits for volume decreases. FIRM7 is now over two and one half years into the contract and many of these items are still undefined.

4.7.3.2 Outcome and Consequences of FIRM7's Second Decision

At the close of 1988, FIRM7 signed the contract with the vendor and almost immediately all of FIRM7's information systems professionals relinquished their corporate identification cards and became vendor employees. The only FIRM7 information systems professionals that remained on staff were several vice presidents of the operating divisions and several IS managers. These individuals belong to a team that monitor the contract and provide a liaison between users and the vendor.

At the same time, the outsourcing vendor purchased FIRM7's assets, such as computers, PCs, I/O equipment, printers, and microfiches machines, for several million dollars. These cash infusions are typical of outsourcing deals. All in all, the deal is supposed to save FIRM7 several hundred million over the next ten years.

The two outsourcing decisions are now interpreted through the political and transaction cost perspectives. The first decision can be interpreted as a defensive mechanism initiated by IS professionals. For the second decision, case participants felt that the CEO tried to make a rational, economically justified decision, but due to his lack of knowledge about information systems, he negotiated a poor deal.

4.7.4 FIRM7's Decisions from a Political Perspective

The first decision seems to be politically motivated. Due to FIRM7's acquisitions, the demand for IS services was growing at a considerable pace. Since senior management viewed IS as a cost pit, they were unwilling to invest the money needed to upgrade the data center to meet this additional demand. The IS department wondered if its management would turn to an outsourcer to meet additional demand.

Therefore, one interpretation of the actions of the IS professionals who initiated the outsourcing evaluation is that they needed additional resources to accommodate the acquisitions. Fearing that the resource requests would trigger senior management to investigate outsourcing, they decided to evaluate the option on their own. By enacting political tactics designed to sway the decision in their favor, they hoped to acquire the upgrade and prevent outsourcing. From Trevor's report, it is obvious that they failed to economically justify their decision. They merely presented qualitative reasons for not outsourcing, such as the risks of not being able to forecast demand and the loss of control that comes with outsourcing to a third party. Apparently, the efforts of these IS professionals failed to impress their management, since the CEO decided to outsource just six months after the first outsourcing evaluation.

Since more information was gathered about the second outsourcing decision, our analysis probes more deeply into this situation. The general consensus is that the CEO and members of the executive team made an economic decision to save money—even though the decision was a poor one. Therefore, the second decision is more appropriately scrutinized from the transaction cost perspective. There is one relevant political construct, however, that adds insight into this second decision, namely power. When a decision-maker possesses all the power, he or she does not have to resort to political tactics to influence the decision outcome. This second outsourcing decision demonstrates the trite but fitting adage, "Those who have the gold make the rules."

In particular, an analysis of the power structure reveals that FIRM7's holding company makes most of the operating decisions. In the case of outsourcing, the CEO and members of the executive committee pushed outsourcing on its operating companies without gaining consensus.

4.7.4.1   *FIRM7's Power Structure*

FIRM7 possesses a great deal of power over its operating companies. To FIRM7, the outsourcing arrangement is beneficial since it is the recipient of the several hundred million in savings. The operating companies were forced to accept the outsourcing arrangement signed by the CEO of FIRM7. They apparently received no savings or benefits from the arrangement. Dennis explains how the deal was structured:

> "Financially, the way the deal was structured, it was more to FIRM7's holding company benefit than it was to each of the operating companies. So the individual companies didn't see the benefit to their bottom line. In other words, all the savings accrued at the corporate level so that the people down here who are living with it don't get a chance to see the benefits."

Since senior management—the CEO, CFO, and the President—possesses a great deal of power, it was able to outsource without selling the deal to the operating divisions. Indeed, the operating companies were not even represented in the outsourcing negotiations, yet they are contractually bound to pay the cost. Dennis notes that the operating companies are extremely dissatisfied with the arrangement:

> "See, before they didn't have to pay for anything. So it was very much—this deal was a vision and a negotiation from the highest level of FIRM7 without buy-in and not an understanding from the operating companies who will eventually have to pay for it."

In summary, we see that politics do shed some insights into the outsourcing decisions. In the first decision, we see an IS staff, who possess little power, trying to acquire upgrades and prevent outsourcing through a cursory evaluation process. In the second case, we see that FIRM7's corporate management team is so powerful that they are able to push decisions on their underlings without resorting to political tactics to sell the decision.

The second outsourcing decision is now evaluated from the lens of the transaction cost model. In particular, this decision underscores the importance of Williamson's attention to the threat of opportunism.

4.7.5 FIRM7's Decision from a Transaction Cost Perspective

FIRM7's CEO was searching for alternatives to reduce his information systems costs. What prompted this decision was the aggregation of all the information systems dollars into one budget. This figure amounted to an estimated $1 billion dollars that would be spent on information services over the next ten years. When the CEO hired a consultant to assess the effectiveness of their organization, they told him that he could cut IS costs by outsourcing. The CEO responded to the consultant's report by initiating discussions with an outside vendor.

4.7.5.1 Costs

The vendor promised to save FIRM7 20% off their projected IS budgets if the CEO would turn over his entire organization to them. The deal was also sweetened by a multi-million dollar check for information assets. In addition, the vendor offered an attractive payment schedule. Trevor explained that FIRM7 is charged very little fees for the baseline services during the first four years. Most of the payments occur at the back end, making the net present value of this deal extremely desirable to FIRM7.

Thus, from the CEO's vantage point, he made an economically sound decision. However, others counter that the total cost of information systems in the long run will cost more with outsourcing. This comes from the simple equation that FIRM7's total costs equal the fixed fees on the baseline bundle of services plus the excess charges for the incremental growth (TOTAL COST = BASELINE CHARGES + EXCESS CHARGES).

Gary explains that "top management thinks it's a super deal." This is because they are confident that they will realize the projected savings on the *baseline* services. However, many feel that the excess charges for incremental growth will cancel out the benefit of this deal.

The CEO signed a contract that had minimal provisions for growth. FIRM7 is allowed a 5% growth for the first four years and 3% growth for the remaining seven years at no additional charge. FIRM7's demand for services, however, continues to increase 30 to 35% annually. They pay a stiff excess charge for additional computer resources. One manager from the remaining IS group claims excess charges are in the neighborhood of five to six digit figures per month.

Thus, the savings on the baseline "bundle of services" are expected to be realized, even though the excess charges may eventually cancel out the net benefit.

Some users portray an even darker picture. They claim that the savings actually come from cuts in services, not through the vendor's inherent natural efficiencies. Gary complains:

> "From the information systems function types, like myself, I say, 'No, it's not a good deal. You didn't even get the X [figure omitted for confidentiality reasons] in savings. In fact, it costs you that and you are getting less than what you got before, so how the hell can you say it's a good deal?'"

We have already stated that the CEO attended to costs, but he did not question how the vendor could provide a cheaper service than his internal IS department. Transaction cost theory suggests that vendors pass savings from economies of scale to their customers. The remaining IS staff, however, contends outsourcing vendors do not necessarily have inherent natural advantages.

Economies of scale. The trade literature suggests that outsourcing vendors achieve economies of scale by running multiple clients from one data center. On the hardware side, Walter notes that FIRM7 is so big that they can achieve similar hardware discounts as an outsourcing vendor. On the software side, Trevor feels that the economies of scale a vendor used to enjoy no longer exist because software vendors have changed their licensing fees:

> "They are changing their license agreements. Many were site licenses and today they are changing to CPU licenses and being able to move software from one CPU to another one, they are giving you a hard time. Some are willing to play ball with you, others are not. [A major software vendor], we have had a significant amount of disputes."

Outsourcing vendors now have to pay licensing fees based on volumes. They no longer enjoy the savings of running multiple clients through the same software.

Gary offers an alternative explanation why the outsourcing vendor does not pass savings to the customer. He points out that when the decision was made in 1988, the software vendors were still administering site licenses. He says that during the negotiations, they determined that the vendor could save them 15% on software licensing fees since the vendor runs multiple clients out of one data center. These projected savings were not realized, however, because most of FIRM7's software was not supported by the vendor. Thus, FIRM7 pays for any non-standard software such as its database management system, CASE tools and programming languages. During negotiations, Gary claims the vendor said much of this non- standard software would eventually be adopted as more clients ran through its data center. To date, none of FIRM7's non-standard software has been adopted as a standard by the vendor.

Thus, we see at least three explanations on why FIRM7 has comparable economies of scale as the vendor. First, FIRM7 is large and therefore receives similar hardware discounts as a vendor. Second, the change in the structure of software licensing fees makes vendors pay on a volume basis. Third, vendors pass discounts to clients only on their standard technology platform. Non-standard software elicits excess charges. This covers economies of scale for data processing, but what about applications development and maintenance? According to Trevor, the outsourcing vendor has not been able to achieve economies of scale in software development.

As a final note on cost, it seems that the CEO made a superficial decision based on some seductive numbers, without questioning how the vendor is able to reduce costs. Senior management at FIRM7 still considers the deal a success because of the savings on baseline services. Walter, who worked on this account during the transition, says the CEO told him, "They bitched about IS before outsourcing, they bitch now—but at least it's costing me a lot less."

4.7.5.2 *Threat of Opportunism*

Williamson argues that vendors will behave opportunistically when their customers have no other service alternatives. He suggests that power can be balanced by negotiating a tight contract. At FIRM7, we see that the CEO signed a poor contract because he did not understand the complexities of information systems. As a result, many disputes have occurred between FIRM7 and the vendor.

In particular, the operating companies accuse the vendor of providing sub-standard services. Users complain about the degradation of service, lack of vendor responsiveness, time wasted pointing "the finger of blame" rather than fixing problems, excess charges for services they assumed were covered in the contract, and loss of IS expertise. The vendor rightfully counters that they are only responsible for providing the same level of service that FIRM7 users received prior to outsourcing. Although FIRM7 claims certain services were performed at a certain level prior to outsourcing, the vendor has no way of verifying it because FIRM7 failed to measure these services during the baseline period. Although the vendor promised to develop service levels and performance measures after the contract went into effect, they have neglected to do so. As time passes, it becomes more and more difficult to retroactively determine exactly what services FIRM7's IS department delivered to users.

Examples of disputes that have occurred because of the incomplete contract are numerous. Seven examples are provided below: security requests, database administration, report distribution, storage management, loss of IS expertise, FIRM7's right to request bids for additional work, and the infamous "change of character" clause.

Security requests. The users claim that the vendor provides very poor service in the area of security requests. Trevor claims:

> "We have, at one time, in excess of seventeen working days to get somebody through security. We have a big problem with that."

Trevor is referring to the elapsed time from requesting a logon ID or access to data to implementing the request in ACF2. The vendor counters that requests do not take this long, but that some take longer because users fill out request forms incorrectly. After hours of negotiations, the vendor agreed to process 90% of the security requests in five days. Note that there is no agreement when the vendor must process the remaining 10% of requests. Some users believe that this service level is still below industry standard.

Database administration. Another example that users point to as an alleged degradation in services is database administration. The vendor claims that the contract only covers physical database services, which boils down to SYSGENs. The vendor notes that prior to outsourcing, database applications were just coming on-line so the baseline period covers minimal database services. FIRM7 users claim that logical database services, such as database design, consulting, and logical views were provided during the baseline period and are thus included in the contract. Gary explains the problem:

> "[In 1988] we had consolidated much of our database design into a simple group, and basically it was to provide logical database design and that sort of thing to our projects on a consulting basis. And then also do the physical database design and management, what I call data base administration. And that has really been a problem. Part of the problem is that [the vendor] looked at this [in 1988] and decided they could do it with less people. Therefore, less people is money in their pocket. It turned out that it has actually taken them more people. When it took them more people—for whatever reason: they didn't have the skills, they didn't have the management, whether they don't know what the hell they are doing—they want to charge us. Now we say, 'Wait a minute. We were doing this before, we want it now, we don't want to pay for it.'"

After many battles, the vendor won. Since FIRM7 could not prove that logical database design was part of the baseline services, the vendor was only obligated to cover physical database design.

Report distribution service. The users are also dissatisfied with their report distribution service. Users claim that reports are often late, delivered to the wrong bins, or lost altogether. Since there are no baseline measures, the vendor is not contractually bound to deliver the reports in any specified time period.

Over two years into the contract, however, the vendor agreed to strive to meet a service level of delivering 95% of the reports by the target date. When FIRM7 responded, "Okay, but that 95% better be delivered to the right place," the vendor countered, "Let's have two measures—one for having the reports on time and one for having them accurately delivered." By having two measures, the vendor actually negotiated a lower level of service. The probability of a report being on time *and* accurate is only 90.25%—the probability of being delivered on time (0.95) times the probability of being accurately delivered (0.95).

Storage management. Since only a certain amount of storage was used during the baseline period, FIRM7 must pay for additional DASD and tape storage. Upon inspection, one consultant found that DASD utilization was under 50%. The users felt they were being charged for excess storage when it wasn't needed. One of FIRM7's IS managers stated, "That's the trouble with [the vendor], they have no motivation to be efficient." The vendor counters that processing efficiency decreases when disks are jammed with data.

Loss of IS expertise. In addition to complaining about the degradation in service, users claim they have lost their IS expertise. The vendor transferred 100 of FIRM7's transitioned employees to other accounts. The vice president of information systems for one of the operating divisions feels that FIRM7 suffered a great loss:

> "We did lose people. But of the managers that we had, we lost the three best managers that were transferred. Has the caliber improved or changed radically? The nature of the people has changed. They are more technical, less user-oriented, they are more technically-oriented and less functionally-oriented, less industry-oriented. So if you were to grade them overall, yes, I lost."

Dennis, who is now speaking as an account manager for the vendor, claims this allegation is unfair. He retorts:

> "The guy running the business, he says, 'Wait a minute. You can't take Mary Jo away from me, she's been with me seventeen years.' Well now is that being fair to Mary Jo? So we get a lot of criticism from customers about how we are always turning people over. And yet that is one of our strengths."

Dennis makes a poignant point: senior management at FIRM7 claim they wanted better career opportunities for their people—but are annoyed when those opportunities mean transferring people off the account. If FIRM7 wanted to retain control over IS expertise, perhaps they should have managed the IS function themselves.

Right to request bids for additional work. Another area that users complain about is the right to request bids from other vendors for additional work. Users accuse the vendor of violating the spirit of the contract clause which allows FIRM7 to hire other vendors to develop applications. Gary explained that he was so displeased with the outsourcing vendor that he used funds from his discretionary budget to hire an outside consulting firm to develop a particular system. When he tried to hire someone to support the system, the outsourcing vendor contested on the grounds that no non-vendor employees could alter production code. The maintenance contract, therefore, went to the outsourcing vendor. From the vendor's standpoint, they don't want to be liable for errors another company's employees may make to their production code. From the users' standpoint, they feel that the vendor has eliminated their right to seek competitive bids.

Change of character. Yet another bone of contention between FIRM7 and the vendor is the change of character clause in the contract. This provision states that FIRM7 is to be charged for any changes in functionality. This clause has triggered several disputes. For example, the vendor wanted to charge FIRM7 for changing its word processing software from one package to another. The vendor argues that a change in word processing packages represents a change of character since this product was not supported in the baseline. FIRM7 argues that this is not a change of character since the function—word processing—has not changed, only the software. At the time of this writing, this dispute has not been resolved.

The area of personal computers is another point of contention. The contract says that the vendor will service all personal computers for a fixed price. However, the number of computers has doubled since 1989, and many PCs are now connected to LANs. The vendor claims that LAN technology is a change in character, whereas FIRM7 claims it's only a difference in technology. In addition, the outsourcing vendor wants to charge a set dollar amount for each additional PC supported. Trevor claims that "volumes do not equal costs." In other words, doubling the number of PCs does not require double the cost to support them. This issue remains unresolved.

In summary, the transaction cost view offers an interpretation of the CEO's and vendor's behaviors. The CEO tried to conduct a rational decision aimed at reducing the costs of his information systems function. His lack of understanding of information technology, however, resulted in a poor contract. Disputes between the vendor and FIRM7 are understandable since each interprets the contract differently.

4.7.6 FIRM7—Conclusion

Both the political and transaction cost perspectives offer useful insights into the intentional actions of decision-makers. In the first outsourcing decision, the IS staff may have initiated an outsourcing evaluation as a defensive maneuver. Due to their lack of power, however, their strategy was ineffective.

In the second outsourcing decision, the CEO was able to push outsourcing on the operating companies because he is more powerful than his underlings. The CEO was free to make his outsourcing decision without interference from the people who would be forced to live with the consequences. The following quote from Dennis captures the general consensus of the operating companies:

> "What generally happens is senior managers way up here at the 40 000 foot level cut the deal. The people who have to implement it are down here. They are really faced with a different set of problems. And when you try to work through all of those, it is not a one or two week solution."

Although the CEO may have been implementing an economically sound decision, was he wise not to get concurrence from the operating companies? Perhaps outsourcing failed at FIRM7 because the operating companies refused to make it work. The animosity between users and the outsourcing vendor is readily apparent. The question remains, however, whether this animosity would exist if users had been involved in negotiations. Perhaps then a tighter contract would have been signed and disputes minimized.

If one was forced to choose which theory offers the more insightful interpretation, transaction cost would rise the victor. The attention to costs and the threat of opportunism correspond well with Williamson's theory. However, once again, we witness that a richer interpretation arises when both theories are incorporated in the analysis. Perhaps the CEO's second outsourcing decision would have been more successful if he had attended to the political aspects of implementing his decision.

We conclude this case by offering Trevor's analysis of the outsourcing decision. He shares three lessons from the mistakes FIRM7 has made. First, be honest about your goals. "I think that you better understand your goals prior to the contract." He felt the goal should have been meeting the long run information needs of the company in a cost effective manner, not "save me 20%." Anybody can save money by cutting corners. Second, Trevor suggests that companies define service levels in the contract. Currently, FIRM7 has no repercussions for poor service since service levels were never agreed upon. Third, Trevor says if he was to do this again, he would only outsource the data center. "I think, if we did it all over again, we would have kept the applications development and applications maintenance. I would have kept data base administration, I would have kept PC services, and workstation architecture and technology."

4.8 FIRM8

FIRM8's IS director, Barry, evaluated outsourcing the data center on two occasions. In late 1989, when Barry was first hired from a competitor, he requested bids from five outsourcing vendors. All five declined to submit bids because they could not undercut FIRM8's extremely low data processing costs. Within a year, Barry evaluated the outsourcing option again. This time, the evaluation resulted in a five-year outsourcing contract. Barry interprets his outsourcing decisions as a rational action to improve FIRM8's financial position. Other participants, however, contend that Barry outsourced to gain departmental and personal recognition.

Six people were interviewed at FIRM8 (see Table 4.10).

4.8.1 Historical Background of FIRM8

The CEO and founder of FIRM8 has a vision to make his company one of the largest producers of oil and natural gas in the United States. In an internal memorandum distributed to his corporate officers in 1989, he states three strategies to support his vision: production growth through acquisition, production growth through an aggressive drilling program, and marketing growth through

Table 4.10 FIRM8 participants

Name used in this case	Job title	Involvement in outsourcing
Barry	Director of IS	Barry championed both outsourcing decisions.
Mike	Controller	Mike is Barry's boss. He supported Barry's second outsourcing decision.
Tim	Manager of Computer & Network Services	Tim provided the financial analysis for the second outsourcing decision.
Stephen	Data Center Manager	Stephen lost his job as result of outsourcing.
Dan	Supervisor of Technical Support	Dan was promoted as a result of outsourcing and will help monitor the contract.
Norman	Manager of Applications	Norman lost his job as a result of outsourcing.

the expansion of international customers. The first strategy in particular—growth through acquisitions—impacts FIRM8's information systems director, Barry. He is expected to integrate information from acquired companies into FIRM8's systems with virtually no additional resources.

> "All of us measure ourselves in terms of percentage of company revenues. We are about 1.4% [of revenues]. Now with the acquisition, we are way under 1% [of revenues]. And I like to remind my boss of that sometimes. We are running skinny."

Thus, Barry operates in a volatile climate. He is expected to accommodate great changes in business without additional resources.

4.8.2   FIRM8's First Outsourcing Decision

In the spring of 1990, Barry took the first initiative to look at outsourcing. When asked why he decided to investigate an outsourcing alternative, he says he was searching for ways to save FIRM8 money:

> "I think I got the feeling from John [Barry's previous boss] that there was an intolerance by our management about having a big computer operation. It was viewed as a big boat anchor even though it was a vital service. And they kept asking questions if there were other ways to do this and I took that hint from there."

Barry requested bids from several vendors, but all declined to submit bids. The vendors claimed that they could not save FIRM8 money. The results of this study were not presented to senior management. The general feeling is that senior management was not interested in outsourcing.

4.8.3   FIRM8's Second Outsourcing Decision

In April 1991, Barry initiated a second look at outsourcing. Again, he claims that his decision was economically motivated. When he discovered that company headquarters was moving, he feared that FIRM8 would incur a huge expense to relocate the data center:

> "What are we going to do when we move? I had studied this [outsourcing] a year ago and said that FIRM8's costs were lower than service bureau/outsider costs. We demonstrated that back in 1990. If we had to face what I call a cataclysmic event—such as a relocation of a

company—a major acquisition, then we ought to seriously recommend outsourcing our data center."

Thus, Barry convinced his boss—at that time, the CFO—to take another look at outsourcing.

4.8.3.1 *FIRM8's Second Outsourcing Decision Process*

Barry began the process by confiding in Tim, his manager of computer and network services, and the two of them put together a request for proposal in May. This proposal was very detailed: hardware, software, headcounts, and transaction volumes were included in the proposal. In addition to this technical data, the vendors were given cost figures for each component of data center operations. Sound business practice suggests that cost figures should not be given to vendors because it conditions their bids. Barry says he:

> "struggled about giving them cost data. But I said, 'they need to know our measuring base'. . . . I dropped all of our data in front of them and said, 'Can you beat this?'"

He asked for bids back from five vendors in 30 days. He was in a hurry because he either had to outsource by August of 1991 or upgrade his mainframe to accommodate a new acquisition. Two bids came back. In a comparison of these bids with the cost figures for the internal bid, Vendor A's bid resulted in cost savings of 16%, while Vendor B's bid yielded cost savings of 3%. These savings are based on a three-year comparison rather than a five-year comparison. Barry based the evaluation on a three-year forecast because he wanted an option to terminate or renegotiate the contract in three years.

The lower of the two submitted bids was accepted. Contract negotiations resumed with Vendor A during June. Barry hired a lawyer and a consultant, both experts in outsourcing contracts. Even though the contract was negotiated in a very short time, Barry feels, "this is a good contract." Indeed, compared with other contracts encountered during this research, this contract appears airtight. Barry included service level measures, service level reporting, cash penalties for non-performance, credits for a drop in volumes due to a change in business, and discount prices for excess charges in case of a growth in volumes. In June 1991, the five-year (with a three-year out-option) contract was signed.

4.8.3.2 Outcome and Consequences of FIRM7's Second Decision

The long term consequences of this outsourcing decision cannot be determined. Barry feels confident he will save money; he estimates a saving of 16% over a five-year period. In the short term, his main concern is the transfer of data center operations over to the vendor.

Barry retained the entire staff through December 1991. He tried to help them find other jobs and had offered each an attractive severance package. His other immediate concern is how to success-fully transfer processing to the new data center. The main issue so far seems to be telecommunications.

In summary, Barry's first attempt to outsource the data center failed because no vendors could provide a cheaper service. The second outsourcing decision concluded in a five-year contract with an outsourcing vendor. Below, the outsourcing decisions at FIRM8 are analyzed through the lens of the political and transaction cost models of organizational decision-making.

4.8.4 FIRM8's Decision from a Political Perspective

Two political issues are relevant in this case. The first is the issue of power and the second is the political tactics used to sway the decision in favor of outsourcing.

4.8.4.1 Power of FIRM8's IS Department

There are several indications that the IS department has little power within FIRM8. First, a company reorganization in April 1991 added an extra layer between Barry and the CEO. Second, senior management seems to view the entire IS function as a cost pit. Third, the IS department has no concrete measures to demonstrate its value to senior management. Fourth, IS is not involved in corporate planning, nor are IS plans aligned with stated corporate objectives. These four indicants of power are examined.

Authority: IS reporting level. Prior to April 1991, Barry reported to the CFO. In April, an extra layer of management was added so that Barry now reports to the controller, Mike.

According to the political model, this change in Barry's reporting level indicates a loss of departmental power. When Mike, Barry's current boss, was questioned about the reorganization, he stated:

"Unfortunately, most people in IS, and the textbooks are totally wrong, they get hung up on the position that IS reports to versus the individual. In other words, the textbook says that IS should report to the directors if possible. They forget that it's not so much the function they report to as the personality of the person they are reporting to. My personality, I am involved in things, I have a key interest in the things I do, I am probably a workaholic. I get very involved in the departments, what they are doing, how we can provide services."

Mike implies that position is not an indicant of power. He states that IS is better off—that is, has more power—because he is now responsible for the department. Mike offers the following as an example of this alleged increase in power. He had Barry come to lunch for the first time with the CEO of FIRM8 so that "Barry could hear first-hand how [the CEO] feels about IS."

Senior management's view of information systems. Another indicant of power—senior management's view of the information systems function—suggests that the IS department is not influential within FIRM8. Mike admits that the CEO views IS as a necessary overhead rather than a valuable resource, "No question about it." Barry also concurs with the opinion that IS was viewed as a necessary overhead by senior management. Throughout Barry's interview, he expressed senior management's primary agenda for information systems: contain costs.

The inability to demonstrate IS's contribution. A third indicant that the IS department has little power is that there are no concrete measures to demonstrate the value of IS to senior management. Unlike the production and marketing departments that can tie their contribution to the bottom line, FIRM8's IS department is ill-equipped to prove its efficiency and effectiveness to senior management. The only "objective" proof of its efficiency came from a vendor's study in 1990 that the data center was extremely cost-effective. That is a moot point, given the function was outsourced. There is no chargeback system, so the user groups view IS as a free resource. The only other measures they use are (a) the IS expenditures as a percentage of revenue and (b) total headcounts compared to other IS shops. These measures, however, provide no evidence of efficiency or effectiveness.

IS department's lack of involvement in corporate planning. A final note on power: the IS department is not involved in any sort of corporate planning. There is no attempt to develop a strategic plan for information systems that is even remotely tied to the corporate objectives. The users decide what systems will be developed. There is no attempt to justify systems based on contribution to the bottom line.

Given these indicants of power—reporting level from the CEO, perceptions of upper management, the inability to demonstrate contribution, the lack of involvement in corporate planning—the IS department is not deemed as powerful as other departments within FIRM8.

One interpretation of this case is as follows. Given the lack of departmental power, Barry may have used the outsourcing decision to bolster IS credibility. Through outsourcing, IS proves its commitment to higher corporate objectives—so much so that IS is willing to abandon part of their territory for the good of the kingdom. One may ask, "But isn't this an economic interpretation?" Not when one considers the political tactics used to sway the decision in favor of outsourcing.

4.8.4.2 *Political Tactics*

Three political tactics in particular are evident: the selective use of information, the selective use of decision alternatives, and delegation to a biased subordinate.

Selective use of information. The objectivity of the numbers used in the analysis is suspect. Dan, the supervisor of technical support, who was promoted as a result of the outsourcing decision, notes:

> "We made some sort of biased analysis so it would show that we were going to save money, but that's not the case, I don't believe it to be the case."

Tim corroborates that the numbers were biased in favor of outsourcing:

> "We put in the one time cost of relocating the data center, but we didn't put some one time costs on the other side."

For example, the costs to de-install the data center, ship the equipment back to the vendors, and transport the tape library were not included in the bids.

The major point of contention is the one million dollar charge included in the internal bid for building a new data center. Tim and the data center manager, Stephen, are confident they can build a data center for $600 000. Since they relocated the data center in 1987, they had experienced first-hand the costs associated with such a move. They were never permitted to formally analyze the cost of building a new data center. This brings us to the second political tactic—selective use of decision alternatives.

Selective use of decision alternatives. One option that seems glaringly absent from the analysis is keeping the data center where it was. When asked why management did not consider this option, Dan, the supervisor of technical support, responds:

> "They were basically thinking—and this is twisted logic—that the data center belonged. . .they couldn't imagine the data center being here and corporate offices being elsewhere, but it's okay to have the data center in an alternative site [in the instance of outsourcing]? They are still going to have to make a phone call to have something done."

When Barry's boss, Mike, was asked why keeping the data center where it was had not been considered, he responded:

> "Because I wanted 100%—if that is theoretically possible—I want 100% of Barry's time going to what people view as providing service to our clients in this company. For example, if we had a power plant in this company and devoted ten people to providing power for the lights, as long as I turn on the switch and get light, I don't care where it comes from. Within this business environment, people don't care where the computer processing comes from."

Barry's boss, one will note, did not answer the question. When it was put to him that "A lot of people feel you could run your own data center cheaper than [the outsourcing vendor]." He responded:

> "Let me put it to you this way. When you ask the people whose jobs are affected to evaluate the numbers, they tell you it's a push. If you have any sense at all, you know they are stacking the deck. They accuse me of stacking the deck, I KNOW they are stacking the deck."

Thus, one obvious alternative that FIRM8 failed to consider is keeping the data center where it was. Both Tim and Stephen were convinced that this alternative was ignored because it would have been the low cost choice. Another tactic that may have been employed is delegating the data gathering task to a biased subordinate.

Delegation to a biased subordinate. Barry delegated the data analysis and financial justification tasks to Tim, the manager of computer and network operations. Barry was asked, "He did all this help, knowing he would help eliminate his position?" Barry answered:

> "I'd ask him about that. He claims that I lied to him. He is sore about this, but I am giving him a very handsome severance package. I kind of led Tim to believe that he would be the person to manage all of this. . . . I lost a lot of sleep over this."

According to Tim, however, Barry promised him an even better job if FIRM8 outsourced.

> "Barry as much as said that [that Tim would be offered a great job]. When they were talking about moving, he told Norman and I, 'You guys will be invited to move, no question about it.' And beyond that, Barry and I talked about the effect on staff. He assured me that my job would be intact."

By Tim's own admission, he manipulated the numbers because he knew his boss wanted to outsource:

> "That kind of ties in with when you know the answer that your boss wants, the smart thing is to give him that answer. And actually it was a close call, but we had a trump card. . .this whole locating to the new city wild card. That is the item that swung the deal from costing you money to saving you money."

The day before the contract was signed, Tim was fired. Tim is still furious:

> "The point is, all along Barry led me to believe that a job would still exist for me. So I have to admit that I feel betrayed and led on."

In summary, one interpretation of the outsourcing decisions at FIRM8 is that Barry used political tactics to sway the decision in favor of outsourcing to increase his departmental and personal credibility. One participant noted of Barry:

> "I can only speak from my own observations. I got the feeling that he just wanted to make a mark. To give the illusion that he proactively made a decision. I don't think it was a business-oriented decision. It

was a project that was highly visible. He got some press, that sort of thing. That's really what I felt the agenda was."

One may dismiss this response, given that this participant was bitter about helping Barry to outsource, only to lose his job. It is interesting to note, however, that Barry's outsourcing decision was the only time that Barry was invited to speak to FIRM8's senior executives. A second interpretation arises, however, when analyzed through the lens of transaction cost theory.

4.8.5 FIRM8's Decision from a Transaction Cost Perspective

From the previous discussion, some evidence suggests that the outsourcing decision was political. By analyzing some of Barry's other decisions, we see an IS manager who strives to be a corporate player. In particular, he tries to provide low cost services since that is the agenda set for him by his management. In addition, he attended to the threat of opportunism.

4.8.5.1 Costs

Barry insists that outsourcing was only one of several cost-saving measures he initiated to satisfy his management. Another strategy Barry pursues to contain costs is to use outdated equipment. Barry has been able to reduce his equipment costs every year by renegotiating his lease on the company mainframe. When Barry arrived at FIRM8, this lease cost $60 000; It now costs only $4 000. Barry notes:

> "And I said as long as we stay on the trailing edge of technology—and I've been pushing this concept to senior management—we have an opportunity to capitalize on cheaper computing costs."

Barry also tried to forecast future IS demand so that he could plan for future IS expenditures. He asked his boss, then the CFO, in early 1990:

> "Tell me what we are doing in 1993, 1994. He said, 'I don't know but I can bet you again we are going to do this again in 1993.'. . . that is, a one half billion dollar acquisition. That's why I started out with company strategies. What is the company going to be doing? So this whole [outsourcing] decision was based on company strategy. I would never have done this, because our costs were already low and declining, you can see that."

Thus, Barry contends that part of the reason he considered outsourcing—besides the relocation issue—is that it is cheaper to buy resources from a vendor when IS demand is unpredictable. Vendors allow you to purchase computer resources "as you need them," thus eliminating the risks of over- or underspending. Since he could not forecast demand, outsourcing offered him a way to reduce risk, and thus costs.

4.8.5.2 *Threat of Opportunism*

Williamson proposes that an employee is motivated through rewards and punishments to contribute to profitability. This is why vendors may behave opportunistically—vendor employees are motivated to maximize the vendor's profits, not their client's profits. In order to reduce the threat of opportunism, contracts should be used.

Barry seems to concur with the transaction cost view of organizational reality. He feels that he is trying to do the best for his company, just as a vendor manager will do the best for his company. Therefore, to prevent the vendor manager from increasing vendor profits by extracting funds from FIRM8, Barry signed an airtight contract. The contract was so favorable to FIRM8, that the outsourcing vendor expressed many reservations. According to Barry:

> "A lot of people at [the outsourcing vendor] were uncomfortable with this [the contract]. In fact, their VP said, 'Barry, can't we put this thing in the drawer?' I said, 'Yeah, but this is still the operating agreement.'"

In summary, from the transaction cost perspective, Barry's outsourcing decision was economically sound, given a risk-averse attitude. Knowing that he had to contain costs in an unpredictable business environment, he outsourced to predict with certainty the costs of information systems regardless of growth. With an outsourcing vendor, Barry does not have to buy new equipment when his company grows, he merely spends a predetermined amount for additional MIPS and storage. This way, Barry saves his company "up front capital expenditures."

4.8.6 FIRM8—Conclusion

The outsourcing decisions at FIRM8 can be interpreted from many vantage points. Clearly, Barry feels he made an economic decision. One point to his credit is that he allowed the interviewing of employees who he knew were bitter about the decision. This indicates that Barry stands confident that he made the right decision. Throughout the three-hour interview, he discussed the issues of cost, inability to predict demand, the cost of the relocation, and the need for upgrades—all economic justifications for outsourcing.

However, the political interpretation of the decision cannot be ignored. Much evidence suggests that the decision-making process was really an exercise to justify management's preference for outsourcing. First, the deck was stacked in favor of outsourcing by including a figure of $1 million for the cost of a data center. Recall that the first outsourcing decision resulted in five vendors declining to submit bids since none could provide a cheaper service. Only when this $1 million was added to the internal bid could vendors offer a cheaper alternative. Second, the obvious alternative of keeping the data center where it was, was not evaluated. Many felt this was a lower cost alternative than outsourcing. Third, when Barry delegated the task to Tim, he clearly indicated his preference for outsourcing. Tim notes that when you know what your boss wants, the smart thing is to give him that answer. Another piece of evidence to suggest that the outsourcing decision was not based solely on costs is a that a consultant measured the data processing operations and reported that FIRM8's operations were extremely cost-effective. Tim notes that his staff was very proud of this report, since it showed that an outsider could not provide a cheaper service:

> "We had consultant XYZ come in for a data center assessment when Barry first came here. And we thought, well, he just wants to get a perspective on what kind of job we are doing. He doesn't know any of us too well, and the study said, 'Hey you are doing a great job.' In many cases, they couldn't believe how we were able to do what we were doing with the resources that we had. So we were all real proud of that. We thought we were kind of protected by that. And so it was real surprising to us when we went forward to look at outsourcing."

Once again, we see that the intentional actions of individuals can be interpreted in many ways. The transaction cost perspective sees a man trying to save his company money. The political perspective sees a man trying to gain recognition for himself and his department. Perhaps Dan offers a way to reconcile these competing interpretations. Dan feels that IS directors, like Barry, want to make an economic decision, but end up making a political decision because they fail to trust their instincts. Society keeps telling them that outsourcing saves them money, so they had better do it whether their own analysis justifies it or not:

"I think that people should analyze it, but analyze it like any other business deal. A lot of people are doing it because it is fashionable. They read about it in the magazines and they don't even trust their own analysis. You know, they say even if the internal is cheaper, like ours did, they don't trust it. They say, 'now wait a minute—all the articles said people are saving money, we must be doing something wrong.'"

4.9   FIRM9

Although most companies state cost reductions as their primary motivation for outsourcing, managers at FIRM9 said they outsourced to eliminate personnel and technical problems. FIRM9's IS staff was poorly trained, systems were antiquated, and users felt the entire department was unresponsive to their needs. Because FIRM9 was strapped for cash, it would not invest the money necessary to overhaul the IS department. FIRM9's senior executives fired the IS manager and charged his replacement with the task of improving customer service with existing resources. This new IS manager decided the best way to meet this challenge was to outsource almost every IS function to a third party vendor. The contract has been in effect since December 1990, and at time of writing, FIRM9 is pleased with its outsourcing arrangement.

Five individuals were interviewed at FIRM9 (see Table 4.11).

Table 4.11   *FIRM9 participants*

Name used in this case	Job title	Involvement in outsourcing
Robert	Manager of Information Systems	Robert initiated the outsourcing decision.
Henry	Manager of Systems Development	Henry provided financial analysis for the decision.
Al	Manager of Purchasing	Al is a major user of information services. He initially opposed outsourcing.
Marvin	Account Manager	Marvin recruited FIRM9's staff during negotiations. He currently manages the account.
Richard	IS Consultant	Richard helped negotiate the contract and provided transition services.

4.9.1   Historical Background of FIRM9

The CEO of FIRM9 worked hard during the 1980s to make his company one of the largest mining companies in the United States. His primary strategy for accomplishing this goal was growth through acquisition. In 1988, for example, FIRM9 acquired thirteen companies. Through such acquisitions, revenues grew threefold between 1984 and 1989. These acquisitions reeked havoc on FIRM9's information systems staff. They were expected to integrate new companies into their current systems with few additional resources. Senior management became dissatisfied with the level of service provided by this over-burdened IS staff. In 1988, they fired their Manager of Information Systems and hired Robert as his replacement.

Robert was courted away from his previous job as IS Director. In that job, Robert experienced outsourcing first hand when his company evaluated outsourcing. Although they decided not to outsource, Robert learned about the outsourcing marketplace, how to develop an RFP, and the risk associated with outsourcing the entire IS function to a third party. These outsourcing lessons simmered in the back of his mind as he faced new challenges at FIRM9.

Robert soon discovered that the IS department was ill-equipped to handle FIRM9's information processing needs. The IS department was under-staffed—there were only forty IS professionals servicing 7000 users. The staff that was on board was poorly trained and possessed only remedial technical skills. The data processing center ran antiquated hardware and the mainframe required an immediate upgrade since it was running at full capacity. Robert wondered how he was going to bring his people and technology into the twenty-first century when senior management didn't want him to hire additional people or increase spending.

Al, the Manager of Purchasing, explains why senior management was opposed to hiring additional staff:

> "Hiring is not very palatable to FIRM9 because the mining industry typically has highs and lows and they felt with the highs they could justify additional manpower, but with the lows they couldn't. They would have to go through a lay-off cycle."

Prices in the mining industry fluctuate dramatically. For example, the price of copper fluctuates between 50 cents and $1.50 a pound. When prices drop below a certain level, production is halted. Henry, the Manager of Systems Development, explains the impact of price fluctuations on FIRM9's operations:

"At $1.50, you can do all kinds of wonderful things. At 70 cents, you start cutting to the bare bones."

Because of the price volatility, FIRM9's senior management are cautious about hiring additional personnel to meet erratic, possibly short term demand.

4.9.2 FIRM9's Outsourcing Decision

Given senior management's position on hiring, Robert decided that outsourcing could potentially provide flexibility in managing FIRM9's human and computer resources. In 1989, he discussed the possibility of outsourcing with his boss, the CFO. The CFO encouraged Robert to proceed with an outsourcing evaluation.

4.9.2.1 *FIRM9's Decision Process*

Robert contacted the same vendor who submitted a bid to his former employer. He was confident that this vendor could provide the necessary human and computer resources. During the initial stages of contact, Robert told the vendor he only wanted a bid for data center operations. Rather than upgrade to a new mainframe, Robert felt that this vendor could offer additional capacity at a much lower cost. The vendor expressed interest in managing other IS functions as well. Robert decided to get some expert help with evaluating the vendor's proposal, so he hired Richard, an information systems outsourcing consultant.

Richard was concerned that Robert had not contacted any other vendors. He immediately made Robert request a bid from another vendor. Henry says, "[this other vendor] became a part of the process and they were instrumental in letting us negotiate a better contract because there was competition." Richard strung both vendors along, playing one against the other until the original vendor clearly rose as the better candidate. Marvin, the vendor account manager, claims they won the contract because they were willing to invest in FIRM9. He notes:

"Well, in my opinion, we were willing to invest some money to develop within our company a mining center of expertise. Where [the other vendor] was not willing to do that."

Indeed, the vendor is providing several analysts free of charge so that they can learn the mining business.

During the negotiations with the vendor, Robert decided he wanted a pricing structure that mirrored changes in the business. Unlike most outsourcing arrangements, he did not want to pay a fixed fee for a fixed bundle of services. Responding to Robert's wishes, Richard crafted a unique pricing mechanism for the data processing piece of the contract. Richard explains that he developed a measure that tied the volume of mine activity to CPU charges:

> "We developed a mine equivalent. Okay, it was really neat. And we didn't have any technical data to do this with. What we did is develop a mine equivalent based on the type of mine, number of people that worked in the mine, the shifts that were worked in the mine, the tonnage that was removed, and the quality of that tonnage. And what we did was we developed these models where we related the amount of transactions run through their GL [general ledger] based on the type of mine. And we actually were able to come up with that there actually is a mine equivalent."

Richard then separated variable data processing costs from fixed data processing costs. For any change in the number of mines supported, the vendor immediately adjusts the price. Thus, if the number of mines supported is reduced, FIRM9 receives an immediate credit equal to the variable cost. If the number of mines increases, FIRM9 pays for the marginal cost. This unique feature of the contract allows FIRM9 to immediately adjust their data processing costs to fluctuations in the business environment.

Al, however, notes that data processing costs are minor compared to the people costs. He feels that total IS costs will not really mirror business fluctuations. Al explains:

> "One of the primary reasons for outsourcing being considered, one of the primary things I always heard was that it gave us some cyclical ability to have whatever staff we need during the times when we have a lot of activity and being able to bear down. I don't buy that rationale in this particular case because even if you cut your operations in half, you still do purchasing, you still do accounting, you still do maintenance, all the reporting associated with those activities. The volume may be down, but the support is still there. I don't see a one-to-one relationship between volume of activity at a site to the level of activity in the IS to support it."

Al has a valid point. The data processing costs, measured in CPU minutes, will fluctuate based on the mine equivalent, but will the vendor actually reduce staff if a mine closes?

Richard also included a penalty clause for not meeting a number of data processing service levels, such as response time and availability.

Although the data processing piece of the contract is well defined, other service areas were neglected. There are no objective performance standards for applications development, support, or IS-related services. Henry claims that the contract merely stipulates that the vendor performs these services: "It doesn't matter how long it takes them to do it. It is just an obligation of the contract." When asked whether FIRM9 was afraid that the vendor would take advantage of the lack of measures, Henry claims no. He explains Robert's attitude towards the contract:

> "I think Robert approached that whole contract on the basis of evaluating [the vendor] as a company and what they would deliver regardless of what the contract had to say. If you had to go to the contract every-day to make an interpretation of it then he didn't want to outsource at all."

Prior to signing the contract, Robert informed his staff that FIRM9 was going to outsource with the vendor. This caused a virtual panic in his IS organization—a number of people immediately resigned. Al explains:

> "The IS employees were bailing out in droves. I think that was something that there was an honest attempt in trying to prevent, but it wasn't very successful. They just didn't want to work for [the outsourcing vendor]."

4.9.2.2   Outcome and Consequences of FIRM9's Decision

When the ten-year contract was finally signed in December 1990, only half of FIRM9's employees transferred over to the vendor. Robert expected the vendor to restaff the function and migrate processing over to the vendor's data center. The outsourcing vendor came through on both counts. The vendor immediately brought in qualified employees from other accounts. FIRM9 was very pleased with the professionalism of the vendor's staff. Al, for example, has this to say about the new staff:

> "I think we lost a lot of mediocre talent. We lost a lot of lightweights and filled those positions with a lot of heavyweights."

The data center transition was also accomplished in only three months. This migration was critical since FIRM9 needed to increase its capacity. Robert has been very pleased with the vendor's ability to bring the people and computer resources up to speed in only a few months. In an interview published in FIRM9's employee newsletter, Robert discusses the vendor's performance during the transition:

> "FIRM9 had a significant amount of turnover immediately after the transition. I was impressed with the ability of [the vendor] to fill vacancies with quality people. [The vendor] has been able to pick up the pieces and keep on going. I was also impressed with the preparation activities and the actual execution of the migration to their data center. There were few interruptions in service to the users, and [the vendor] made this very detailed, complex move look like it wasn't difficult at all."

In the long term, FIRM9 expects to save 16% on data processing costs. Henry feels the vendor is able to reduce data processing costs because they run multiple clients through its 300 MIP shop. Before outsourcing, FIRM9 had to pay an entire operations staff to run a small 17 MIP shop.

In the area of applications development and maintenance, however, there are no projected savings. When asked why FIRM9 would outsource such a vital function when there are no savings, Henry responded, "Their level of technical support." The vendor employees are much more technically competent than the previous staff. Al notes:

> "A lot of areas needed some new software capabilities to stay competitive. There wasn't a chance in the world that the current staff was going to be able to provide support necessary to get those things on-line."

Al says the vendor is implementing bar-coding based systems, an executive information system, and some additional automation in the purchasing function. Al notes that the prior staff did not have the technical skills to implement these systems.

All in all, Robert feels he will realize the two goals of outsourcing: increase the skill level of the staff and manage the computer resource through fluctuations in the business. The 16% data processing savings is an additional bonus. All five people who were interviewed expressed satisfaction—and in Al's case, gratitude—with their outsourcing decision.

FIRM9's outsourcing decision is now analyzed through the political and transaction cost perspectives. The latter offers a better understanding of the decision, primarily because case participants did not discuss political aspects of the decision.

4.9.3 FIRM9's Decision from a Political Perspective

The political model offers very few insights into FIRM9's decision, primarily because participants seemed reticent. In particular, Robert and Richard are polished businessmen. They spent most of their interviews talking about the success of their outsourcing arrangement. Marvin, the vendor's account manager, was uncooperative because he feared violating customer/vendor confidentiality—an understandable and respectable position. Henry and Al were more open, Al in particular. From these two, inklings of the political aspects of the decision emerged.

They felt that Robert was basically hired as a hatchet man. FIRM9's senior management felt that a stranger would be better able to implement radical changes than the previous IS director. Robert's previous outsourcing experience would also be helpful. From this perspective, Robert did not conduct a rational decision process where the decision-maker studies the problem, generates alternatives, and picks the low cost solution. Rather, the decision is construed as political because he was merely commissioned to perform a task.

Basically, the situation at FIRM9 was that the IS function simply did not meet the needs of the organization. The following quote from Al attests to the poor quality of the applications portfolio and IS staff prior to outsourcing:

> "The level of technical expertise, as I said, in the department was very, very low. And another area that lended itself to outsourcing was that we were in a mode where some very old systems existed and were being supported and there was a need to upgrade a lot of capacity in materials, maintenance, operations, and transportation. A lot of areas needed some new software capabilities to stay competitive. There wasn't a chance in the world that the current staff was going to be able to provide support necessary to get those things on-line."

Because the IS department possessed little power, it was unable to acquire the resources to revamp the department on its own. Therefore, outsourcing seemed a viable way to eliminate the headaches of managing an ineffective function.

In conclusion, the political model provides little insight into FIRM9's decision. The reason may be (a) politics did not play a role in the decision, or (b) participants refused to discuss any issues that may be viewed as pejorative.

4.9.4 FIRM9's Decision from a Transaction Cost Perspective

The meaning behind the intentional actions of decision-makers is better explained through the lens of transaction cost theory. Robert was given a seemingly impossible task: upgrade the mainframe, overhaul the current application portfolio, and obtain a qualified IS staff. Given that he was expected to accomplish this without the use of additional resources, Robert was prudent to turn to outsourcing. As prescribed by Williamson, he attended to transaction type and costs to determine which functions he should outsource. He failed, however, to realize that vendors may behave opportunistically. As a result, some provisions in his contract leave him vulnerable to stiff excess charges in the applications area.

4.9.4.1 *Transaction Type*

Transaction cost theory postulates that companies can manage certain functions more efficiently on their own. In particular, transactions that are idiosyncratic can be cheaper to produce internally because companies do not have to waste time explaining their unique requirements to an outsider. Williamson, however, ignores the concept that some transactions (or functions) are strategic in nature and thus should not be farmed out to a vendor. In those cases, it is not so much a cost issue as a competitive advantage issue.

For Robert, he considered that there were some functions that he did not want to turn over to the vendor. In particular, Robert feels that "you don't outsource the management of IS." Robert decided to keep strategic applications and IS planning in-house. Richard says that Robert wanted to keep the strategic mining systems because he was worried that the vendor didn't know enough about the mining industry:

> "He wanted to make sure that [the outsourcing vendor] could do it on some of the more uncomplicated applications before they handed over their life blood to them."

Richard believes Robert may eventually turn the support of the mining systems over to the vendor "after they prove themselves."

Robert, however, will never turn over IS planning. Henry explains FIRM9's position on this issue:

> "I guess the most significant problem we face—and we are trying to compensate for it—is the loss of FIRM9's perspective relative to running

the business. For that risk, we determined that we would never turn over the strategic planning and decision-making direction part of the business to [the outsourcing vendor]."

Of course, another reason why Robert may never turn planning over to a vendor is that it would obviate his job.

4.9.4.2   Costs

Cost was a major consideration in the decision because Robert was able to access a more qualified staff and upgrade his mainframe without asking management for more money. In addition, Robert projects that he will save 16% on his base bundle of services. However, FIRM9 potentially faces the same situation as FIRM7 as far as excess charges. Al feels that FIRM9 pays a premium for services over and above the baseline bundle:

"None of it is cheap. I guess there is a perception that once you have an outsourcer hooked in that you have a conduit to all this expertise, but you pay."

To Robert's credit, he did question how the vendor was able to provide cheaper information services. He and Henry feel that since the vendor's operations are much larger than FIRM9, they are able to achieve economies of scale.

Economies of scale.   Robert and Henry feel that the vendor achieves economies of scale in three areas: operations personnel, software licensing fees, and hardware discounts. Henry feels that the vendor is able to achieve economies of scale on the people and hardware side of data center operations:

"The economy of the way they run the data center, they have fifty customers and it takes one person—they don't have fifty people on the night shift, they have maybe three. So there is savings. They also have buying power capability that we may not have. And within the machine area, and more significantly, within the software. The operating things such as COBOL, and then on top of that, in the applications area, there are contracts that give them the ability to get lower rates."

He also stated that the vendor will reduce FIRM9's hardware costs because FIRM9 will only pay for the capacity they use. He claims that small shops can never be efficient because they always pay for unused capacity:

"Every time you upgrade, hopefully you run a machine up to the point where it is beginning to falter under the load you are adding. So for X period of time when you buy a new machine, you are paying for excess capacity and not getting use out of it. You never have an optimum and you cause business units problems because you can't provide them the optimal capacity. They have to pay more significantly than what the company is using at the present time."

While costs played a significant role in the decision, Robert's failure to attend to the threat of opportunism may negate the projected savings.

4.9.4.3 Threat of Opportunism

Robert did not attend to the threat of opportunism because he was looking for a business partner. He feels that the outsourcing vendor will not behave opportunistically because they are "committed to making this work." This may be a rather naive assumption. When Richard was hired as a consultant to help negotiate the contract, he made Robert solicit another bid. Richard tried to convince Robert that outsourcing vendors aren't your friends, they are your supplier.

Richard's advice is prudent. Outsourcing vendors are not partners because they do not share the same profit motive. The outsourcing account manager is responsible for his own profit and loss. Every additional dollar he squeezes from FIRM9 ends up on his income statement. Therefore, FIRM9 should have designed a contract to protect themselves.

FIRM9 negotiated an adequate deal for data processing, but they may have left themselves vulnerable to excess charges in other service areas. Henry notes that there are no measures for training, processing security requests, or PC maintenance because this is antithetical to the concept of a business partner:

"There isn't anything in there that says that they have to meet a certain number of statistics in a period of time. More that they fill a position within an organization. I guess what we have been trying to achieve more than anything else is that they are functioning as if they were an employee. They just happen to get paid from someone else."

This optimism may prove misguided. FIRM9 may be happy with outsourcing because this is still the trial—otherwise called the honeymoon—phase. There are few contractual provisions, however, that protect FIRM9 from potential excess charges in the applications area.

Henry reports that the vendor told FIRM9 that they were

uncomfortable with defining application measures in the contract—
they couldn't find "the right set of words to be put in the contract."
Therefore, this issue will allegedly be resolved after the contract is
in effect. In the meantime, the vendor assigned the same number
of employees that FIRM9 had prior to the contract. FIRM9 will pay
an excess charge for additional personnel. When Henry was asked
how he would know if the vendor really needed to hire additional
help, he revealed a major contractual flaw. If the vendor cannot
meet its deadlines, they get to charge FIRM9 for additional personnel.
Henry explains the situation in his own words:

> "We determine whether the objective completion date meets with
> business requirements. If they don't, then we hire additional resources."

In other words—the vendor is actually motivated to miss its
deadlines because they get to charge extra for more employees!

4.9.5   FIRM9—Conclusion

In conclusion, the transaction cost perspective offers an apt
interpretation of Robert's outsourcing decision. Given resource
constraints, he was able to upgrade the mainframe, access a better
IS staff, and improve the current systems by outsourcing. However,
his questionable assumption that the vendor is his "partner" may
result in excessive charges in the future. Henry sums up the gist
of FIRM9's outsourcing decision: "Costs aside, risks aside, we are
better off than before."

4.10   FIRM10

FIRM10 is part of a large service conglomerate. It provides
information services for its parent and sister companies. It also
supports over 200 outside customers on its computerized reservation
system. Given that FIRM10's business is information systems, some
may question the rationale for signing a ten-year, multi-hundred
million dollar contract with an outsourcing vendor. The answer is
rather simple: the entire conglomerate is bankrupt. FIRM10's
outsourcing arrangement brought in a multi-million dollar cash
infusion, protected information assets from creditors, transferred
almost 2000 employees to a more stable company, and possibly
diverted liquidation. From all indications, the outsourcing decision
at FIRM10 was based solely on economic considerations.

Executives at FIRM10 are struggling to survive bankruptcy. Therefore, only one individual, the CFO, was available for an interview (see Table 4.12). The CFO, however, was responsible for the outsourcing decision and spent three hours sharing his knowledge during the interview.

4.10.1 Historical Background of FIRM10

In 1988, FIRM10 belonged to a large service conglomerate. Pseudonyms have also been assigned to other companies in this conglomerate—the parent company is called HOLDING, and the other three subsidiaries are SERVICE1, SERVICE2, and FIRM10. SERVICE1 and SERVICE2 were the major subsidiaries that generated most of the profits for the conglomerate.

FIRM10 provided information services for HOLDING, SERVICE1, SERVICE2, and also supported 219 other outside companies on its computer reservation system. In simpler terms, FIRM10 can be thought of as the IS department for the conglomerate. Jack describes its comprehensive service:

> "We provide reservation systems, CRS information, payroll, inventory, engineering, maintenance, scheduling—anything that you would need from data processing or telecommunications."

FIRM10 differs from more traditional IS departments because it is organized as an independent company. It is not considered a profit center since it operates its own support functions such as finance, marketing, and legal. Jack describes the structure of FIRM10 as follows:

> "As an entity, FIRM10 is independent, separate, free-standing. We have our own management structure, our own president, our own corporate offices, our own lines of credit, we have our own banking sources, separate general ledger, separate P&L responsibilities."

Table 4.12 *FIRM10 participants*

Name used in this case	Job title	Involvement in outsourcing
Jack	Chief Financial Officer	Champion of the outsourcing decision.

Although FIRM10 is basically a large information systems company, it sees itself as a marketing company, not a technology company. It considers its marketing department as the true strategic thrust of the company. As such, Jack, the newly appointed CFO, questioned whether two-thirds of FIRM10's costs should be tied up in the technology department. Jack explains:

> "The start of the facilities management review really came from us. We said, two-thirds of our costs is data processing/telecommunications. Is there a better way to provide that?"

As Jack was scrutinizing technology expenses, a large outsourcing vendor contacted FIRM10's CEO in December of 1988. This vendor had read in the trade literature that FIRM10 abandoned its new global network strategy because of the cost. They asked to bid on the network. After a few initial meetings, Jack, his CEO and the general council decided to expand the scope of the outsourcing evaluation to include the entire technology department.

4.10.2 FIRM10's Outsourcing Decision

Jack also contacted other vendors, but soon realized most were too small to handle FIRM10's data processing needs. Therefore, very early in the process, he decided to commit to the one vendor. Next, Jack determined how he was going to conduct contract negotiations with this vendor. He believed that outsourcing decisions take one of two forms. The first he called the "CEO handshake" deals where the CEO signs the deal with the understanding that details will be worked out later. The second approach is when all the details are specified in the contract before anything is signed. Jack rejected the first approach:

> "We heard the horror stories, the problems of those type of situations. Clearly, the receiver of the service, the buyer of the vendor's products, you clearly have no leverage in the negotiations after that point."

Instead, Jack wanted a tight contractual agreement:

> "We said we are going to have everything done up front. We would have no issues to be resolved later. No pricing to be determined later. No analysis to be done later. No operations manuals to be done later. Everything to be resolved up front."

He thus entered into negotiations in early 1989 with the strategy that all services would be specified before the contract would be signed.

4.10.2.1 FIRM10's Outsourcing Decision Process

FIRM10's outsourcing decision process required almost two years because of fighting within the conglomerate. During the early phase of negotiations, HOLDING wanted the vendor to make them a loan as part of the deal. The vendor finally agreed to lend HOLDING millions of dollars at a very low interest rate. FIRM10 would see none of this money. The next battle ensued among the sister companies. Each fought to absorb their share of the savings. Jack explains:

> "The various pricing methodologies, the allocation costs between FIRM10, SERVICE1, and SERVICE2 was raised as an issue. Where are the cost savings? Aside from the very thorny issues of cost accounting, another slice was then added that said, 'If you didn't give as much savings to FIRM10, could you give more savings to SERVICE2?'"

Finally, the three subsidiaries agreed to an equitable share of both savings and costs. Just when the deal was about to be finalized, SERVICE1 filed for bankruptcy. The deal was halted. Jack explains:

> "All of a sudden in the middle of this process, SERVICE1 goes into bankruptcy...BOOM! SERVICE1 creditors come along and say, 'Under bankruptcy law, there can be no change in the normal course of the company. So if you want to do something that is not in the ordinary operating course of the company, you have to get our permission.'"

The creditors unraveled the intercompany pricing agreement. After months of negotiations and pleas to the judge, Jack got a modified deal approved. Before this contract was signed, however, SERVICE2 filed for bankruptcy in the fall of 1990. The outsourcing vendor decided to halt negotiations to determine its liability if FIRM10 went bankrupt. The vendor may have been prudent to wait, since FIRM10 went bankrupt in November of 1990. Now the entire contract had to be approved in bankruptcy court.

Just when the judge was about to approve the contract, another outsourcing vendor submitted a surprise bid for the outsourcing contract. Jack appeared before the judge and pleaded with him to grant FIRM10 permission to sign with the original vendor. This second vendor asked and received an injunction to prevent FIRM10 from signing the deal. Jack was forced to evaluate the other vendor's proposal and to submit his findings to the judge. Jack remained committed to the first vendor:

> "We told [the second vendor] that we have been looking at this deal for two years and they bring certain things to the transaction that you do not bring such as they will make us a loan, they will buy a portion of our business which we no longer have a need for, they will invest in our business.' And [this second vendor] did not want to make a loan and they did not want to buy the [name omitted] division."

After careful consideration, the judge agreed to let FIRM10 sign with the first vendor. The judge's decision was based on the first vendor's willingness to transition all the IS employees—the second vendor would only transition 250 employees. In the end, three contracts were signed between the vendor and SERVICE2, the vendor and HOLDING, and the vendor and FIRM10. FIRM10 signed their contract in May of 1991.

4.10.2.2   Outcome and Consequences of FIRM10's Decision

FIRM10's contract amounts to hundreds of millions of dollars and covers ten years of service. The contract encompasses data processing, telecommunications, applications development, and applications support. Although Jack declined to give an exact figure, he says the contract will save FIRM10 20% on IS costs. He is confident that he will realize the savings because of his "three foot contract." The contract includes service definitions, service measures, penalty clauses, incremental prices, volume fluctuations, and the right to purchase outside IS resources. Jack feels his biggest insurance is the penalty clauses. He explained that millions of dollars in revenue is booked in their reservation system everyday. Since downtime equates to lost revenue, the outsourcing vendor is charged about 1% of daily revenues for every downtime occurrence. Although this is not enough to compensate FIRM10, Jack feels it is enough to make the vendor attend to disasters.

Risks of outsourcing.   Jack feels good about his outsourcing contract, although he acknowledges four risks of outsourcing: loss of control over assets and people, loss of flexibility to make changes in direction, inability to rebuild an internal IS shop, and inability to foresee advances in new technology. In particular, Jack is concerned about the loss of control. FIRM10 no longer makes hiring decisions about IS personnel, it no longer determines what technology to buy, nor determines how resources will be allocated. FIRM10 must abide by the vendor's decisions on these issues.

Jack's decision is now evaluated from the political and transaction cost perspectives.

4.10.3 FIRM10's Decision from a Political Perspective

In the other twelve cases, the power of the IS department is analyzed vis-à-vis the other departments. In the case of FIRM10, the coalitions formed along company lines, rather than departmental lines. Surprisingly, there was little opposition to outsourcing within FIRM10. The IS employees, who typically feel threatened by outsourcing, were glad to transition to a more stable company. Indeed, every IS employee from FIRM10's technology department transitioned to the vendor. Their fate with FIRM10 would have been tenuous at best.

The politics that did occur, occurred between the three subsidiaries and the creditors. These entities were all vying for their share of the savings from outsourcing. Since the outsourcing deal was viewed as a zero sum game, each coalition fought for their slice of the pie. At first, HOLDING possessed most of the power and succeeded in acquiring the money the vendor lent to the conglomerate. After it acquired the monetary prize, HOLDING let the sister companies battle over the cost allocation. Jack describes the process as follows:

> "There was a fair amount of internecine, brother/sister argument. 'You're screwing me.' 'I'm screwing you.' 'We didn't get a good deal here.' 'You got all the savings.' 'I didn't get enough savings.' 'Raise your price.' A lot of squabbles along those lines."

By the time SERVICE1, SERVICE2, and FIRM10 agreed on the cost and pricing structure, everybody went bankrupt. The power then transferred from HOLDING to the bankruptcy judges who had final say on the outsourcing decision.

Given the financial turmoil, it is difficult to view Jack's behavior as political. He had nothing personal to gain by outsourcing. During the entire negotiation process, he was aware that he may be on the streets regardless of the decision outcome. He lost many nights of sleep during bankruptcy hearings. When Jack was asked how he fared through this tumultuous time, he replied in grave humor, "I'm really only twenty-six years old, I just look fifty." His behavior is better understood from the transaction cost perspective.

4.10.4 FIRM10's Decision from a Transaction Cost Perspective

During Jack's interview, he used the financial lingo typical of a chief financial officer. His concerns during the contract negotiations centered around the selection of value-consuming functions (analogous to Williamson's transaction type), costs as assessed by net present value calculations, and the prevention of opportunism. By attending to these considerations, he made a decision that improved the financial position of his company.

4.10.4.1 Transaction Type

During negotiations, Jack wanted to identify value-consuming functions as candidates for outsourcing. He felt that a vendor could provide these services for a lower price. He explains:

> "In general, if I were writing a book or giving a speech, I would say the way to do these things is to define value-added versus commodity resources. Now those resources may be people, computers, space, technology—whatever. Just look at what you are giving away and make sure you are only giving away commodity type transactions."

One may question whether Jack only outsourced his commodity resources, given that information services are FIRM10's business. The response is that FIRM10 does not see itself as an information systems company, rather it sees itself as a marketing company. Since FIRM10 maintained its marketing function, Jack feels it did not give away its assets. On the technology side, Jack said he tried to keep as many value-added people as possible:

> "And we kept a certain amount of what I'll call value-added people. There are some pieces of a facility management contract that are pure commodity. And you ought to outsource those. Everybody ought to. There is no reason to keep the computer. They are not going to be able to run it as efficiently as [an outsourcing vendor]. However, things like systems analysts, application programmers, things like business people develop, capacity planning people. People like distributed processing planners. Those are the people that really know your business. They add value."

4.10.4.2 Costs

From a financial standpoint, the outsourcing vendor offered FIRM10 a very attractive deal. It gave FIRM10 a substantial loan at low interest rates, it paid cash for FIRM10's information assets, it pushed FIRM10's expenses to the later part of the contract, and it bought a share of one of their divisions for about a quarter of a million dollars. Thus, the net present value of the cash flows was very favorable for FIRM10. Modest estimates project 20% savings over a ten-year period.

The vendor offered FIRM10 an attractive package because it wanted an entrée into the industry. The vendor seems to possess few inherent economies of scale that enable it to provide services at a lower cost. Since FIRM10 runs 800 MIPS, one assumes that it has achieved economies of scale in data processing. FIRM10 and the vendor also receive similar discounts on hardware purchases. From a functional standpoint, FIRM10 and the vendor should experience comparable operating costs.

Thus, the savings come from the manipulation of payment schedules, rather than the vendor's inherent ability to provide services for less money. But from FIRM10's perspective, it cares little about the source of savings as long as savings are realized.

4.10.4.3 Threat of Opportunism

The threat of opportunism is an important consideration since the costs of outsourcing arrangements will increase if vendors behave opportunistically. Jack was well aware of this possibility:

> "Once you sign with a vendor, you have no options other than onerous contract terms, so when you get into that situation it's a lose/lose for both parties. What are you going to do? Sue them? Fire them? Stop buying services? There is nobody else, in a short period of time, who you can buy services from."

Jack feels, however, that the vendor will not behave opportunistically in this case because of his three foot contract and because the vendor has a vested interest in FIRM10. He likes to think of his outsourcing vendor as a partner. When Jack was asked, "How can a vendor be a partner when there is no shared P&L?," he explained that the outsourcing vendor is using this account as an entrée into the industry. Their future revenues depend on the success of this account. Therefore, they do share common goals. Jack explains:

> "How important are we to them? Didn't we give them an entrée into a new industry? Didn't we give them special skills—which is one of the reasons they wanted the transaction. What would their image be if the

deal were to collapse? What besides just financial benefits is there that they are getting out of the deal? And if there are a lot of yeses, where there is some meat to those things, then you really have a partnership where there is a shared risk, shared goals, shared vision. They are really a partner as opposed to a vendor."

Although Jack believes that common goals help mediate opportunistic behavior, he took other preventative measures. He says most companies neglect to retain staff to monitor the bill:

"You get a bill, it's sent to the controller or the CEO. He doesn't know whether the bill is right or wrong. He's not watching technology going forward. He's not on top of technological changes. So he has a problem getting himself satisfied that he is getting the savings and the most efficient way to produce a service...We, on the other hand, kept a significant portion of our technology people. And we have a contract administration group that monitors things like monthly performance, efficient configuration of data centers to ensure that before we get into incremental costs and out of baseline, that we maximize every last little MIP."

4.10.5 FIRM10—Conclusion

FIRM10's outsourcing decision appears to be based on economics. Through outsourcing, FIRM10 received a cash infusion from the sale of information assets, it negotiated a multi-million dollar loan at an attractive interest rate, it sold a portion of its service division for cash, and it suspended payments until the later part of the contract. Politics came into play during contract negotiations when coalitions fought for their share of the savings. The entire power structure changed, however, after the conglomerate filed for bankruptcy. The bankruptcy judges ultimately decided the fate of the outsourcing decision.

4.11 FIRM11

FIRM11 is another example of a successful outsourcing arrangement. FIRM11 claims it outsourced because the IS department was staffed with unqualified personnel and the users viewed them as non-responsive. Through outsourcing, FIRM11 accessed a qualified staff, upgraded technology, and improved customer service.

Although much of this research seems to admonish readers about the potential for opportunism, FIRM11's account manager, Lawrence, offers a welcome exception. He envisions changing the culture of his outsourcing firm to be more customer oriented and less ruthless. FIRM11 placed so much faith in Lawrence that it included a clause in the contract stipulating that he must remain the account manager for three years. Under Lawrence's direction, the IS department has gained the credibility and power that eluded the previous IS director.

The controller, who made the outsourcing decision, and Lawrence were interviewed for this case (see Table 4.13).

4.11.1 Historical Background of FIRM11

FIRM11 is a large coal producer in the United States. It runs a rather lean operation with under 2000 people. Prior to outsourcing, the information systems department comprised 45 people and reported to the controller who in turn reported to the CFO. The IS department, which operated a 12 MIP machine, was located thirty miles from company headquarters. Customer service was viewed as dismal. Systems analysts rarely communicated with their users in person. In fact, analysts needed permission even to visit company headquarters. This arrangement isolated the information systems department from the users it was to serve.

Paul, the controller, claims that the distance was not the only problem, but rather his primary concern was the exorbitant cost of information services. In 1987, the IS budget was about 7 millon dollars. Paul felt that "the level of service did not support the dollars involved."

In 1987, FIRM11 suffered a major loss in net revenues. This prompted the CEO to search for cost-cutting measures. Paul explains:

"About five years ago, FIRM11 went on a cost reduction program. And that cost reduction program was felt by every department without

Table 4.13 *FIRM11 participants*

Name used in this case	Job title	Involvement in outsourcing
Paul	Controller	Paul initiated the outsourcing decision, contacted the vendor, and negotiated the contract.
Lawrence	Account Manager	Lawrence negotiated the contract for the vendor and now serves as account manager.

exception. One of the focuses on it was naturally information services. It was viewed strictly as overhead. There was constant pressure on information services to reduce costs over a period of five years, and they did reduce their costs significantly. But we still felt we weren't getting the best bang for the buck."

Indeed, the prior IS director managed to reduce his budget by 2 million dollars by 1989. The controller was still not pleased with the IS department primarily because of "the people problems." The turnover rate of IS professionals was very high:

"We were constantly having turnover. As small shops do, people leave for better opportunities with bigger companies. So by the time you get somebody trained in your system, they get up and leave."

Paul wanted somehow to reduce the personnel costs associated with the high turnover rate.

4.11.2 FIRM11's Outsourcing Decision

In 1989, Paul attended a National Coal Association conference. This was his first exposure to information systems outsourcing:

"I was talking to some of my peers in the industry. We were talking about data processing costs, comparing notes. I was amazed what this other company's costs were. They were so much lower than ours and they were approximately the same size company as us. So I asked him, 'What is your secret?' He said, 'We outsourced.'"

After that meeting, Paul told his boss (the CFO) about outsourcing and both agreed, "it was worth exploring."

4.11.2.1 *FIRM11's Outsourcing Decision Process*

Paul contacted the same vendor his peer told him about at the conference. He said he also contacted two other vendors, but they were only interested in running the data center. Paul was determined to outsource the applications development and support as well as data center operations.

In December 1989, Paul and his boss decided to outsource with the only vendor who agreed to takeover the entire IS function. From December 1989 to April 1990, Paul entered into private negotiations with the vendor. He decided not to involve anyone from the information systems department, not even the IS director:

"It was our intention not to make it public to the IS people. In case something went wrong in the negotiations, we didn't want to cause a lot of disruption in the mean time."

Paul hired a lawyer and a consultant to help him negotiate the contract. His primary concern was that he had no understanding of information systems: "I mean, I am not a technician. MIPS? Bytes? Who knows?"

According to Paul, the consultant was valuable because "he helped supplement our ignorance as far as the design of the contract." The consultant stressed the importance of defining service levels and measures in the baseline period (December through May), at least in the data processing area. The consultant added one unique feature to the contract—the baseline measures would be readjusted after the first six months of the contract. He was rightfully concerned that the CPU minutes running on the old computer would not translate to the machines running at the vendor's data center. This preventative measure saved FIRM11 significant money. When the vendor transferred many systems from tape to DASD, for example, the baseline measure was recalculated, thus preventing excess charges.

The consultant also included provisions in the contract for "significant changes in the business." If volumes exceed a certain variance—either increases or decreases in growth, the contract is opened for renegotiation. Paul feels this provision will reduce FIRM11's longterm risks.

The performance measures for applications, however, are not defined in the contract. Paul merely prioritized which systems should receive attention first:

> "If there is a specific problem with a specific system, depending on degree of importance, there are certain criteria that they have to respond to in a certain period of time. Other than that, there are not a lot of criteria for measuring performance."

Despite the consultant's contribution to improving the contract, he missed one vital area. The contract is weak because of the absence of cash penalties for non-performance. Thus, FIRM11 has no recourse if services are sub-standard.

In April 1990, two weeks prior to signing the contract, the IS director discovered that Paul was about to outsource:

> "His involvement came in the end when it was brought to his attention that we were in the process of doing this. He had put together a

proposal of his own. It was a weak proposal, it was not very formal. He said he could do everything that [the vendor] could do for the same price. But we didn't place that much faith in his proposal."

Paul felt that if the IS director was truly capable of reducing costs and improving service, he would have already accomplished it. In all, the IS director's proposal was "too little, too late" to prevent outsourcing.

4.11.2.2 *Outcome and Consequences of FIRM11's Decision*

In May 1990, FIRM11 and the vendor signed a ten-year, forty-five page contract. On that day, the entire IS staff was offered a position with the vendor; 75% of the staff accepted, including the IS director who now provides marking research and consulting for the vendor on another account.

Paul estimates that the contract will save him $600 000 annually. Despite the weakness of the contract, Paul has not paid a single dollar in excess charges to the vendor. This is one of the few cases encountered where the client has not been blind-sided by a monthly bill for services above baseline. In addition to the cost savings, Paul is convinced that customer service has improved. We will see that the success of this outsourcing arrangement is largely attributed to Lawrence.

Attention now returns to Paul and his perceptions on the keys to success of outsourcing. Paul feels that Lawrence is the number one key to success because of his significant talent. Paul's second key to success was negotiating what he perceives to be a sound contract by hiring the lawyer and the consultant:

> "They initially gave us their standard off-the-shelf contract, but during negotiations, we hired a legal counsel who specialized in dealing with outsourcing. We also hired an expert consultant who had dealt with outsourcing. They assisted us in negotiations and framing the contract. So really, the final contract resembled very little to the original contract."

Paul thinks the biggest risks of outsourcing are (1) changes in technology, and (2) the prohibitive cost of ever rebuilding an internal IS department. Paul explains these risks:

> "Ten years. . .that's a long time. Technology will change drastically over ten years. So it is a gamble. Maybe because of technological changes, we could have saved more doing it in-house. Increase use in microcomputers, what have you. I really don't know, I'm no futurist. I can't predict those things easily. But I think it is worth the gamble."

This contract is a gamble because Paul feels the outsourcing decision is permanent since the cost of rebuilding a shop is prohibitive. Paul describes the outsourcing decision in this way: "It's like being half pregnant when you outsource—it's all or nothing." But all in all, Paul is very pleased with the outsourcing arrangement. He notes: "It has been more of a pleasurable experience than a disappointment at this time."

Now that the outsourcing decision has been described, the decision is analyzed from the political and transaction cost perspectives.

4.11.3   FIRM11's Decision from a Political Perspective

The previous IS director would be someone who could shed significant insights into the political climate surrounding the outsourcing decision. Unfortunately, he was unavailable for an interview. Therefore, the pertinent political constructs are inferred from Paul and Lawrence's interviews.

Since Paul was obviously more powerful than his only potential opposition, the IS director, he did not need to enact political tactics to sway the decision in his favor. The previous director's lack of power is assessed below.

4.11.3.1   Power of FIRM11's IS Department

From the political perspective, three indicants suggest that the IS department was powerless and ineffective. According to case participants, the IS director commanded a mediocre budget, he was not involved in corporate plans, and his staff was viewed as technically unqualified and non-responsive.

FIRM11's IS budget.   During the interview, Paul expressed several times that he thought he was paying too much for information services. As a controller, he is understandably cost conscious, but by industry standards, the IS department was not over-budgeted. In 1987, the IS budget was 1% of revenues. By 1989, the IS budget had shrunk to 0.8% of revenues. Even though the IS budget was somewhat lean, Paul had the perception that "we weren't getting the best bang for the buck."

IS director's lack of involvement in planning.   Another indicant of power is the ability to influence decisions and company goals. The previous IS director was not only non-influential, he never developed a comprehensive systems plan. When Lawrence took over the IS department through the outsourcing contract, he was determined to align his IS plans to FIRM11's corporate plan. To his horror, however, FIRM11 did not have a well articulated corporate plan, let alone an IS plan. Lawrence explains:

> "The sophistication of planning by senior management was quite low. Even when it was there, it centered around financial forecasts and it was not communicated throughout the company."

Lawrence subsequently had the CEO explain the corporate objectives to him. From that conversation, he developed a comprehensive business plan. The main focus of this plan was to integrate the current information systems. Paul describes the need for integration:

> "Another recommendation that came out of the business plan was to get our systems to talk to each other. The communications between the systems need to be improved. Along with the fact that a lot of applications are kept on microcomputers, that information is not being shared among users. As a result, we need to establish communication links in that area. As a result of all that, information will be exchanged more freely between users to achieve the goals of customer satisfaction."

Whereas the previous IS director had failed to develop a systems plan, Lawrence succeeded not only in creating an IS plan, but he also helped the CEO develop and communicate a corporate plan.

Lack of dependency. Another indicant of power is dependency— the extent to which other departments depend on the outputs of your department. In the case of FIRM11's IS department, users felt that they could not depend on the IS staff. Not only were they physically removed from the users, they had remedial technical skills and were not customer-oriented. Lawrence describes that he had to retrain FIRM11's IS staff:

> "The people development—I put an emphasis on training. God knows the FIRM11 folks that were here were severely curtailed. We needed to get them back to speed."

Users have grown much more dependent on the IS department under Lawrence's direction.

In summary, we see that the previous IS director had little power—he operated with a small budget, he was not privy to corporate plans, and he was unable to maintain a qualified staff. One also must question the IS director's political savvy since he did not learn of the outsourcing arrangement until three weeks prior to signing the contract. Paul, the consultant, and the vendor were able to run reports, tour the data center, and determine technical requirements without the IS director's knowledge. His last-ditch attempt to prevent outsourcing just prior to the close of negotiations was ineffective. His lack of power made him extremely vulnerable to outsourcing and any political tactics he may have enacted were perceived by Paul as "too little too late."

In addition to analyzing the power of the IS department prior to outsourcing, it is interesting to see how the power structure has changed under Lawrence's expert reign. Whereas the prior IS director possessed little power, Lawrence has been able to increase the user's dependency on systems, align the IS plan with the corporate plan, and decrease the user's ability to substitute his services for an outside vendor.

Whereas the previous director was isolated in an office thirty miles from headquarters, Lawrence is actively involved with FIRM11's senior management. He not only commands an audience with the CEO, he assists him in corporate planning.

To Paul's surprise, his CEO was willing to pay the vendor extra money to implement the recommendations from the business information plan (BIP). The CEO told him, "Okay. I understand that as long as I can see the benefit of it." Thus, Lawrence was able to achieve something his predecessor was unable to do: sell the value of IT to the CEO. Lawrence said it was simple, "If you show a guy value, he is willing to pay for it."

Another indicant that Lawrence has increased the power of the IS department is that he has decreased the users' desire to acquire substitute services. When a user hired another vendor to implement a network that subsequently failed to work, Lawrence stepped in and told him:

"We have never been good at the one-sy, two-sy, Mickey Mouse deals. There will always be people to beat that sort of thing on price. But if you are looking for an infrastructure-wide issue to be dealt with, then we are able to deliver the best long-term solution. . .By the time we were done the conversation, he said, 'Yeah, I think you are right. Nothing you said was wrong. I did maximize my savings in the short run. But I must admit, I didn't think about some of these issues that you brought up.' I said, 'Well let's learn a lesson from that.'"

Lawrence challenges a basic assumption of the political model. The political model feels that power is largely a structural phenomenon. But Lawrence was able to increase power, as indicated by dependency, non-substitutability, and his influence on the CEO— without any corresponding change in authority. The IS department still reports to the controller. This provides some evidence that personality is also another significant source of power.

4.11.4 FIRM11's Decision from a Transaction Cost Perspective

Upon meeting Paul, the overwhelming impression he exudes is that of a rational decision-maker. Equipped with his spreadsheets, MBA in Finance, and lifelong career as a controller, he lives and breathes financial models. He never discussed IS in terms of strategic advantage, but rather focused attention on the costs of providing what he perceives to be a utility service. He claims that his decision was motivated by the desire to reduce costs.

4.11.4.1 *Costs*

Paul was charged by the CEO to cut costs. He naturally turned his attention to his troublesome IS department. Although he had succeeded in reducing the IS budget by two million dollars, he was concerned how he was going to contain costs given the need for an upgrade, the high turnover rate, and the need for technical training. He found his solution when he attended the National Coal Association's seminar in 1989. Excited about the possibility of outsourcing as a means to reduce costs, he contacted the vendor.

After months of negotiations, Paul is convinced that he will save his company 6 million dollars over the course of a ten-year contact.

One question that all the participants were asked was whether they investigated the possibility of reducing costs on their own. Paul felt that his previous IS director was given ample opportunity, but failed to deliver. Paul believes that the outsourcing vendor is able to reduce costs because of its economies of scale on hardware and people.

Economies of scale. In the area of hardware, Paul feels that the vendor is able to achieve these savings by running eighteen customers from their data center:

> "One thing is the economies of scale of the processing. They leverage software by running a lot of customers from that utility."

In particular, Paul notes that the vendor is able to support his needs with a leaner staff:

> "Their staff that they support us with now is smaller than what we had. And because of the depth of their organization, they are able to support us with a smaller staff."

Paul claims the vendor's staff is "heads and shoulders over what we had before." When Paul's statement was challenged by pointing out that 75% of his staff were the same people he had before, he responded:

> "Not all of them stayed once they went over. Most of them are still supporting our account, but at the same time Lawrence supplemented our staff with some [of the vendor's] people."

Indeed, Lawrence was able to access people resources less expensively than FIRM11. He brought in experts to support the payroll package and a small DEC system, which prior to outsourcing went unsupported because FIRM11 could not retain qualified personnel.

Thus, Paul feels that the vendor's ability to achieve hardware and people economies of scale is the source of his cost savings— savings he could not achieve on his own.

4.11.4.2 *Transaction Type*

Transaction cost theory suggests that only non-specific transactions should be outsourced. Since such functions are viewed as a commodity, vendors that specialize are able to produce goods and services cheaper than a company can produce themselves. Paul seemed to concur with this theory. Since he perceived the entire IS function as a utility, he felt an outsourcer could provide a cheaper service. When he was asked why he didn't consider keeping applications in-house, he responded:

> "People say you should keep applications. I ask them, 'Why would you want to do that? That's the biggest headache. Anybody can run a machine, it's the applications that are a headache.'"

He basically felt that his previous staff was so poorly trained that he could not provide a cost-effective applications team. Therefore, he outsourced this as well.

4.11.4.3 Threat of Opportunism

The flaws in the outsourcing contract were discussed in a preceding section. Since Paul failed to develop application service measures or penalties for non-performance, the transaction cost theory would suggest that he is vulnerable to the threat of opportunism. However, after a year and a half of service, the vendor has never charged FIRM11 for excess services. The threat of opportunism seems largely improbable because of Lawrence's unique background.

Prior to working for the vendor, Lawrence was actually one of its customers. When he was working as a manager for a large manufacturing company, his management decided to outsource the information systems department to a vendor. Lawrence constantly complained about the level of service the vendor provided. He claims the vendor charged his department for services he felt were covered in the contract. He felt the vendor's account manager was a "money grubber" only concerned with his P&L. He complained so much that the vendor offered him a job, stating, "You are right— so how would you like to come join us and try to make us a better company?" After much thought, Lawrence decided to work for the vendor on a trial basis. Six years later, he continues to implement cultural changes. His goal is to make his company reward its account managers for customer service first, people development second, and profitability third:

> "It is very simple in my mind. The profitability is absolutely the number three thing on my list of priorities. The first one is customer satisfaction, the second one is development of people. . .If you can achieve that, the gains you are going to make in terms of new business, whether that be with existing customers or new customers, far outweighs some of their little operational concerns. And certainly on an account this size, so we lose a few thousand dollars doing something, if I can win a customer that's going to reference another 35 million dollar deal, surely that's smarter business."

One may suspect his statements as pure platitudes, but he has succeeded in instilling these priorities on his account. In the area of customer service, he put his staff back in contact with the users. His analysts now frequent the base office and are evaluated on how well they respond to user needs. In the area of people development, he provided each analyst with three weeks of technical training as well as reorienting the staff to the concept of serving the customer. He also tries to motivate his staff by being a "leader" rather than a "manager." He explains the difference between the styles:

"I think when you lead people, you are talking about a motivational aspect of management. Having the belief that people inherently will excel—do the best job they can—if they are given two things. The first is the skill set to do the job. The second is a reason to do the job. If you give them those two things, I believe people will do the best they can. So, to provide those two things is to lead. They are motivated, they believe in what they do, and they see life beyond Friday. Managing people says, 'Let's focus on the tasks to be accomplished.' And using people like chattels, assigning them to tasks and saying, 'Let me know when you are finished. When you are done, I'll give you something else to do.' That makes people feel expendable. It doesn't give them a long-term reason for being here. So I think it's a difference in culture and approach—that's the difference between leading and managing."

Paul placed so much faith in Lawrence's ability that he decided to consummate the deal only if Lawrence was guaranteed to manage the account. Paul explains:

"In our contract, we stated that Lawrence had to remain for a certain number of years. After that, he can be replaced, but it will be a major decision who will replace him. We had expert help in negotiating that into the contract."

Thus, although Paul failed to attend to the threat of opportunism, the risk that the vendor will behave opportunistically is minimized by Lawrence's presence.

In summary, Paul's outsourcing decision seems economically motivated. His major concern as a controller was to provide the cheapest service possible. Because he views IS as a utility, he outsourced to an expert who could provide a lower cost service through its ability to achieve economies of scale.

4.11.5 FIRM11—Conclusion

The political and transaction costs models offer a rich picture of Paul's outsourcing decision. By analyzing the power of the previous IS director, we see that the IS department was vulnerable to outsourcing. Since Paul, the controller, possessed a significant amount of power, he was able to implement his decision without resorting to political tactics. He conducted an economic analysis of outsourcing and determined that he could save 6 million dollars while improving customer service at the same time.

The power of the IS department has increased as a result of Lawrence's abilities. His users are happy, they no longer acquire resources from other sources, and the CEO hired Lawrence to develop a corporate plan. Lawrence sums up the change in power, "We are finally recognized at the corporate level of this company." It seems unlikely that Lawrence will abuse his power since he is committed to changing the vendor's corporate culture. Paul does note, however, that the situation may change:

> "Right now, after one and one half years experience—I might speak differently in year five than in year one—this is still the honeymoon. I haven't noted anything that we would do different."

One suspects that if the previous IS director had Lawrence's business acumen, that FIRM11 may not have outsourced. Thus, we witness once again how the political climate influenced what seems to be an economically motivated outsourcing decision.

4.12 FIRM12

FIRM12 offers a unique opportunity to evaluate the long term consequences of outsourcing. The decision to outsource the entire IS function was made in 1984. After seven years of poor service, FIRM12 is slowly rebuilding an internal information systems organization.

Because negotiations are still in process between FIRM12 and the vendor, the manager of data processing (see Table 4.14) did not permit his staff to be interviewed. Since he has been with FIRM12 since 1982, he was privy to all the major outsourcing decisions made at his company and was willing to discuss these decisions in the interview.

4.12.1 Historical Background of FIRM12

Before 1981, FIRM12 was a subsidiary of a large energy holding company. In 1981, the entire energy company and its subsidiaries were bought in a hostile takeover. The new owners had little

Table 4.14 *FIRM12 participants*

Name used in this case	Job title	Involvement in outsourcing
Gary	Manager of Data Processing since 1988	Responsible for rebuilding an internal IS department.

interest in FIRM12 because it produced specialty chemicals, which is considered a low margin product line. They tried unsuccessfully to sell the company for three years. In 1984, FIRM12's management finally bought FIRM12 in a leveraged buyout (LBO) that left the company riddled with debt. This LBO triggered the outsourcing decision.

As part of the LBO deal, FIRM12 signed a six month support agreement with its prior owners. During this time, the prior owners would continue to run FIRM12's systems. During this transition period, FIRM12's senior management decided not to build an internal IS department because (a) the company was in too much debt to justify building a multi-million dollar IS shop and (b) it was not sure it could feasibly build an internal IS organization in only six months. Instead, FIRM12's management decided to contact three outsourcing vendors.

4.12.2 FIRM12's First Outsourcing Decision

Of the three vendors solicited, FIRM12's management felt that only one vendor was capable of handling all its information needs. This vendor was willing to provide services for applications development, support, telecommunications, and data processing. FIRM12's senior management hastily signed the vendor's generic, seven-year contract in August 1984. This contract stipulated that the vendor would provide the same level of service that FIRM12 was receiving in 1984. Once again, the first problem encountered was defining the current service level. During the six-month support agreement, the prior owners refused to divulge information about data processing services to the vendor. Gary describes their position:

> "The [previous owner] that was doing the work wanted to be cautious and not underestimate the amount of work so they wouldn't have a liability coming back from [the vendor] or us in case there were some differences. So the vendor had no idea what the services were for sure. So everybody was hedging their bets."

The negative consequences of this hasty outsourcing decision quickly became apparent. Senior management feared it would not realize the savings after receiving its first monthly bill. The excess charges exceeded the fixed monthly fee. Gary explains:

> "Time share costs were a lot larger than expected, connect fees, port fees, things that you had no idea about. They were never mentioned in the contract. They just started showing up."

Excess charges were not the only problem. Gary claims the vendor provided terrible service. He feels the major problem is that outsourcing vendors do not share common goals with their customers. FIRM12 wants a cost-effective service; the outsourcer wants to make a profit. The discrepancy in goals manifests itself in a decline in customer service. Gary offers three areas where he claims customer service suffered: (a) loss of IS expertise, (b) antiquated technology, and (c) an overworked applications team.

Loss of IS expertise. Gary claims FIRM12 paid the vendor to train the vendor staff only to lose its IS expertise to another vendor account:

> "You pay for them to learn your business, then they move those people to court other companies in your industry. They transfer skills to get new business, now the learning curve is yours to pay for again."

One will note the same complaint echoed by FIRM7 users. However, outsourcing vendors are free to assign staff where they see fit. If customers want to retain key talent, they should consider keeping these people on staff rather than outsource.

Antiquated technology. Gary also claims that most people are under the illusion that outsourcing provides accessibility to new technology. "Their [meaning the vendor's] best bet is to get a ten-year contract and just grind it. . .no new technology, just try to make you happy and take your money." Gary explains why the vendor does not implement technical innovations:

> "I think you find with outsourcing that any innovation in technology comes from your own people. Requirements from users on your staff. But basically the [outsourcing vendors] just crank it. And so we were operating old software. Some of it was written in the 1960s. All batch."

Even when the users at FIRM12 identified technological innovations, the vendor was hesitant to implement them. For example, Gary's users wanted to buy a packaged manufacturing software product. When Gary was trying to calculate the costs and benefits, he asked the vendor, "How much will this cost me to run at your data center?" The vendor refused to provide a number. They did, however, offer to sell FIRM12 a similar product. Gary explains:

> "It gets back to the point: you don't know what it will cost you to run new software on their mainframe. And so their primary way to solve

that problem is to say, 'Okay, we can't really say what it will cost you.' So right away you are hesitant. So they say, 'Well, here's what we will do. We have a software package that we own, we know what it takes to run because we are running it for XYZ company over at Dodge City. You implement it on our machine, and it will save you a huge amount of money.' If you do that, you run on software that you don't even own. And that's what you call hook, line, and sinker, as far as I am concerned."

Overworked staff. Gary says another consequence of outsourcing was poor application support service. The contract entitles FIRM12 to 1000 hours of enhancements per month. Gary claims that FIRM12 meets that number by overworking its staff. He claims the vendor sent many members of his staff on temporary duty assignments, leaving the remaining staff to pick up their workload.

"Well, in order to meet their 1000 hour deal, let's say they had an opportunity for some other people, like one guy was a chemical engineer. They want to take a shot at some new business with a chemical plant in Ohio, so they send him out there for six months. He was in my base, I was paying for the 1000 hours. Now they charge $10 000 dollars a month for this guy at the other site. You know what they do with the remaining people that were here? They pick up the slack so that I get my 1000 hours so contractually I couldn't do anything about it. The programmers, so they have to pick up more hours, they are tired, sick, they make mistakes."

The lack of customer service motivated many user groups to seek information solutions elsewhere. In particular, FIRM12 users started using personal computers linked by local area networks. The users pay for these systems from their discretionary budgets. The vendor offered to provide PC support services, but Gary says, "That was one area of control we never turned over to them after we saw what was going on."

4.12.3 FIRM12's Second Outsourcing Decision

Gary says that all these problems—loss of IS expertise, no new technology, poor application support, and users seeking alternative solutions—led his senior management to appoint him as the manager of data processing in 1988. His major responsibility was to "clean up this mess," although management did not dictate a particular course of action.

4.12.3.1 *FIRM12's Second Outsourcing Decision Process*

Gary did not conduct a formal evaluation of the situation. He decided immediately to terminate the outsourcing relationship. Gary's strategy was to proceed slowly, however, since he knew he could not obtain the capital necessary to construct an entire IS organization in a few months. His first challenge was to counterpoise the balance of power between FIRM12 and the vendor. This way, he could use some of the vendor's resources to gradually recover control over the IS function.

Gary reopened the outsourcing contract in late 1988—two years before the contract expired:

> "I opened negotiations early, to renegotiate the contract to get me out. If you wait until the end—it's like you'll never get there. I started negotiating for six, seven months in 1989 so there was over two years left in the contract, so they knew we had options. If you don't do that you are dead because they know you can't build a data center in a week."

Since the vendor was apprehensive that they would lose FIRM12 as a customer, they agreed to alter several contract provisions. In particular, Gary negotiated more favorable terms by: (1) requiring the vendor to assign costs to specific functions, (2) prohibiting vendor meetings on Gary's time, and (3) eliminating temporary duty assignments.

Assign costs to functions. Under the previous deal, FIRM12 paid a lump sum for services. Now the vendor allocates costs to specific functions. Gary needed this provision so that "as functions go away, monthly billing goes down." He knew that he could not recover the entire department at once, so this arrangement allows him to gradually assume services.

Reduce overhead charges: vendor staff meetings. Gary claims that his overhead charges were excessive because the vendor held meetings on FIRM12's time. Gary calculated that each meeting cost him one quarter of a man-year. In addition, Gary says, "My users call in, no one is working, they can't get a hold of anybody." The revised contract prohibits the vendor from holding staff meetings during FIRM12's time.

Eliminate temporary duty assignments. The last issue re-negotiated was the temporary duty assignments. The vendor is no longer permitted to send members of Gary's staff to other accounts without his permission.

When Gary was asked whether the outsourcer resisted these new contract provisions, he said no, but the vendor vowed to improve service if FIRM12 decided on another long term contract. He describes the situation: "It's like when you were a little kid. Two weeks before Christmas, you suddenly cleaned up your act and behaved a whole lot better."

With these new provisions, Gary restored the balance of power between FIRM12 and the vendor. The vendor was aware that Gary might permanently terminate their relationship. Therefore, it was willing to help Gary re-establish an internal IS department—for a price. First, the vendor helped Gary build his own data center last year. Second, they relocated 35 programmers from the vendor site to FIRM12's headquarters. Gary says he paid the vendor "an extra arm and a leg to get their programming staff on site." He hired the vendor's staff, for now, until he can gradually accumulate an internal applications staff of his own.

4.12.3.2   Outcome and Consequences of FIRM12's Second Decision

Thus, the outcome of Gary's decision was to rebuild his own IS department. Although the task is incomplete, he has managed to move IS personnel and data center processing to FIRM12's headquarters. Eventually, he will terminate all ties with the vendor, but he must first create an infrastructure to support his users. Gary claims that an infrastructure must be built in phases:

> "You do this in stages. You start formalizing the organization, you start to see what you get."

He needs to determine the headcount, job titles, and salary structures of IS employees, as well as establish operating procedures. Gary's most recent effort was to create a chargeback system for programming services. Since his users are anxious to develop some new software, he felt a chargeback system would help prioritize the tremendous demand for new systems.

In summary, the experiences at FIRM12 illustrate some of the dangers of making an outsourcing decision out of desperation. Again, the key ingredient missing from the decision was the negotiation of a sound contract. Without baseline measures, service levels, or penalty clauses, FIRM12 was at the mercy of its outsourcing vendor. The result: no savings were realized and customer service suffered. Gary is confident, however, that rebuilding its own IS organization will remedy these problems.

Gary's decision to rebuild is now evaluated from the political and transaction cost perspectives. The first decision, made in 1984, is not evaluated since it is difficult to interpret the behavior of individuals from Gary's recollections. Given that FIRM12 only had six months to build an IS department, Gary says that "outsourcing seemed like the only logical solution." Perhaps this first decision can be viewed as a rational decision with devastating consequences.

4.12.4 FIRM12's Decisions from a Political Perspective

Several indicants suggest that Gary's behavior was political. When he became the data processing manager, his only agenda was to rebuild an empire. He did not consider other alternatives, such as establishing a better rapport with the vendor on a permanent basis or contracting with other outsourcing vendors. He spent two years trying to rally enough support to convince his management that all functions should be brought in-house. In particular, two additional tactics Gary may have used to sway the decision in his favor are use of outside experts and the building of coalitions.

Selective use of decision alternatives. A rational decision process dictates that the decision-maker generate alternatives, then pick the low cost solution. Noticeably absent from Gary's decision was outsourcing with another vendor. Gary admits, however, that outsourcing can save a company money:

> "I'm sure there are astute people out there doing it, and looking at it, and I think Kodak spent a lot of time to make sure they have the right structure there. And they didn't give one person the whole apple cart. And I felt that they set up committees to look at quality and they had benchmarks and standards. It was well thought out and the right way to do it."

Given that Gary feels that outsourcing can save money, the question is why he never considered another outsourcing alternative. He seemed adamant about building his own data center. Since the current service was outrageously expensive, justifying an in-house shop was facile.

Use of outside experts. Although Gary's agenda may have been to build his own shop, he realized he needed financial justification to sell the idea to management. He hired a consultant to help him present the economic case for building an internal IS department. The consultant concluded that FIRM12 could save one million dollars by building its own data center—as long as it used mid-range technology. Gary did not share a copy of the consultant's report, nor did he specify the payback period of such an investment. The numbers must have been compelling since FIRM12 spent millions of dollars on new hardware.

Building coalitions. Another strategy that Gary pursued was to build coalitions with key users so that they could present a united front to management. Users were very anxious to have information services back in-house. They continually complained to management about the vendor:

> "I think they [senior management] had an awful lot of feedback from the users that they didn't like the systems. In other words, they were not supported in the manner that they needed to be supported to run the business. That was the kind of feedback they got. Also, the issues of quality came up, customer service, no new technology."

Gary's coalition of users was very successful. When Gary was asked whether his senior management would have permitted rebuilding the data center if the cost savings were not evident, he replied:

> "Yes. I think there are enough issues from the aspect of having your own hardware and software at your own location."

So, from the political perspective, we see that Gary's behavior may have been motivated by his preference to run his own department. Through the tactics of selective use of alternatives, use of outside experts, and building coalitions, he was able to convince management that insourcing was the preferred solution to their service problems.

4.12.5 FIRM12's Decisions from a Transaction Cost Perspective

Gary may have preferred insourcing because it was genuinely the most economical solution for FIRM12. Throughout Gary's interview, he discussed three of Williamson's hypothesized decision criteria: costs, transaction type, and the threat of opportunism.

4.12.5.1   Costs

Since the consultant's report was unavailable, there is no evidence to suspect that the projected annual savings of one million dollars is fallacious. Since FIRM12 was getting hammered by the monthly excess charges, Gary may be able to realize savings by providing services in-house.

4.12.5.2   Transaction Type

Another indicant that Gary based his decision on economic considerations is his attention to transaction types. He claims that he believes outsourcing is a viable alternative for certain functions:

> "I'm not totally against outsourcing. I mean, I just re-bid our communications network and outsourced it because I don't have a big enough shop to have my own communications specialists. So I wouldn't say I am opposed to outsourcing in all cases."

4.12.5.3   Threat of Opportunism

Perhaps Gary's main reason for wanting his own IS department is to regain control over services. With outsourcing, Gary experienced the negative effect of outsourcing. The threat of opportunism was readily apparent in the excess charges, degradation of services, loss of IS expertise, antiquated technology, and overworked staff. The vendor is able to increase its revenues by exploiting the contract loopholes. By terminating the relationship, Gary prevents such behavior in the future.

Another note on vendor opportunism: Gary was asked what he thinks when he reads the positive reports of outsourcing in the trade literature. He merely replied, "I laugh."

A final piece of evidence suggests that Gary feels that outsourcing decisions should be based on economics. He believed that FIRM12's original decision to outsource was prudent, since it was the only way to provide IS services with limited time and resources. Although, he would have structured the outsourcing arrangement differently:

> "Well, I would have done it differently and for a shorter period of time. We would have been more careful about the gray areas, volume-related issues. We would not have left such a long window. I might have done more of an effort to keep applications."

4.12.6   FIRM12—Conclusion

Gary's behavior can be interpreted from a political as well as transaction cost perspective. From the political vantage, Gary spent two years rallying support to rebuild his IS shop. Through the use of outside experts and the coalition formation, he was able to convince his senior management that insourcing would save his company money. The fact that Gary never considered other alternatives suggests that his agenda was created rather early in the decision process. However, the numbers are compelling to suggest that insourcing was a more economical solution than repairing the business relationship with the vendor—it's hard to argue with an annual savings of one million dollars.

4.13   FIRM13

FIRM13 is the second of the thirteen cases where a company decided to terminate an outsourcing contract. Unlike FIRM12, however, FIRM13 never made a proactive decision to outsource—it acquired a company that had previously signed a seven-year outsourcing contract. After the acquisition, FIRM13 learned that the out-sourcing vendor was providing poor service and charging excessive prices for systems that simply did not work. At the time of the interview, FIRM13 had only brought data processing and applications support back in-house. Applications development will be absorbed after the vendor completes the development of several large projects.

Terrence, the Vice President of IS, explained the historical background of the acquisition and subsequent decision to terminate the outsourcing contract (see Table 4.15). None of the original managers who made the outsourcing decision were retained after the acquisition, so Terrence was the only individual interviewed

Table 4.15   *FIRM13 participants*

Name used in this case	Job title	Involvement in outsourcing
Terrence	Vice President of IS	Decided to terminate outsourcing contract.

for this case. The outsourcing vendor declined to participate in this research.

4.13.1   Historical Background of FIRM13

FIRM13 is a large company with over 50 000 employees world-wide. FIRM13's operating companies produce industrial and consumer products in five business segments. During the past ten years, FIRM13 has achieved profitable growth, in spite of the progressive deterioration in the general economy. In 1990, FIRM13 achieved sales of over 6 billion dollars and earned a net income over 600 million dollars.

Terrence, Vice President of IS, explains FIRM13's two-phased approach to constantly improve shareholder wealth:

> "We have a two staged approach: one is acquisition, the other is manufacturing improvement after the acquisition that is a quality product at a lower cost. That's the name of the game. That's why we have been successful."

This philosophy has led to a rather decentralized organizational structure. The five operating companies function as independent units. Each company controls its own production and marketing functions. Each company also operates its own information services department. These IS departments develop and maintain their own systems as well as run their own data centers. Currently, the five operating companies employ approximately 1000 IS personnel.

At corporate headquarters, Terrence manages a small centralized IS group. The three major responsibilities of this group are (1) financial administration, (2) office and computer-integrated manufacturing (CIM) system support, and (3) technology standards. Of these, Terrence describes financial administration as his primary role:

> "I have responsibility for just about all the IS functions with FIRM13—planning, capital budgets, stewardship. I don't have responsibility for any day-to-day operations. It's more of a consulting role."

When it comes to standards, Terrence also considers his role to be more of a consultant than a law enforcer. He encourages all the decentralized IS employees to adhere to corporate technology standards where it is economically feasible:

> "We try to standardize on application software, where possible. You know, we don't force people to do that because it's expensive. When

[an acquired company] comes in here looking for money because they have outgrown their CPU, at that point we say, 'Let's take a look at the IBM solution.' But we wait until they've outgrown their system mainframe."

In summary, FIRM13's strategy of growth through acquisition has led to a decentralized organizational structure where the operating companies run their own businesses—including their own IS shops. Although Terrence manages a centralized IS department, he considers himself a consultant and rarely interferes in the operations of the decentralized IS departments. One exception, however, is when Terrence became actively involved in a newly acquired company that had outsourced its entire IS department to a third party vendor.

4.13.2 FIRM13's Outsourcing Decision

In the late 1980s, FIRM13 acquired a large industrial parts company. This acquisition contributes a hearty 10% of the overall business for FIRM13. As part of this deal, FIRM13 was also obligated to honor the seven-year outsourcing contract that this company had signed with the vendor in 1987. Terrence became actively involved in this acquisition when FIRM13's senior management discovered that the company had obtained legal counsel to try—unsuccessfully— to break the agreement.

Terrence feels that the primary problem was that the previous senior managers "outsourced out of desperation":

"Basically, they were a DOS-V shop. They were faced with a conversion to MVS. They had outgrown their operating system. They had no expertise in-house. I think the IS staff was a little frightened of it [the conversion]. So they had retained [the vendor] to come in and do a study. Then senior management said, when the IS staff was reluctant to go through this conversion, they basically said to the vendor, 'How would you like to do this conversion for us then run our IS staff?'"

These senior managers, who knew nothing about IS, signed the vendor's standard, seven-year contract. Terrence describes this contract as "very, very strange." He says:

"In the agreement, I don't know if they had any people review it legally, if folks reviewed that agreement, but it was very one-sided in favor of [the vendor]."

In the contract, the vendor was to provide all the services related to information systems. They ran the entire IS department— applications development, support, data center operations, telecommunications, and related IS services. However, the contract did not stipulate performance standards, service level measures, or penalties for non-performance. The company had no recourse other than to accept any level of service that the vendor provided them—and Terrence claims that service was poor.

When asked to cite specific service level problems, Terrence explained that the vendor's conversion from DOS to MVS failed. The reason, according to Terrence, is that the original employees ended up doing the conversion. He explains:

> "[The vendor] took over all the people, as they usually do. So what happens in that environment is that your unqualified IS people that you had become your unqualified [vendor] people. So you are not better off. And what have you picked up? You know, they installed the new software, but it just did not work."

Terrence also offered the following story as another example of poor service:

> "One of the things that really soured [the parts company] was a warehouse system that [the outsourcing vendor] had committed to getting from another client. And about six months into the project, the other client says, 'Hey these guys are our competitors. They are not getting our systems.' So [the outsourcing vendor] came back hat-in-hand and said they couldn't deliver what they had committed to deliver."

Besides poor service, another result of this poorly negotiated contract was excessive IS costs.

4.13.2.1 *FIRM13's Outsourcing Decision Process*

Getting out, however, was not as easy as Terrence anticipated. After reviewing the contract with his legal staff, Terrence concluded, "It looked pretty binding to us and so I basically arranged for a meeting with the top guys at [the outsourcing vendor]." He describes his first encounter with the vendor as a battle:

> "Basically, they had set up the battlegrounds. [The outsourcing vendor] was on one side and the [parts] people were on the other side—very unhappy campers. [The outsourcing vendor] came in here and we said to them, 'We are going to use you like we use any other of our IS

organizations and we are going to make this sucker work. I mean, so the battlelines are down and you are either an asset or a liability. We'll let you decide which that is, based on your performance.'"

Terrence said after that meeting, the outsourcing vendor agreed to renegotiate the contract. Within a year, Terrence migrated data processing off of the vendor's data center, he transferred application support to another IS group, and he managed to reduce the contract length from seven years to five years. Those measures reduced the total cost of the contract by two-thirds. Currently, the vendor's only remaining function is applications development. After these systems are completed, FIRM13 will sever all ties to the vendor.

When Terrence was asked how he was able to terminate the contract when his predecessors at the company could not, he smiled and said:

"They didn't want FIRM13 badmouthing them, giving them a poor reference, because basically there were some real non-performance issues. They also didn't want to get into a legal hassle. And it would have cost them a lot of money, and it would have cost us a lot of money. And I guess they recognize that they lost."

In conclusion, this case reinforces the lessons learned in the other cases: don't outsource out of desperation and don't sign the vendor's standard contract.

FIRM13's decision to rescind the contract is now analyzed from the political and transaction cost perspectives.

4.13.3   FIRM13's Decision from a Political Perspective

From the information gathered, FIRM13's decision does not appear to be political. After the acquisition of the parts company, FIRM13 terminated the outsourcing contract because the outsourcer's prices exceeded internal IS costs. The only interesting insight that arises from the political perspective is that the outsourcing failure protects FIRM13's IS department from an outsourcing threat. From an assessment of the power structure within FIRM13, we see that the decentralized companies have the power to outsource and have been approached by outsourcing vendors. Thus far, Terrence has been able to prevent a formal outsourcing investigation by referring to the parts company's outsourcing calamity.

Power is assessed for three coalitions within FIRM13: senior management at corporate headquarters, Terrence's centralized IS staff, and senior managers in the operating divisions.

Power of the senior management at corporate headquarters. Compared to most large organizations, senior management at FIRM13's corporate headquarters are not very powerful. They purposefully delegate decision-making to their operating companies. The CEO partly attributes FIRM13's strong financial success to their philosophy of autonomous operating divisions.

Terrence confirms that senior management at corporate headquarters would not impose an outsourcing initiative on the operating divisions. He states, "Basically, that is not our culture."

Power of the centralized IS department. Terrence does not possess much power to influence decisions at FIRM13 for several reasons. First, his department is accounted for as an overhead account. Second, he is two reporting levels from the CEO, buried in a support function. Third, since he belongs to the centralized headquarters, he is viewed as a technology consultant rather than a ruler. Most IS decisions are made in the decentralized operating companies, not at company headquarters.

Terrence, however, is currently developing some CIM systems that will be tied to profitability. In FIRM13's 1991 Management Philosophy brochure, the CEO describes CIM as: "essential to the future of the company." The success of these systems will bolster the credibility of the IS department. In addition, the outsourcing failure has also secured the IS role within FIRM13.

Power of the managers with the operating divisions. The senior managers in the operating divisions have significant power over their operations—including their IS departments. The major divisions run their own data centers and manage their own applications development and support. Given the inclination, they would be powerful enough to outsource. In fact, several of these managers have approached Terrence about outsourcing:

> "I think they see it in the press, they get letters from every CEO of an outsourcing organization telling them how great they are and how much money they could save...we've had that asked, "Should we do outsourcing?" by our management folks here. And I just keep quoting the [parts company's] experience."

Terrence feels that the reference to the outsourcing experiences at the parts company extinguishes their hopes that outsourcing will ever save them money. He also explained to these operating managers that outsourcing vendors would not respond to their business needs:

> "Change seems to take an awfully long time with an outsourcing vendor basically because it takes a long time to explain your business to the folks. They aren't a part of it. It's like anything else—if you have some strategic issues, you don't know if you want to give them to an outsourcer."

Thus, Terrence used the outsourcing failure to actually increase the security of IS's position within FIRM13. By referring to its previous experience with outsourcing, he had prevented FIRM13's operating companies from formally evaluating outsourcing.

4.13.4 FIRM13's Decision from a Transaction Cost Perspective

The transaction cost perspective offers a useful interpretation of FIRM13's decision to terminate the outsourcing relationship. Terrence claims the decision to rescind the contract was based on costs. Although Terrence did not conduct a formal analysis that compared the vendor's costs with FIRM13's costs, his anecdotal evidence was enough to convince management to terminate the relationship. In particular, his justification centered around overall IS budgets, the economies of scale myth, and service degradation.

In regards to costs, Terrence compared the IS costs of the vendor with FIRM13's IS costs:

> "Our IS costs average about one and a half of a percentage of sales. The outsourcing costs average about 4% of sales at [the parts company]. We don't feel that is a good business decision, that's why we are getting out of it. We can do it a lot less expensively."

In regards to the economies of scale issue, Terrence argues that the vendor has no inherent advantage. He says, because of its size, FIRM13 is able to negotiate similar hardware and software discounts as an outsourcing vendor. Therefore, an outsourcing vendor cannot provide a cheaper service. In addition, outsourcing costs more because the vendor is expected to make a profit whereas the internal IS shop does not:

> "They [the outsourcing vendor] are not a small company by any stretch of the imagination. But, you know, let's just assume that they have a certain amount of cost. But those guys look for a gross margin of 50 to 60%. So can they do it cheaper? I guess if they are willing to reduce

their sights they might. But I have a hard time thinking that they would."

So Terrence feels that even if an outsourcer had inherent natural cost advantages, it doesn't pass these savings on to its clients. So from a total cost perspective, FIRM13 would not save money with outsourcing.

The anecdotal evidence that Terrence used to support his argument of service degradation included the failed MVS conversion, the vendor's broken promises on delivering "free" systems, and the lack of business perspective.

4.13.5   FIRM13—Conclusion

FIRM13's decision to terminate the outsourcing contract is best understood from a transaction cost perspective. The vendor's IS costs and poor service record was enough to convince FIRM13 that it could reduce costs by rescinding the relationship. The expense to bring systems in-house was minimal since it used an existing data center.

The lesson learned from the political perspective is that the Vice President of IS uses the outsourcing failure to prevent other divisions from evaluating the option. Indeed, when an operating division expresses interest in outsourcing, Terrence merely summarizes the excess fees and service degradation its parts company suffered. The failure is indeed enough to deter further investigation.

4.14   CONCLUSION

Thirteen cases, thirteen unique outsourcing stories. Some decisions were initiated by IS managers, others by senior executives. Some decided to outsource nothing, others decided to outsource everything—two even decided to rebuild internal IS departments. Some decisions appeared rational, others political, most both. Some loved their outsourcing vendors, others displayed vile repulsion. Some companies saved money, some companies lost money, and some companies appeared to do nothing as a result of their outsourcing evaluations.

At this point the reader may be demanding a higher level gestalt. Indeed, what do all these outsourcing stories *mean*? Can we make sense out of thirteen different stories to generate any meaningful insights into the whole outsourcing phenomenon? The answer is a resounding "yes." In the next chapters, we attempt to summarize the major themes arising out of the cases. In particular, the next chapter explores senior management's view of IS and suggests why their view plays an important role in the outsourcing decision. Chapter 6 then zeroes in on what seem to be the fundamental reasons for initiating outsourcing evaluations. Chapter 7 presents an outsourcing evaluation process, which is a direct result of the insights gained from the thirteen case studies.

5
Senior Management's View of Information Systems

5.0 INTRODUCTION

This chapter addresses the question: How is senior management's view of the IS function related to IS outsourcing evaluations? This question is important because research findings presented in subsequent chapters are best understood by exposing the relationship between outsourcing evaluations and senior management's view of IS. In particular, participants' motives for initiating outsourcing evaluations seem to be couched in the greater problem of demonstrating the value of IS to senior management.

As IS practitioners and academics, we espouse the importance of IS to the survival of a corporation. If systems fail, we claim that companies would falter within days, hours, or even minutes. Readers might be disappointed to learn that only two of the thirteen companies that participated in the study agree that their IS departments are critical to corporate success. The remaining eleven companies all see their IS departments as necessary, but burdensome, cost pits.

In this chapter, the evidence to support the conclusion that most senior managers in the participating companies do not value their information systems is presented. The evidence includes qualitative assessments articulated by the participants as well as indicants of senior management's views such as the accounting structure of the IS function, the IS manager's number of reporting levels from the CEO, and a measure of IS departmental power extracted from the questionnaire.

5.1 QUALITATIVE ASSESSMENTS OF SENIOR MANAGEMENT'S VIEWS OF THE IS FUNCTION

During the interviews, many participants expressed that senior managers within their organizations fail to support their IS departments. Because of this lack of support, IS managers have difficulty selling the worth of their services, acquiring new resources, or getting promoted into the upper echelons of management. The following quotes by participants from FIRM1, FIRM2, FIRM8, FIRM4, and FIRM5 provide a sample that attests to these conclusions.

FIRM1. FIRM1 is a prosperous company—in 1991 they were identified as one of the most profitable companies in the United States. Despite the excess cash reserve, FIRM1's senior managers are reluctant to spend money on information systems. Gordon, FIRM1's IS Manager, laments that he often has trouble acquiring funds from top management to meet the increase in demand for IS services:

> "Recognize that in their mind, computers are not strategic. So making investments in large computers or computer systems are not what they are comfortable with doing."

FIRM2. Similar sentiments were expressed by a member of FIRM2. Anthony, FIRM2's Director of Advanced Technology, stated that his senior management does not consider the IS department to be a critical contributor to the organization's success. He notes:

> "It was not in the eyes of executive management—and I think in the eyes of a lot of IS folks as well—we are not in an information intensive business."

FIRM8. Barry, FIRM8's Director of IS, echoes a similar attitude to Anthony when he states that senior management sees information systems as a drain on resources:

> "I think I got the feeling from John [the CFO] that there was an intolerance by our management about having a big computer operation. It was viewed as a big boat anchor even though it was a vital service."

FIRM5. Even though the IS trade literature devotes much space to the concept of strategic systems, few participants saw their systems as competitive weapons. At FIRM5, for example, the Treasurer states that systems in his company were never viewed as a strategic resource:

"FIRM5 does not have a desire to be a leader from a technological standpoint. We merely see systems as a way to process data. Competitive advantage and things like that did not enter into the reason for data processing."

FIRM4. James, the Director of Corporate Planning at FIRM4, paints an even bleaker picture. Senior management not only perceives of information systems as non-strategic, they see IS as a money vortex:

"All they [senior management] see is this amount of money that they have to write a check for every year. Year after year after year. Where is the benefit? IS says, 'Well we process data faster than we did last year.' They say, 'So what?' IS says, 'Well, we can close the ledger faster.' And they say, 'So what? Where have you increased revenue? All you do is increase costs, year after year and I am sick of it. All I get are these esoteric benefits and a bunch of baloney on how much technology has advanced. Show me where you put one more dollar on the income statement.'"

Many other quotes could be extracted from the interviews to illustrate that the senior management of the participating companies view their IS departments as value-consuming functions. The two exceptions were the senior management at FIRM3 and FIRM10. Because their IS departments are set up as profit centers and because information systems are tied to corporate strategies, they see systems as contributing to profitability.

5.2 INFORMATION SYSTEMS STRUCTURED AS OVERHEAD ACCOUNTS

Another indicator that senior management in the participating companies do not value information systems is the way they account for the function. In eleven of the thirteen companies, the IS departments are set up as overhead accounts. As an overhead account, the IS function is viewed as a necessary cost, but one that does not add value directly to the company.

The objective for managing overhead functions is typically to keep costs at a minimum (Quinn, Doorley, & Paquette, 1990). In recent times, the trend in business is to maintain value-added functions while outsourcing value-consuming functions (Quinn, Doorley, & Paquette, 1990). Since overhead accounts fall into the value-consuming category, they become prime candidates for outsourcing evaluations. The theory of outsourcing overhead accounts is that a vendor, through economies of scale, can produce a service cheaper. This also allegedly frees management from focusing on tedious overhead activities so they can expend their energies on more strategic issues.

The relationship between senior management's view of IS and the accounting structure of the IS department may best be illustrated by looking at the two exceptions, namely, FIRM3 and FIRM10.

FIRM3. From FIRM3, we can compare senior management's view of IS while it was an overhead account to senior management's view of IS when it became a profit center. We learned from Ronald, the Vice President of IS, that this accounting transformation required years of hard work. Ronald felt that the IS department must be accounted for as a profit center in order to prove that his department was a value-added resource, not a cost-consuming one.

Before FIRM3's IS department became a profit center, Ronald was exposed to the same pressures as the IS managers in the other participating companies—he was constantly questioned about his rising IS costs:

> "He [the Chairman of the Board] would sit there and pistol whip me to death about my expenses and I had to answer to every one of them. I wasn't making him happy because he wasn't getting me to agree to reduce my costs. I said I'd be glad to cut expenses. . .anything that my user organization doesn't need, just let me know. If the Marketing guy doesn't want me to do invoicing, we'll shut her down tomorrow."

According to Ronald, the Chairman didn't realize that IS costs were increasing because the IS department was automating functions in other departments. For example, the transportation department reduced its costs because Ronald automated sixteen of its truck fueling terminals. The computers now handled dispatching, security, and invoicing. Through Ronald's efforts, the transportation manager reduced headcount by 40 people. Ronald proved to the Chairman that he was contributing to FIRM3's bottom line but that the accounting mechanism camouflaged his profitability. This demonstration was a great victory for the IS department—they were finally made a profit center. Once the function was a profit center, the Chairman told Ronald, "You are not part of the problem, you are part of the solution."

The lesson at FIRM3 is this: overhead functions are not seen as strategic. Rather, the accounting structure of an overhead account only allows management to focus on costs rather than benefits. When senior managers focus on rising IS costs, they seem less likely to hold a favorable view of the IS department. Now, the question remains whether senior management's view of IS determines the accounting structure or visa versa. Either way, a relationship is apparent.

FIRM10. At FIRM10, a twist to the relationship emerges. FIRM10's information systems department was the only company besides FIRM3 that was accounted for as a profit center. They were also the only other company where senior management viewed systems as contributors to corporate success. FIRM10's IS department charged fees to their users in their subsidiary companies as well as outside companies from within their industry. Despite the obvious contribution to profitability, FIRM10 outsourced their entire IS department. The outsourcing decision was unquestionably pre-cipitated by FIRM10's impending bankruptcy. Ironically, the CFO at FIRM10 feels that the profitability of the IS department allowed FIRM10 to negotiate a better deal with the vendor. FIRM10 proved to the vendor that their systems commanded respectable fees from global customers. One could argue that the information systems assets were sold to the vendor because these were the only assets that could generate enough cash to save the company.

In summary, the accounting structure of the IS department is related to senior management's view of the function. When IS departments are accounted for as overhead functions, senior management tends to view IS as cost pits. When IS departments are set up as profit centers, senior managers are more likely to recognize their value.

5.3 NUMBER OF REPORTING LEVELS FROM CEO

The number of reporting levels the head of a department is from the CEO is often used as an indicant of the importance of that department to the company (Pfeffer, 1981). As IS academics, we have proposed that the strategic importance of information systems warrants a reporting level directly to the CEO (Mensching & Adams, 1991). In the participating companies, however, the IS manager typically reported to the Controller or Chief Financial Officer (see Table 5.1).

Only one IS department manager in the study reported directly to the CEO/President: FIRM10. At one time, FIRM3 reported to the Chairman, but an extra layer of senior vice-presidents was added to the organization in 1972.

In five of the thirteen companies, the head of the IS department is two reporting levels from the CEO. It may seem that the CEO is

Table 5.1 *Number of reporting levels of the head of the IS department from the CEO*

Company	IS reports to:	# of reporting levels from CEO
FIRM10	CEO	1
FIRM3	Senior Vice President	2
FIRM2	CFO	2
FIRM7	Director, Corporate Staff	2
FIRM9	CFO	2
FIRM13	Senior VP of Manufacturing Services	2
FIRM1	Controller	3
FIRM4	Controller	3
FIRM5	Treasurer	3
FIRM6	Senior VP of Operations	3
FIRM8	Controller	3
FIRM11	Controller	3
FIRM12	Controller	3

accessible to the IS director, but many participants stated that they rarely participated in meetings with the CEO. The exception was FIRM3—the IS manager typically visits with the CEO once a month.

In seven of the thirteen companies, the head of the IS department was three reporting levels from the CEO. IS managers typically reported to the Controller—a position often held by a cost-conscious individual. Stanley, FIRM1's Manager of Data Processing, for example, echoes the sentiment that IS's direct boss notoriously ignores the IS department—he just wants costs minimized:

> "I guess Tom is the controller and vice president of the corporation, who is an accountant. My perception of him is that he could not care less what we do over here as long as the dollars are the cheapest."

In summary, the reporting level of the head of the IS department serves as an indicant of senior management's view of the IS function. The greater number of reporting levels between IS and the CEO, the less likely senior management sees the value of IS services.

5.4 MEASURE OF INFORMATION SYSTEMS DEPARTMENTAL POWER

As a last indicant of senior management's view of IS, the power of the IS department compared with other departments in the

Table 5.2 *Relative power of the IS department*

Department	Mean
Production/Operations	3.8021
Marketing	3.5986
Accounting	3.2667
Engineering	3.0852
Information Systems	2.9697

organization was assessed. The power instrument developed by Hickson et al. (1971) and used by Lucas (1984) and Saunders and Scamell (1986) was administered to participants. These questions measure five dimensions of departmental power: criticality, uncertainty absorption, pervasiveness, substitutability, and influence of that department within the organization. After participants indicate the relative power on a five-item Likert scale, the departments are ranked based upon the average mean scores for each dimension.

The results of this calculation are consistent with Lucas's and Saunder's previous measures of departmental power—production and operations is perceived as the most powerful department while IS is perceived as the least powerful department (see Table 5.2). Although many criticisms can be launched against this power measure—such as the bias towards manufacturing firms, preponderance of IS responses which yielded a blank response for some questions—the rating does provide another piece of evidence that IS is not deemed very favorably by participants.

5.5 CONCLUSION

Four pieces of evidence were offered to illustrate that senior management in eleven of the thirteen companies perceive of their IS functions as cost burdens. The evidence includes participants' qualitative assessments of senior management's perceptions, the accounting structure of the IS function, the number of reporting levels between IS and the CEO, and a measure of departmental power.

Now that the evidence has been presented, we are equipped to understand how senior management's view of IS relates to participants' motivations for initiating outsourcing decisions. These motivations are categorized into a framework presented in the next chapter.

6
Participants' Reasons for Initiating Outsourcing Evaluations

6.0   INTRODUCTION

This chapter addresses the question: What were the organizational members' intentions for evaluating outsourcing alternatives? In other words, what were they trying to accomplish? The participants identified reasons that are related to senior management's view of IS discussed in the previous chapter. Since senior managers do not value IS, IS managers have difficulty justifying their existence, acquiring capital and labor resources to meet increasing IS demand, and gaining personal credibility. As will be shown, outsourcing evaluations temper these pressures in several ways.

It is important to note that the reasons presented in this chapter reflect the participants' views of their company's outsourcing intentions. Participants expressed a plethora of financial, political and personal reasons for initiating outsourcing evaluations—we merely categorized them into a framework.

Before explaining the framework, two caveats are warranted. The first caveat is that the framework does not identify mutually exclusive categories since participants express multiple reasons for initiating outsourcing decisions. Second, although some of the reasons identified by participants may seem pejorative, they are not meant to be criticisms of behavior, merely descriptions of behavior. These caveats are explained below.

Caveat One: The framework does not identify mutually exclusive categories. Participants' intentions cannot be compartmentalized into tidy, non-overlapping, discreet categories. Participants rarely identified one superordinate reason for initiating an outsourcing decision, but rather they identified multiple motivations. For example, one participant first expressed that he thought outsourcing would save his company money. In the next breath he admitted he initiated the outsourcing evaluation to prove to his management that his IS department is cost-efficient. Later in the interview, the participant confessed that he doesn't know why he studied outsourcing, other than "everyone else is looking at it." So which was the real reason for initiating an outsourcing evaluation? The argument posed here is that all reasons are equally valid. Since human behavior is complex, participants' intentions cannot be assigned to mutually-exclusive categories.

Caveat Two: The framework does not criticize behavior. The second caveat is that the framework is not to be construed as criticisms of behavior. Many people may interpret the themes as pejorative— senior executives trying to eliminate information systems headaches, IS managers pursuing career boosts, etc. The reader is urged to view these behaviors through the participants' eyes.

With this said, the framework is introduced below (see Table 6.1).

Reaction to the efficiency imperative. The first reason participants cited for initiating outsourcing evaluations was reaction to the efficiency imperative. Since eleven of the thirteen companies are accounted for as an overhead function, senior managers tend to evaluate the function solely on cost efficiency (Quinn, Doorley, & Paquette, 1990). Since no concrete measure of *actual* efficiency exists, senior managers formulate only a *perception* of efficiency. When senior managers perceive that IS is inefficient, they initiate outsourcing evaluations to improve efficiency. In a similar vein, IS managers themselves initiate outsourcing evaluations. This way, IS managers

Table 6.1 *IS outsourcing framework*

Participants' reasons for initiating outsourcing evaluations
1. Reaction to the efficiency imperative
2. The need to acquire resources
3. Reaction to the bandwagon
4. Reduce uncertainty
5. Eliminate a troublesome function
6. Enhance credibility

"prove" that the IS department is already efficient or is making strides to become efficient.

The need to acquire new resources. The second reason that participants initiated outsourcing decisions was to acquire new resources, such as machine upgrades, additional personnel, or cash. Outsourcing evaluations helped participants acquire resources in two ways. First, if the participant showed that outsourcers could not provide the additional resources at a lower cost, the participant was usually granted the resource. Second, the participant may truly have used outsourcing to acquire new resources. This was particularly evident in cases where participants needed skilled labor or cash.

Reaction to the bandwagon. The third reason identified was the reaction to the proverbial bandwagon. Favorable outsourcing reports triggered participants to initiate outsourcing for two reasons. First, participants—especially senior managers—wanted to duplicate the success stories they read in the literature. Since these senior managers didn't truly value the IS function anyway, they hoped to at least reduce costs to the levels their competitors allegedly achieved through outsourcing. Second, participants—particularly IS managers—feared that the favorable reports would seduce their managers into outsourcing. By taking the initiative, participants used outsourcing evaluations to temper the many exaggerated claims made in public information sources.

Reduce uncertainty. The fourth reason cited was the desire to reduce uncertainty. Because IS demand is erratic, IS managers have difficulty planning for IS services. Rather than react to demand fluctuations, IS managers outsourced. By including a clause that varies fees with volumes, IS managers effectively dispensed with the risks associated with uncertainty.

Eliminate a troublesome function. The fifth reason identified was the desire of participants to eliminate a troublesome function. Since senior executives do not fully value IS, IS administrators receive few accolades for managing the function. When the function runs smoothly, senior executives do not notice. When the function experiences problems, senior management screams. Participants in the research felt, quite frankly, who needs the aggravation? Since no one cares about the function, why not outsource it and let the vendor worry about it?

Enhance credibility. The sixth and final reason identified was the use of outsourcing evaluations to enhance personal or departmental credibility. Since senior managers don't fully value the services of the IS department, they may not value the contribution of the people who run the function. Studies have repeatedly shown that IS personnel rarely break into the upper echelons of management. Several participants initiated outsourcing decisions to enhance their credibility. By showing that they are willing to outsource their kingdom for the good of the company, they prove to management that they are corporate players.

Throughout these introductory paragraphs, the motivations behind outsourcing decisions have been tied in some way to senior management's view of the IS function. The proceeding sections explain these reasons in full. In addition, the evidence from the cases is also presented so that the user can assess the validity of the framework. (See Figure 6.1 to determine how the thirteen cases fit into the framework.)

6.1 REACTION TO THE EFFICIENCY IMPERATIVE

The issue of efficiency is particularly pertinent for the management of IS departments. Since the majority of the companies viewed IS as a cost burden, IS managers cannot appeal to effectiveness or strategic importance to justify IS dollars. Instead, IS managers must somehow demonstrate cost efficiency. But how does the manager of an IS department that is accounted for as overhead cost, swallows increasingly more resources, requires highly-trained and highly-paid personnel, and produces services that elude measures supposed to demonstrate efficiency? How does one prove that applications development is efficient? Applications Support? End User Support? Telecommunications? The argument made here is this: actual *IS efficiency cannot be assessed, therefore senior management formulates only a* perception *of IS efficiency.* This assertion is relevant to the outsourcing phenomenon in two ways:

> *Case 1:* IS managers used outsourcing evaluations to create the perception that IS is efficient by showing that outside vendors cannot provide the service more efficiently.

> *Case 2:* When senior managers perceived that the current IS service was inefficient, they initiated outsourcing evaluations to assess whether changing the governance structure of the department would decrease costs. For companies that currently ran their own departments, senior managers considered outsourcing. For companies that currently outsource, senior managers con-

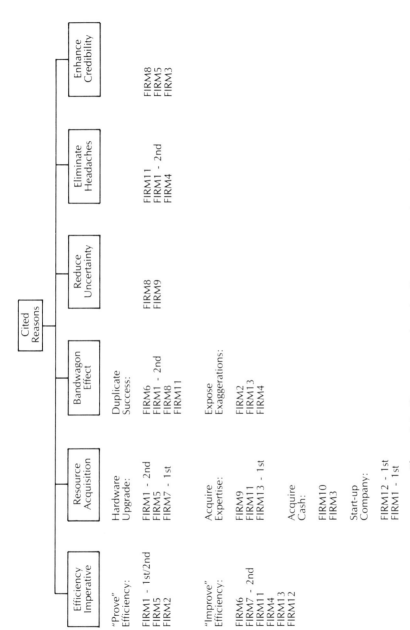

Figure 6.1 *Cases mapped to the IS outsourcing framework*

sidered terminating the relationship when they perceived that the vendor's service was too expensive.

These two uses of outsourcing evaluations are explored below.

6.1.1 Case 1: IS Managers Used Outsourcing to "Prove" Efficiency

Surprisingly, when most participants were asked how the IS department demonstrated efficiency, they responded that they compared their budgets with other IS budgets in their industry. In particular, they look at the IS budget as a percentage of sales. Mike, the Controller at FIRM8, provides one example. When Mike was asked how he demonstrates the efficiency of his IS department (which is under his jurisdiction), Mike replied, "I have a good understanding about what other people's total headcounts are, what their costs are." Headcounts and budgets, however, are NOT measures of efficiency. Efficiency measures are calculated by dividing outputs by inputs. Comparing IS budgets gives no indication whether those dollars are spent wisely.

The problem is that meaningful measures of departmental efficiency do not exist for IS. When efficiency measures are calculated at all, they are confined to the data processing domain. For example, IS managers at FIRM2, FIRM8, FIRM3, and FIRM6 hired industry consultants to assess the efficiency of their data centers. These consultants measure data processing costs per MIP, normalize the measures, and compare them with similar sized IS departments. These efficiency audits are viewed as unbiased because they are conducted by outside experts and because the organization is compared with hundreds of other companies. The reader may note, however, that in one case we found a glaring error in one consultant's efficiency report: his pie chart showing the percentage of IS costs by function summed to 130%! Regardless of their validity, efficiency audits often command credibility by providing an illusion of objectivity.

Outsourcing evaluations provide a similar function as efficiency audits, which leads us to the first way in which outsourcing evaluations are tied to the need to demonstrate efficiency: Like efficiency audits, *outsourcing evaluations provide a powerful demonstration of IS efficiency*. By comparing internal IS costs with vendor bids, IS managers can hold up their reports and say, "See, no one can provide services cheaper than us." The hard numbers also give the illusion of objectivity and, therefore, add credibility to their efficiency claims.

In addition, outsourcing evaluations provide IS managers with several advantages over efficiency audits. First, IS managers can selectively pick vendors rather than be compared to an entire database of companies. Second, IS managers can selectively pick functions that they feel the vendor cannot underbid. In other words, they can select one of their best-managed functions as a "candidate" for outsourcing while eliminating poorly-managed functions from the scope of the evaluation. Third, outsourcing evaluations are less expensive than efficiency audits. Whereas consultants may command exorbitant fees to measure efficiency, vendors usually submit bids free of charge. The only expense incurred is the opportunity cost of the manager's time.

The three companies in this research that illustrate the use of outsourcing to "prove" efficiency are FIRM1, FIRM5, and FIRM2.

FIRM1. Gordon, the IS Manager at FIRM1, initiated outsourcing evaluations on two occasions. The first occasion was when FIRM1 was first spawned off from a large petroleum company back in 1985. At that time, the senior management at FIRM1 hired Gordon to build an IS department. He considered outsourcing data center operations rather than build a data center. The evaluation resulted in the decision not to outsource. Gordon claims that one impetus for the evaluation was as follows:

> "I did this because I was scared to death that if I didn't take the initiative that it was going to be there. In a start-up operation I had to satisfy my management that I was not building an empire."

By showing that outside vendors could not provide the service less expensively, Gordon "proved" his data center plans were efficient. Gordon's control over the evaluation process may have biased the outcome in his favor. First, he only acquired a bid from one vendor. Gordon contends that he only acquired one bid because at the time, viable vendors were not as plentiful as today. Second, he limited the scope of the outsourcing evaluation to a subset of data processing. Since the vendor submitted a bid that included the cost of unneeded analysts, programmers and managers, the vendor's bid was higher than FIRM1's internal bid. As an added bonus, Gordon did not have to pay for the vendor's bid (other than the opportunity cost of his time).

FIRM1's second outsourcing decision also falls under this category. Both Gordon and Stanley, the Data Processing Manager in charge of the evaluation, claimed that they initiated the evaluation to see if they could be more efficient. With senior management constantly scrutinizing their expenses, they decided to see whether outsourcing could reduce costs. They solicited five bids from lesser-known outsourcing vendors. Although one bid showed 7% savings, they decided not to pursue the outsourcing option. Gordon and Stanley felt that the study, once again, proved to management that their IS department—at least the data center—is efficient. Gordon notes: "The good news is that I am really comfortable that we have a very effective and very efficient mainframe computer operation."

FIRM5. FIRM5 provides a particularly poignant example where the IS Manager initiated an outsourcing evaluation on a function he already knew was efficient. Thomas, FIRM5's Director of IS at the time, initiated an outsourcing investigation that pertained only to the data processing function, a service he felt was efficient and excellent. The following quotes stand testimony to the confidence he had in his data center operations:

> "We were running the CPU with 99% availability, less than two second response time all the time, less than one second response time 90% of the time. We were providing a great level of computing service."

> "We knew that we were running efficiently. We had low lease rents on our processors. We don't have a large staff. There are four people on our tech support group. We weren't spending an incredible amount."

Ironically, applications development and support were perceived as non-responsive and over-burdened, but Thomas did not allow vendors to bid on these items. When asked why these functions were not included, Thomas responded: "I feel that the service level has to be provided internally from an applications standpoint."

As far as data processing, the outsourcing evaluation was effective at demonstrating efficiency. Thomas wrote a memo to his Chairman saying: "We've evaluated this now and there is no economic benefit to the company for doing outsourcing right now. Similar levels of service would cost us more money."

FIRM5's outsourcing evaluation epitomizes the use of outsourcing evaluations to demonstrate efficiency. By limiting the scope of the decision to a function he knows is managed well, Thomas gathers objective evidence that his operation is efficient. When senior executives read about outsourcing or are solicited by outsourcing vendors, they think, "Oh yeah, we already looked at that—we don't need to outsource because we are efficient."

FIRM2. The IS Manager at FIRM2 decided to initiate an outsourcing evaluation to supplement the findings from his data center efficiency audit. Although the efficiency audit demonstrated that the function was very efficient compared to similar sized shops, the IS Manager felt it prudent to look at the outsourcing market. Anthony, the Director of Advanced Technology at FIRM2, explains why the outsourcing evaluation was conducted:

> "Once we had those numbers in hand [from the efficiency audit], we were pretty comfortable with where we were. We were comfortable that a third party coming in with an outsourcing pitch would have a tough sell. But we also felt that it made an awful lot of sense to understand the outsourcing market and the kind of pitches people could hit us with."

Anthony hopes that the efficiency audit, supplemented by the outsourcing evaluation, will prove to management that the IS Department—or at least the data center—is efficient.

In summary, some IS managers may initiate outsourcing evaluations to demonstrate the efficiency of their departments. Since management views IS as a cost burden, IS managers need some way to prove that their IS costs are competitive. Outsourcing evaluations provide a convincing argument that internal IS departments are cost-efficient.

To drive the point home even more forcefully, consider what was mentioned to us by a former outsourcing vendor sales representative. The former saleswoman said that her company did not seriously consider bid requests initiated by IS managers. She claimed that IS managers requested bids for two reasons: to get a free efficiency assessment or to prevent their senior managers from outsourcing. When the vendor did indicate savings, the IS manager often implemented cost reductions without the vendor's assistance. The practice was so common that the vendor started charging IS managers $20 000 for bid submissions.

The question remains, however, whether this strategy is effective. In FIRM1's first decision, the evaluation was effective because Gordon was allowed to build his data center. His second evaluation, however, was viewed with skepticism by senior management. FIRM5's evaluation seemed very effective—the Chairman congratulated Thomas on his commitment to efficiency. At FIRM2, the jury is still out. Rumors within the company suggest that outsourcing vendors are wooing senior management. Whether FIRM2's efficiency audit, coupled with the outsourcing report, will be effective enough to prevent outsourcing remains undetermined.

Thus, some IS managers used outsourcing as a means to demonstrate efficiency. Other participants used efficiency audits, efficiency measures (although these measures seem suspect) and qualitative appeals to convince senior management. What happens, however, when IS managers fail to justify their existence to upper management? Their senior executives may initiate their own plans to make the IS department more efficient. Outsourcing may be one option they elect to explore.

6.1.2   Case 2: Senior Managers who Perceived that IS is Inefficient Used Outsourcing Evaluations to Increase Efficiency

When senior managers perceived that the current IS service was inefficient, they initiated outsourcing evaluations to assess whether changing the governance structure of the department would decrease costs. For companies that currently ran their own departments, senior managers considered outsourcing. This situation is evident in FIRM6, FIRM7, FIRM11 and FIRM4. For companies that currently outsourced, senior managers considered terminating the relationship when they perceived that the vendor's service was too expensive. This situation is evident in FIRM13 and FIRM12.

FIRM6. During a financial crunch at FIRM6, the Senior Vice President of Operations decided to scrutinize IS expenditures. He hired a consultant to assess the efficiency of the entire department. Although systems applications was deemed efficient, data center operations was judged outdated. Although the consultant claimed FIRM6 had the resources and talent to improve efficiency, the Senior VP and the IS Manager decided to outsource. Both perceived that vendors are inherently more efficient:

> "Number one, they [vendors] have the automation tools, their equipment is less expensive, over time they don't pay the same price to run their own systems software and hardware. And they get the benefit of running multiple clients out of one data center."

Thus, FIRM6 members outsourced the data center largely based on their perceptions of vendor efficiency vis-à-vis their own efficiency.

FIRM7. The CEO at FIRM7 decided to outsource after the decentralized IS departments consolidated their budgets. The figures suggested that IS would spend over a billion dollars during the 1990s. Outraged by that amount, the CEO promptly signed an outsourcing agreement. Although the CEO was unavailable for comment, other FIRM7 participants claimed that he felt that the vendor would save him money. Despite the subsequent difficult relationship with the outsourcing vendor, participants claim that the CEO still regards his decision as prudent. One participant heard the CEO exclaim, "They bitched about IS before outsourcing, they bitch now—but at least it's costing me a lot less." Others contend, however, that the CEO inaccurately perceived that the previous IS department was inefficient just as he now inaccurately perceives that the vendor is more efficient.

FIRM11. The Controller at FIRM11 perceived that the IS Department was inefficient—he felt costs were excessive, turnover was high, and service quality was poor. Even though IS expenditures were well under 1% of revenues and the turnover rate among IS professionals is normally 10%, the Controller perceived these levels to be unacceptable. He decided to outsource because he perceived that vendors are more efficient:

> "One thing is the economies of scale of processing. They leverage software by running a lot of customers from that utility. . . . Their staff that they support us with is now smaller than what we had. And because of the depth of their organization, they are able to support us with a smaller staff."

Ironically, FIRM9 is supported by the same staff as before, the analysts merely carry different business cards. But still, the perception persists that the vendor provides efficient service due to their expertise.

FIRM4. According to case participants, FIRM4 senior managers considered outsourcing because they perceived that IS was costing too much money—over $130 million each year. They also perceived that vendors were inherently more efficient—a perception formulated by vendor solicitations and the trade press that purported that outsourcing reduces costs by 25 to 50%. During the evaluation process, however, senior management's perceptions changed. They decided that vendors possessed no inherent advantages that FIRM4 couldn't replicate on their own. In the end, FIRM4 reduced costs by $22 million without vendor assistance.

FIRM13. FIRM13 inadvertently became involved in outsourcing when they acquired a large parts company. This company had previously outsourced the entire IS department to a vendor. The parts company was paying the vendor an amount equivalent to 4% of revenues, whereas FIRM13 spends 1.5% of revenue on IS. The discrepancy was presumed to be indicative of the vendor's inefficiencies. After a preliminary study, FIRM13's senior management decided to terminate the arrangement because they perceived that the vendor's costs were too high.

FIRM12. FIRM12 decided to outsource after a volatile leveraged buyout in the mid-1980s. Crippled by debt, the new owners of

FIRM12 decided to outsource rather than build an IS empire. During the course of the contract, however, management began to question the prudence of their decision. Outsourcing was costing them more money than they had anticipated, primarily due to the excess charges for above baseline services. FIRM12's management now believe that outsourcing vendors offset their inherent efficiency advantages by maximizing their profit margin. After five years of perceived sub-standard service at premium prices, FIRM12 brought their IS department back in-house.

The common element among these six cases is that senior managers perceived (a) their current IS service was inefficient and (b) changing the governance structure would increase efficiency. What is relevant here is that participants initiated outsourcing decisions based on their *perceptions* of IS efficiency. Of the six cases discussed above, only FIRM4 went through the process of gathering detailed data to confirm or invalidate their initial impressions. In the five remaining cases, managers acted on their initial efficiency impressions with cursory corroboration.

6.2 THE ACQUISITION OF NEW RESOURCES

The second reason why participants claimed they initiated an outsourcing investigation was to access new resources. Whereas the previous section dealt with the efficiency of current IS services, this section deals with the efficient acquisition of additional IS services. In this sense, the acquisition of new resources can be considered a variant of the economic imperative. Before senior managers will allocate additional IS resources, they must be convinced that they will acquire the resources at the minimal possible expense. Again, the decision of what and how to allocate additional IS resources is based largely on perceptions.

The problem the IS department has in acquiring new resources reflects senior management's view of the IS function. As a cost overhead, senior managers tended to keep IS budget increases rather flat (0 to 6%). Unfortunately, the demand for information services increases every year—between 10% and 40% in the participating companies. In many cases, internal demand was caused by acquisitions of other companies. Participants from FIRM2, FIRM4, FIRM5, FIRM7, and FIRM8 all expressed frustration over the need to integrate acquired companies into the information architecture without the assistance of additional resources. Thomas, one-time IS Manager for FIRM5, typifies the exasperation these participants felt:

"You know these acquisitions I told you we were doing? You know, they would tell us the day before the contract was signed and say, 'You need to do these people's data processing starting Monday.' I'd say, 'Give me a break. Where am I going to get people to do this?'"

Additional resources that Thomas and other participants needed can be divided into three categories: capital, labor, and cash. Capital resources include hardware upgrades, additional storage capacity, and software products. Labor resources refer to the number of qualified people required to meet demand. Cash resources refer to the need for money or loans during times of severe financial difficulty. In start-up companies, organizations need access to all three types of resources. The need for these resources are tied to outsourcing evaluation in four ways:

Case 1: Justify hardware requests. In the first case, IS managers initiated an outsourcing evaluation to prove to their management that they really needed additional funds. Rather than just present management with resource requests, they bundled their requests with the results of an outsourcing evaluation which confirmed that outsourcing was not a viable alternative. Therefore, IS managers "proved" that they needed the hardware upgrade and that there were no efficient alternatives for acquiring it.

Case 2: Acquire expertise. In the second case, when senior executives in the company perceived that IS personnel lacked needed skills, they outsourced to access a vendor's alleged expertise. Outsourcing was perceived as a less expensive alternative than nurturing these skills in-house.

Case 3: Save my company. The third scenario is when senior managers used outsourcing as a way to reverse a devastating financial situation. Through cash infusions, investment in stocks, and favorable payment schedules, outsourcing vendors can woo a client based on the financial package alone.

Case 4: The start-up company. The last scenario is when newly formed companies consider outsourcing because they are faced with building an entire IS department from scratch. In these cases, companies race against time to erect data centers, buy software and populate an IS department. This requires a significant investment that many new companies cannot afford.

The evidence to support these scenarios is presented below.

6.2.1 Case 1: Justify Hardware Requests

IS managers at FIRM1, FIRM5, and FIRM7 used outsourcing evaluations to justify hardware upgrades. Since senior management in these companies view their IS departments as cost burdens, they are reluctant to provide additional funds for hardware upgrades without substantial justification. By showing that growth cannot be satisfied more efficiently through outsourcing, the IS managers hoped that their resource requests would be granted.

FIRM1. Stanley, FIRM1's Manager of Data Processing, admitted that his outsourcing evaluation was partly motivated by the need to acquire a hardware upgrade. In particular, Stanley wanted to upgrade to a more sophisticated operating system on his mainframe and move to relational databases. Stanley notes:

> "At the same time I was kind of building a base I guess to upgrade to a CPU with a five-year lease on it. That was my thought process at the time. While it was an outsourcing study, it was also designed to enhance my personal credibility when it came time to ask for bucks."

Acquiring additional resources for IS was particularly difficult in FIRM1 because senior management kept IS budget increases to a minimum.

FIRM5. Thomas, who is now the Treasurer of FIRM5, was once in charge of IS. As previously noted, Thomas had trouble meeting the increased demand caused by FIRM5's recent acquisitions. Thomas explains:

> "We have this philosophy at FIRM5 that information systems is here just to do data processing. So needless to say, whenever I would go in and say, 'I need to upgrade the mainframe, we need to add staff, DASD,' it went over like a lead balloon. And it kind of, I experienced that in 1987, 1988, 1989, and then finally last year it got to the point where we had grown as a company, we were acquiring all these small businesses, and you know, it takes many resources. . .to integrate them into the overall company, it requires additional terminals, printers and so forth. So we went through this period of acquisition and I was getting clobbered from a resource standpoint."

In particular, Thomas needed to upgrade his IBM mainframe to the next computer class. Unfortunately, management was reluctant to allocate the funds. Therefore, Thomas looked for alternative ways to acquire the upgrade:

> "The other issue was continued upgrades on the mainframe because we were growing. We were doing more data processing, building more

applications. I needed to determine what was the most cost-effective way to deliver computer resources to the company. . .The next required upgrade takes you into a series of processors and you increase your expenses significantly when you do that. So, what I was looking for, I was looking for a way to avoid the next huge increase in expense."

At first, Thomas attempted to acquire the hardware in a unique way. He asked the IS manager of another company if they could share one data center since both companies needed hardware upgrades. Thomas felt this unique approach would warrant considerable press coverage. Unfortunately, the idea was abandoned after squabbles over who would control the data center. Thomas then turned to outsourcing vendors to submit bids. Since he felt that his data processing operations were efficient, he was confident that the bids would not demonstrate savings. But he could show the bids to management when he asked for the hardware upgrade, thus proving his request is not frivolous. When Thomas was asked whether he succeeded in acquiring funds for the hardware upgrade, he smiled and said, "You bet I did."

FIRM7. During the 1990s, FIRM7 acquired so many businesses that IS could not accommodate the new workload. The Data Processing Manager needed to expand his data center from 60 MIPS to 150 MIPS. At the same time, senior management was trying to reduce IS expenditures. The Data Center Manager lamented:

"That was one of the hardest things for senior management to understand, that you can't shut the budget and control this."

Several IS managers in the divisions initiated a cursory outsourcing evaluation. Without any financial justification, they claimed that outsourcing was not a viable alternative and that they needed the money for the upgrade. In this case, however, senior management was not persuaded—less than a year later, they outsourced all the IS departments.

6.2.2 Case 2: Acquire Expertise

When several senior managers recognized the need for additional skilled labor, they turned to vendors for their technical expertise. In general, participants felt that qualified IS personnel were difficult to acquire. The process of finding, hiring, and training personnel was not only time-consuming but expensive. In addition, management seems paranoid about headcounts. Why not turn to outsourcing vendors to access their skilled labor pool? After all, they are the experts, so why foster these skills internally?

FIRM9, FIRM11, and FIRM13 all cited the need to acquire a better qualified staff as an impetus for outsourcing. Rather than retrain the current staff, eliminate low performers, and/or hire additional personnel, outsourcing seemed a preferred method for meeting labor needs.

FIRM9. Because senior management at FIRM9 viewed IS as a cost burden, they were unwilling to adequately fund the IS department. One strategy for keeping costs low was to keep salaries to a minimum. Unfortunately, when IS salaries fall below market price, few qualified people are attracted to the position. Therefore, FIRM9 hired people with outdated technical skills. Al, Manager of Purchasing, notes the level of technological sophistication of the staff prior to outsourcing:

> "The level of technical expertise, as I said, in the department was very, very low. And another area that lended itself to outsourcing was that we were in a mode where some very old systems existed and were being supported and there was a need to upgrade a lot of capacity in materials, maintenance, operations and transportation. A lot of areas needed some new software capabilities to stay competitive. There wasn't a chance in the world that the current staff was going to be able to provide support necessary to get those things on-line."

Al notes that there was a perception that an outsourcing vendor could provide the needed expertise. In particular, the outsourcing vendor they chose had knowledge of barcoding systems and executive support systems—two areas that interested FIRM9. Overall, Al feels that outsourcing did increase the expertise of the IS staff but that "none of it comes cheap."

FIRM11. FIRM11 was in a similar circumstance as FIRM9: the IS staff was not equipped to meet user needs. Technical skills were rusty—true—but the bigger problem was that the culture of the IS staff was basically one of isolationism. The IS staff were physically as well as psychologically removed from their users; analysts rarely interacted with their users. This attitude made the entire IS function ineffective. Paul, FIRM11's controller, decided to outsource the entire function to an outsourcing vendor. Today, Paul feels that the entire IS is more receptive to the organization's needs. One may note, however, that the same analysts Paul employed prior to outsourcing are now employed by the vendor. The account manager retrained the staff in both technical and customer service skills. Lawrence, the vendor's account manager, describes the level of skills the FIRM11 staff possessed when he took over the account:

"The people development—I put emphasis on training. God knows the FIRM11 folks that were here were severely curtailed. We needed to get them back to speed. And some professional training too. I mean the whole concept of serving a customer, how to deal with customers, how to manage, how to properly analyze their needs versus taking the solution they want to inevitably give you. All those kind of skills to be developed."

Even though the staff is essentially the same, Paul perceives that he acquired considerable expertise from the vendor.

FIRM13. Before FIRM13 acquired a parts company, the parts company outsourced their entire IS department. The primary impetus for outsourcing was to access the technical talent needed to convert to a new computer architecture. In addition, the vendor promised to give the company several transaction processing systems. After outsourcing, the company was dismayed that the conversion failed and that the "free" systems would cost them dearly. The perception that outsourcing was a way to access expertise was deemed largely an illusion; after all, the transferred employees ended up performing the installation anyway. FIRM13's IS manager notes:

"[The vendor] took over all the people, as they usually do. So what happens in that environment is that your unqualified IS people that you had become your unqualified [vendor] people. So you are not better off."

6.2.3 Case 3: Save my Company

Some large outsourcing vendors possess significant cash reserves. Rather than let funds remain idle, vendors use cash to expand their business into other industries. Vendors target companies suffering profit reversals since CEOs are likely to lend a willing ear. FIRM10 and FIRM3 provide two examples where vendors targeted near-bankrupt companies. In these instances, the vendors saw an opportunity for an entrée into a new industry. Each of these companies possessed significant information systems assets and notable IS talent.

FIRM10. FIRM10's situation differs from other case participants because the company was facing bankruptcy. They desperately needed a cash infusion to remain solvent. The outsourcing vendor assembled an outsourcing package that was extremely favorable: purchase millions of dollars worth of FIRM10 stock, loan the company millions of dollars at an attractive interest rate, and pay cash for information systems assets, including a much coveted reservation system.

FIRM3. Like FIRM10, the main reason that FIRM3's CEO even considered outsourcing was because his company was in financial trouble. When bankruptcy was filed in 1987, the public became aware of FIRM3's dire need for cash. This prompted the CEO of an outsourcing company to offer FIRM3's CEO a substantial amount of cash for his information systems assets. After a few discussions with FIRM3's Vice President of Information Systems, the CEO told him to respond negatively to the vendor's offer for two reasons. First, the CEO valued his IS department; second, the money was insignificant compared to the amount needed to salvage FIRM3.

FIRM10 and FIRM3 share a common outsourcing story. Of the thirteen cases, these were the only two where senior managers valued the IS function. Each IS department was established as a profit center. Each generated additional revenue by attracting customers from outside of their companies. Each commanded support and attention from senior management. The only reason why these companies considered outsourcing at all was because of an impending bankruptcy. Outsourcing was only enticing because IS liquidation would generate substantial funds.

6.2.4 Case 4: The Start-up Company

Two companies first considered outsourcing when they were newly formed: FIRM12 and FIRM1. Pressed for cash and time, these companies evaluated outsourcing as a viable alternative to building an internal IS department.

FIRM12. FIRM12's decision to outsource in 1984 was largely due to a hostile raid of FIRM12's parent company. Since the new owners had little interest in the specialty products produced by FIRM12, they placed the company for sale. FIRM12's management subsequently purchased the company in a leveraged buyout. As part of the LBO, FIRM12 signed a six-month contract with the prior owners for support services such as accounting and IS. FIRM12, ridden with debt as a result of the LBO, could not afford to build an internal IS department during the transition period. Instead, they hastily signed a seven-year contract with an outsourcing vendor to provide all their information needs. Although the vendor's subsequent service was pitiful and expensive, FIRM12 had few alternatives at the time the decision was made. Capital investments in technology were simply impractical.

FIRM1. FIRM1 faced a similar situation. In 1985, their parent company bundled several non-profitable businesses to form FIRM1. The new management at FIRM1 considered outsourcing as an alternative to building an internal IS department. The vendor's bid, however, proved more expensive than erecting an IS department. Unlike FIRM12, FIRM1 was able to build an IS department from the hardware and software they inherited from the previous owners. These hand-me-down assets made insourcing less expensive.

In summary, the use of outsourcing evaluations to acquire new resources is largely a reaction to the perception that vendors can efficiently provide capital, expertise and cash to their clients. For hardware upgrades, IS managers proactively evaluated outsourcing to dispel this perception. By showing that vendors cannot provide hardware less expensively, IS managers add credence to their hardware requests. For additional skills, senior managers turned to outsourcing to acquire vendor expertise. The perception that vendors provide cost-efficient labor can be challenged on two points. First, outsourcing clients are usually supported by their previous staff. Second, premium prices are charged for additional talent. For access to financial resources, outsourcing becomes a seductive alternative. Near-bankrupt companies abandon their efficiency perceptions to concentrate on a higher item: survival. For the start-up company, outsourcing is perceived as more efficient than erecting an internal IS department.

6.3 REACTION TO THE PROVERBIAL BANDWAGON

During the interviews, participants identified another reason for initiating outsourcing evaluations: reaction to public outsourcing reports. Some participants, excited by the positive outsourcing reports from other companies, wanted to duplicate these success stories in their own companies. Other participants worried that the overly-optimistic reports might blindly seduce their senior executives into outsourcing. By initiating an investigation themselves, they hoped to separate outsourcing fact from outsourcing fantasy. Thus, public outsourcing reports influenced participants in two ways:

Case 1: Participants initiated evaluations to duplicate outsourcing success stories in their own companies. Who wouldn't want to reduce IS expenditures by 10% to 40%?

Case 2: Participants used evaluations to temper exaggerated claims by exposing the negative consequences of outsourcing.

The evidence to support the cases is presented below.

6.3.1   Case 1: Let's Duplicate the Success Stories

Several case participants initiated outsourcing evaluations because they wanted to duplicate the outsourcing success stories they read in the trade literature, heard at outsourcing seminars or heard from colleagues. Managers at FIRM6, FIRM1, FIRM8, and FIRM11 seemed to have been influenced—at least initially—by these public sources.

FIRM6. Jack, FIRM6's Senior Vice President of Operations, considered outsourcing because he read that many of his competitors were reducing data processing costs through outsourcing. The Vice President of IS describes Jack's motivation for the outsourcing decision:

> "So he really felt, and I think quite correctly, that outsourcing was something people were talking about. Other organizations had done it, especially in banks, that were the same size as us."

When Jack talked to several colleagues in other banks that had recently outsourced, they all reported dramatic *anticipated* savings. Since the bank was in financial trouble, Jack hoped that outsourcing could bail him out the way outsourcing had bailed out his friends.

FIRM1.   Stanley, the Manager of Data Processing, claims that he initiated FIRM1's second outsourcing evaluation partly because he was reading positive reports on outsourcing. This prompted him to attend a seminar on outsourcing. His belief that outsourcing could save him money was corroborated. (When we asked Stanley who participated in the seminar, he said it was outsourcing vendors, which might explain the propagation of outsourcing successes.) He hoped to duplicate these savings at FIRM1. Here is Stanley's account of his reason for initiating an outsourcing investigation:

> "You know, pick up one of these free rags that we get a dozen of every week, you know outsourcing has been a popular topic. Spring of last year, about a year ago, I decided to talk to a few vendors and see if it really was cheaper to do it someplace else."

Stanley felt that since his mainframe operations were small, that a vendor may be able to reduce his processing costs. This idea came from newspaper accounts that purport that vendors reduce costs through economies of scale:

> "Again, from reading in the trade literature and talking to people, I have read and have no reason to dispute that probably the most efficient, cost-effective mainframe shop is somewhere in the 200 MIP range. And a 28 MIP shop is darn small, so if I had a 100 MIP shop or a 200 MIP shop, I would only have one copy of the operating system and so forth, COBOL, and things that you pay for. So it was efficiencies of scale."

The public sources of outsourcing were so adamant that large vendors are more efficient that Stanley began to question his department's own efficiency. After the outsourcing evaluation which "proved" he was efficient, Stanley was more skeptical about vendor economies of scale reported in the literature.

FIRM8. Barry, FIRM8's Manager of Information Systems, spearheaded the data center outsourcing evaluation project that eventually led to a five-year outsourcing contract. Barry's boss, the Controller, fully supported the evaluation and subsequent outsourcing decision. At lower levels of the organization, however, subordinates accuse Barry and his boss of outsourcing because it is fashionable. While backlash from subordinates who lost their positions may be expected, the following criticism comes from an employee who was promoted as a result of outsourcing:

> "I think that people should analyze it, but analyze it like any other business deal. A lot of people are doing it because it is fashionable. They read about it in the magazines and they don't even trust their own analysis. You know, they say even if the internal is cheaper, like ours did, they don't trust it. They say, 'now wait a minute—all the articles said people are saving money, we must be doing something wrong.'"

According to this employee, the written word is powerful enough to undermine any manager's confidence.

FIRM11. Paul, FIRM11's Controller, claims he decided to outsource because he wanted to duplicate the outsourcing success a colleague of his experienced at another company. Here is Paul's explanation:

> "Two years ago I went to a National Coal Association Conference. I was talking to some of my peers in the industry. We were talking about data processing costs, comparing notes. I was amazed what this other company's costs were. They were so much lower than ours and they were approximately the same size company as us. So, I asked him, 'What is your secret?' He said, 'We outsourced.'"

When it was asked of Paul if this was his first encounter with information systems outsourcing, he replied:

> "Yeah, that was the first ever. That was the first time I ever heard of [outsourcing vendor]. So I came back and talked to my boss, Larry, about it. And we both thought it was worth exploring. We had an initial meeting with [a vendor]. Then it was carried through where we are today."

Thus, favorable outsourcing success stories played a significant role in Paul's decision to outsource his entire IS department.

From the above discussion we see that participants partly initiated outsourcing evaluations because they wanted to duplicate outsourcing success stories. This reaction to public outsourcing accounts may be interpreted in two ways. First, the participants may have prudently waited to investigate outsourcing until early-adopters tested the practice. Second, the participants may have blindly jumped on the outsourcing bandwagon.

The first interpretation comes from organizational theories of innovation diffusion. The theory states that practitioners often adopt technologies, managerial practices or other innovations after early-adopters have successfully implemented them. This strategy can be effective since late-adopters do not experience the same level of risks and costs as early-adopters (Rogers, 1983).

The second interpretation can be construed as jumping on the proverbial bandwagon. Whereas the term "late-adopter" suggests a purposeful delay, the term "jump on the bandwagon" connotes an action of uninformed conformity. After talking to participants, the interpretation of their outsourcing intentions makes more sense from this second perspective. Accusing participants of uninformed conformity may seem harsh, but the fault resides with their information sources, not in their inherent shortcomings. Participants reacted to information sources they assumed were reliable—journal articles, newspaper reports, and verbal accounts from colleagues.

Several other participants, however, had an opposite reaction to public outsourcing accounts. Their stories are relayed in the following section.

6.3.2 Case 2: Exposing Exaggerated Claims

Participants from FIRM2, FIRM13, FIRM4 were skeptical about the favorable outsourcing reports purported in the trade literature and seminars. At FIRM2, participants were prompted to write a report on outsourcing that portrayed a more balanced view of outsourcing accounts. At FIRM13, the failure of their outsourcing arrangement succeeded in diminishing management's outsourcing enthusiasm.

At FIRM4, IS managers fought to temper exaggerated vendor claims during an intense outsourcing investigation.

FIRM2. The decision to evaluate outsourcing at FIRM2 was largely in response to favorable outsourcing reports. FIRM2's Vice President of IS assigned his Director of Advanced Technology to write a report on outsourcing. The purpose of this report was to temper senior management's overly-optimistic impression of outsourcing—an impression they formed based on newspaper accounts. The following is an excerpt from the report:

> "Outsourcing has gained considerable notoriety recently not so much because it is a new idea, but because who is doing it. Prominent examples of companies that have chosen to outsource some or all of their functions include Eastman Kodak, American Standard, First City Bancorp, Enron, Purina, Heinz, and Trane. Effective and cost efficient performance are most frequently cited as the motivation behind outsourcing. To date, many of these newsworthy examples of outsourcing have been done by companies that were either in or headed for financial trouble."

Anthony claims that the vogue of outsourcing is primarily attributable to Kodak. Kodak made it acceptable for large companies to outsource their IS departments:

> "In 1987, Eastman Kodak astonished the data processing industry. During that year, Kodak entered into agreements that may ultimately result in the total dismantling of its processing services. The effects that these negotiations and agreements have had on the data processing industry have certainly been startling...the Kodak agreements hit the industry like a bombshell. Kodak had not only decided to outsource, it had determined that data processing is a utility, much the same as electricity."

On the actual savings achieved through outsourcing, Anthony writes:

> "In some cases, costs have actually been lowered by returning to in-house processing from an outsource agreement.... Many companies have also found that while costs for the baseline functions have indeed dropped, increases in other costs have largely offset these savings. Of particular note are costs for time and materials work beyond the scope of the original contract. The work often represents a hidden source of revenue for outsource vendors."

Anthony's report, which exposes many exaggerated outsourcing claims, has the potential to diminish the influence that public outsourcing accounts have had on his senior managers.

FIRM13. Like FIRM8, senior managers at FIRM13 seemed more influenced by public outsourcing information than by their own outsourcing experiences. Despite the sub-standard service and exorbitant prices one of FIRM13's subsidiaries experienced with outsourcing, other division managers are impressed by outsourcing reports. FIRM13's IS manager explains:

> "I think they see it in the press, they get letters from every CEO of an outsourcing organization telling them how great they are and how much money they could save. . . . We've had that asked, 'Should we do outsourcing?', by our management folks here. I just keep quoting the [parts division's] experience."

Even though FIRM13 terminated the contract early, other division heads are still wooed by reported savings.

FIRM4. The Director of Corporate Planning at FIRM4 claims that senior management largely considered outsourcing because they believed vendor claims. He describes vendor solicitations as follows:

> "In steps the white knight saying, 'Mister executive, we can take headaches away from you, and we will not only take the headache away, we will guarantee you without any doubt that we will save you 25% off of what you are spending today.'"

The internal IS managers feared that their senior executives were being seduced by exaggerated vendor promises. Although senior management ultimately rejected vendor bids, the internal IS department went through a nerve-wrenching evaluation process. At one point, the IS manager threw up his hands and exclaimed:

> "Outsource it. . . let's get rid of the headache. . .let them save you the 25% because in three years I guarantee you are going to be bleeding bad."

The Director of Corporate planning claims that enthusiasm over outsourcing reports in the literature is premature:

> "I don't think there has been enough time gone by. Where is Enron going to be 8 years from now? I understand that they already have some problems and have considered litigation. What about Kodak? It looks absolutely fantastic on day 1, but you know, when you are making a ten year contract and you put the fate of your future into the hands of someone else. . . you know I am real curious to see some of these contracts come to their termination and see it then."

In summary, case participants were spawned on by public outsourcing reports in one of two ways. Several participants, excited about the cost savings reported in the literature, wished to duplicate these savings in their own departments. Other participants, however, felt that public accounts of outsourcing are overly-optimistic. They attempted to temper exaggerated claims by exposing the negative consequences of outsourcing.

An apt comment to summarize this theme was made by the IS manager at FIRM12. After seven years of poor outsourcing service, he rebuilt an internal IS shop. When asked what he thought of the trade reports on outsourcing, he merely responded, "I laugh."

6.4 REDUCE UNCERTAINTY

The fourth cited reason for initiating outsourcing decisions was to reduce uncertainty. IS managers abhor uncertainty because they cannot adequately plan for IS services. Severe increases or decreases in IS demand send IS managers in a fury to adjust staffing and resources. Rather than continue this reactionary frenzy, IS managers may outsource to force the vendor to absorb uncertainty by including a clause that fluctuates fees with volumes. The two cases that illustrate this point are FIRM8 and FIRM9.

FIRM8. The IS manager at FIRM8 faced uncertainty from two sources. First, senior management neglects to inform him about acquisitions until deals are consummated. The IS manager is often charged with the risky task of absorbing acquired companies into current systems with virtually no notice (not to mention no additional resources). Second, rumors suggested that company headquarters will be relocated to a new state. The IS manager, who had no experience in moving a data center, stated: "We don't have any business doing this, we ought to take it outside." By outsourcing, he was able to reduce uncertainty associated with the data center move as well as volume fluctuations. A clause in his outsourcing contract obliges the vendor to handle acquisitions efficiently and expediently.

FIRM9. A similar situation exists at FIRM9. They acquired 18 companies in a span of two years. Senior management expected the IS manager to accommodate acquisitions with few additional resources. Furthermore, demand for systems greatly fluctuated with copper prices. When prices were high, users requested many system enhancements. When prices were low, the volume of work decreased. The IS manager could not afford to hire and fire staff to match demand oscillations. He decided instead to outsource. With a similar contract clause as FIRM8, FIRM9's charges now fluctuate with business volumes. This mechanism forces the vendor to absorb uncertainty and thereby reduces the personal risks of FIRM9's IS manager.

In summary, IS managers at FIRM8 and FIRM7 outsourced partly to reduce the risk associated with uncertainty.

6.5 ELIMINATE A BURDENSOME FUNCTION

Most people readily admit that they favor certain job responsibilities over others. For example, a weary faculty member once exclaimed, "this job would be so nice without the students." In this research, several participants expressed displeasure about some of their IS responsibilities. Senior executives who have the IS manager reporting to them often see the IS department as their least favored job duty. IS managers themselves seemed to favor applications over data processing—data processing is a thankless job because service expectations are so high. One lapse in availability and the IS manager is barraged with inquiries. Three companies that seemed willing to outsource their burdensome IS functions include FIRM11, FIRM1, and FIRM4.

FIRM11. The Controller at FIRM11 claims he outsourced to reduce costs. During the interview, however, he identified another motive: eliminate a burdensome function. Even though he felt that the vendor primarily achieved economies of scale for data processing, he also outsourced applications:

> "People say you should keep applications. I ask them, Why would you want to do that? That's the biggest headache. Anybody can run a machine, it's the applications that are a headache."

The Controller simply did not feel comfortable dealing with the IS department. He never understood systems: "I mean I am not a technician. MIPS? Bytes? Who knows?" Through outsourcing, the Controller believes he no longer has to worry about IS. The question remains, however, whether one can actually outsource the *management* of IS.

FIRM1. The IS manager at FIRM1 evaluated outsourcing the data center on two occasions. Although both decisions resulted in a recommendation to keep the function in-house—the IS manager seemed willing to outsource the second time if the numbers so indicated. The data center is a pain to manage because technical people are difficult to retain and because service lapses destroy the IS manager's credibility:

> "If it breaks, it's my fault. If it's late, it's my fault. If response time is lousy, it's my fault. And we do something good every now and then but nobody notices that. . ."

So why not outsource data processing if the numbers dictate? The analysis, however, favored insourcing—perhaps because the data collection task was delegated to employees who would lose their jobs if outsourcing was deemed the favored choice.

FIRM4. As noted in the discussion on the bandwagon effect, FIRM4 senior managers considered outsourcing because they believed vendor claims and because they did not value IS. In fact, the Director of Corporate Planning referred to IS as a "headache" three times. He claims that senior management felt that IS was a burden to manage, so why not outsource it? Fortunately for FIRM4, senior managers realized that you cannot outsource management. Instead, the internal IS department was given the support needed to reduce costs on their own.

In summary, some managers may consider outsourcing to eliminate a burdensome function. Although this intention appears pejorative, it captures a very human desire. Don't we all wish some portion of our job responsibilities would vaporize?

6.6 ENHANCE CREDIBILITY

The final reason, or impetus, that participants cited for the outsourcing evaluation was to enhance credibility. This is particularly true for the participants who held the title of Director of IS. Since IS managers are often viewed as technicians rather than businessmen, they need some mechanism for demonstrating their business savvy to senior management. As will be shown, outsourcing evaluations are one such mechanism.

The first issue to address is why IS managers need their credibility enhanced. In this study, credibility was often questioned because IS managers had little experience outside of the IS world. IS managers typically spent virtually their entire careers in various information systems positions:

> Ronald, Vice President of Information Systems for FIRM3, spent

his entire 35 years with the company in IS-related positions.

Terrence, the current Vice President of IS, has spent his 18 years at FIRM13 in the IS department.

Barry, FIRM8's IS Manager, has spent his 20 plus years working in IS and accounting functions in several large petroleum companies.

Gordon, Manager of Information Systems at FIRM1, has spent his entire career in the IS department of FIRM1 and FIRM1's parent company.

Because IS department heads are born and raised information systems professionals, their senior executives often view them as technocrats. IS managers are the people with the funny acronyms, the people that think technology is the answer to everything, the people that always want more money.

One way that IS managers can increase their credibility is to initiate outsourcing investigations. Outsourcing evaluations can alleviate the misconception that IS managers are myopic; they demonstrate to senior management that they are businessmen committed to corporate goals, not technocrats attempting to build technology empires. According to IS managers, increasing their personal credibility benefits the entire IS organization—upper management support means support for the entire IS team, not just the department head. Some of the IS managers' subordinates, however, contend that outsourcing evaluations were designed for the IS managers' personal gain, not for the good of the whole department. These issues are examined in the following cases: FIRM8, FIRM5 and FIRM3.

FIRM8. Prior to outsourcing the data center and telecommunications, several indicants suggest that Barry, FIRM8's IS Manager, needed to bolster his personal and departmental credibility. First, as a new hire from another company, Barry had to prove himself to upper management. His worth was apparently in question as evidenced by the second indicant, a recent demotion. Barry's position was demoted to reporting to the Controller instead of the CFO. The CFO felt that the Controller could manage IS without his direct intervention. The third indicant was that Barry was having trouble acquiring money to accommodate recent acquisitions. Senior management seemed to question the validity of Barry's resource requests. Thus, we see a newcomer trying to manage a department that is under-valued and under-resourced. Barry had to do something and outsourcing seemed like a wise move.

Barry was quite familiar with outsourcing. His prior position at a firm who had outsourced its IS allowed him to witness firsthand the problems associated with outsourcing. Barry felt, however, that he knew where the mistakes were: they didn't define service levels, they gave away too much functionality, and they signed a weak contract. By compensating for these deficiencies, he could make outsourcing work at FIRM8. As a consequence of outsourcing, Barry captured senior management's attention and respect:

> Barry's first audience with the leaders of his company was when he presented the outsourcing decision to the Board of Directors.

> Mike, Barry's current boss, became Barry's most ardent fan, largely due to outsourcing; Mike now thinks Barry is the best IS manager he has ever met. Mike now invites Barry to his lunches with the CEO.

> The by-line in a respected IS trade publication also enhanced Barry's credibility.

So, in the case of FIRM8, Barry's outsourcing decision was successful at proving to management that he is a corporate player, not a technician. From Barry's perspective, the IS manager's personal credibility is a prerequisite for effectively managing the department. In the future, perhaps senior management will be less likely to question Barry's recommendations and requests.

Barry's subordinates, however, contend that Barry's outsourcing decision was designed for his personal gain, not the good of the organization. Members of Barry's staff claim he used them to help him outsource, then turned around and fired them. They also accuse him of stacking the deck in favor of outsourcing by manipulating the numbers. In his staff's opinion, Barry was determined a priori to outsource the data center for personal gain. One subordinate, for example, stated the following:

> "I can only speak from my own observations. I got the feeling that he just wanted to make his mark. To give the illusion that he proactively made a decision. It was a project that was highly visible. He got some press, that sort of thing. That's really what I felt the agenda was."

Barry, however, does not feel that his motives were selfish, but good business. Being a good businessman can sometimes be heart-wrenching:

> "It was a hard decision. I had too many cooks in the kitchen down there. I lost a lot of sleep over this."

Recall the second caveat stated at the beginning of this chapter: the reasons cited for outsourcing are not criticisms of behavior. Even though outsiders may view the behavior as suspicious or devious, participants do not see themselves in this light. Rather, participants feel their difficult choices are territorial to good business. As researchers, we should strive to see behavior from all sides.

FIRM5. Thomas was FIRM5's Director of IS at the time of the outsourcing decision. He initiated his outsourcing evaluation largely out of frustration. He felt that senior management was demanding too much from his department without providing sufficient resources. Thomas laments:

> "I was getting zero support... I said, 'I cannot get any support from you all in how to allocate these resources. And we cannot be the traffic cop in this whole process because it is not right.' I said, 'I'm trying to satisfy everybody and it's not working.'"

In addition to getting more support for his department, Thomas also admitted that the evaluation was also designed to enhance his personal credibility:

> "You know, I didn't feel any risk that I would personally be out on the streets. Okay?... I'd be lying to you if I thought I would be unemployed. But if you can go in and show something that is clearly right for the company, I don't think that anyone is going to punish you for that, okay? I mean as good corporate citizens, we were trying to do what was right."

According to Thomas, outsourcing did help to increase his personal credibility:

> "So did that help? Since then, I've been to two officer meetings, so I guess it did."

In addition, the Chairman wrote Thomas a memo thanking him for his dedication and conscious efforts to be cost-efficient. One of Thomas's subordinates, however, contends that the outsourcing evaluation was really a charade to increase Thomas's credibility. Although Thomas said that the real objective was to reduce costs, one subordinate claims, "As a result of having done this study, there is no difference now than if we had not done the study."

FIRM3. Ronald, IS Manager at FIRM3, feels that personal credibility is a prerequisite for effective management. Ronald spent his entire career trying to use computer technology as a vehicle for facilitating business objectives. The only jargon that Ronald employs is indigenous to the energy industry, not to computer systems. He feels that his business savvy gave credence to his credibility. Since his CEO trusted his opinion, he consulted Ronald when an outsourcing vendor offered him a substantial cash sum for his IS assets. The CEO promptly listened to Ronald's report on the pros and cons of outsourcing. Together, the CEO and Ronald declined the vendor's offer. Ronald notes:

> "So I think the concept of your IS person being part of the management of the company—not just a technician sitting on the sidelines—is something that keeps you from outsourcing."

Ronald believes that IS managers must become business minded or they become vulnerable to outsourcing. The internal IS manager's business savvy may be the only factor that differentiates him from the sea of outsourcing vendors.

In summary, several IS managers stressed the importance of building a credible reputation. Overcoming the technical guru perception is not easy. Often born and raised in systems, many IS managers are not considered corporate players. Outsourcing evaluations can increase personal credibility by proving to management that organizational goals supersede regional interests.

6.7   CONCLUSION

The reasons presented in this section capture the participants' views of their intentions for initiating outsourcing decisions. Taken as a whole, these reasons represent a mixture of economic and political motives.

The *efficiency imperative* can be analyzed from both an economic and a political perspective. From an economic perspective, participants are well indoctrinated into the capitalist mentality that the bottom line is—so to speak—the bottom line. Legitimate outsourcing decisions in some way reflect the efficiency imperative. The problem, however, is that actual IS efficiency is an ethereal concept. Therefore, efficiency ultimately reduces to a perception. IS managers may be forced to invoke political tactics to create the perception of efficiency; in their hearts they may believe that their departments are efficient, but management must be convinced. In other words, "In God we trust—all others bring data." Outsourcing evaluations provide one mechanism for demonstrating efficiency, but alas these were not always effective. The IS managers' evaluations at FIRM7 and FIRM1, for example, were largely viewed with skepticism. When IS managers fail to convince executives of IS efficiency, executives may initiate cost-saving measures of their own. . .including outsourcing.

The *resource acquisition* theme is a variant of the efficiency imperative. When trying to acquire additional resources, participants must determine the most efficient acquisition method: produce internally or outsource. In the cases of bankrupt firms or start-up companies, outsourcing may yield the only feasible alternative. Politics may come into play when participants merely used outsourcing evaluations to justify hardware upgrades. From the participants' perspective, however, the economic need for upgrades is evident to them, but again—they must provide data to convince management.

The *bandwagon effect* theme may be more indicative of the garbage-can theory of organizational decisions (Huber, 1981). The garbage-can model characterizes decision-makers as primarily reactionary. Not knowing how to manage IS, many participants reacted to reports in the trade press, colleagues in the industry, or consultants to guide IS policy. When reports of IS outsourcing promised tremendous savings, several participants jumped on the bandwagon. Other participants, particularly IS managers, tried to expose some of the exaggerated media claims by evaluating outsourcing. Although some may view these cursory evaluations as political tactics, participants themselves saw their behavior as rational techniques for enlightening senior management.

The *reduce uncertainty* theme can also be viewed from a political as well as an economic perspective. From economic theory, we know that rational decision-makers make choices along their theoretical utility curves. IS managers that outsourced can therefore be viewed as maximizing their utility given a risk-averse propensity. By minimizing the organization's uncertainty, they improve effectiveness. From a political perspective—the IS managers may have been more concerned with the personal risks associated with uncertainty. Rather than risk failure caused by the inability to react to uncertainty—adopt an outsourcing scapegoat.

The *eliminate headache* theme makes more sense from a political perspective. Rather than personally handle a thankless responsibility, why not farm it out?

The *personal credibility* theme can really be viewed from both perspectives. From an economic perspective, IS managers claim that personal credibility must precede departmental credibility. You won't buy the product if you don't trust the spokesperson. From a political perspective, subordinates felt that IS managers only used outsourcing to promote self-interest at the expense of the department.

In summary, the IS outsourcing framework categorized participants' reasons for initiating outsourcing evaluations into six categories. This framework may be viewed as a description of participants' intentions and behaviors. In the next chapter, a prescription is developed based on the subsequent successes and failures the participants experienced as a result of their outsourcing decisions.

7
Proposed Outsourcing Evaluation Process

7.0 INTRODUCTION

This chapter addresses the question: How should practitioners about to face outsourcing decisions conduct their evaluations? The answer is provided in the form of a proposed evaluation process based on the lessons learned from the participants' outsourcing successes and failures.

The proposed process is admittedly value-laden for two reasons. First, the evaluation process is a prescription for potential outsourcing customers, not outsourcing vendors. Whereas vendors are assumed to be capable of protecting their own interests, potential clients seem to need assistance. Second, the evaluation process assumes that the potential clients wish to make rational, financial outsourcing evaluations. Therefore, political reasons for initiating outsourcing evaluations are not addressed. With these biases thus confessed, the chapter begins with lessons learned from the research participants (see Table 7.1).

Using these three lessons, an outsourcing decision tree has been developed (see Table 7.2). The decision tree begins with the comparison of the vendor bid(s) with the internal IS bid. If a vendor bid is more desirable, perhaps in terms of costs, access to resources, or manipulation of payments, then presumably the company will outsource. Right? Wrong! Now is the time to pause and ask the questions: Why was the vendor's bid more desirable? Could my company achieve these results on our own? If we need the vendor, how do we ensure that expectations will be realized?

Table 7.1 *Lessons for practitioners*

An outsourcing vendor may not be inherently more efficient than an internal IS department.

The internal IS department may be able to achieve similar results without vendor assistance.

If a company outsources, the outsourcing contract is the only way to ensure that expectations are realized.

Table 7.2 *Proposed outsourcing evaluation process*

```
┌─────────────────────────────────┐
│ Create a Request for Proposal   │
│ Gather several vendor bids      │
└─────────────────────────────────┘
                 │
                 ▼                    NO   ┌──────────────────┐
┌─────────────────────────────────┐ ────▶│ Keep IS in-house │
│ Is the vendor's bid more        │       └──────────────────┘
│ desirable (in terms of          │
│ costs/resources/finances)       │
│ than the internal IS bid?       │
└─────────────────────────────────┘
                 │ YES
                 ▼
┌─────────────────────────────────┐ YES  ┌──────────────────┐
│ Could the internal IS department│ ────▶│ Keep IS in-house │
│ achieve similar results without │      └──────────────────┘
│ vendor assistance?              │
└─────────────────────────────────┘
                 │ NO
                 ▼
┌─────────────────────────────────┐
│ Negotiate a contract to ensure  │
│ that expectations are realized. │
└─────────────────────────────────┘
```

7.1 THE INTERNAL IS DEPARTMENT MAY BE ABLE TO ACHIEVE SIMILAR RESULTS WITHOUT VENDOR ASSISTANCE

A potential client may receive a vendor bid that is more desirable for three reasons. First, the vendor may offer a financial package whose net present value is extremely attractive. Cash infusions for information assets, postponing payments until the end of the contract, and even purchases of the client's stock may render outsourcing desirable. If this is the sole reason for outsourcing, then the potential client may proceed to negotiate a contract to ensure these financial promises are realized.

Second, the vendor may under-bid current IS costs. The potential outsourcing client should then ask: Why are the vendor's costs lower? If the vendor has inherent efficiencies that the potential client cannot replicate, then outsourcing makes sense from a pragmatic stance. Again, the client should proceed to negotiate a contract to ensure that these savings are realized. In other cases, however, the vendor may implement cost-saving measures that the company could potentially initiate on their own. This includes consolidating data centers, optimizing current resource use, and implementing a charge-back system to deter waste. In these instances, the company may wish to reduce costs on their own, unless their culture or politics makes this option infeasible. Finally, the vendor may offer access to certain resources such as expertise that the potential client feels is too expensive to nurture internally. The potential client should ask whether the vendor truly will provide the technical and business expertise required to meet information needs. In most outsourcing arrangements, the company ends up supported by the same staff since IS employees are transitioned to the vendor. In addition, the vendor may transfer the best talent to attract other clients. In the end, the access to all this expertise may merely be an illusion.

This section presents two guidelines to help potential clients determine whether an outsourcing vendor is truly needed to obtain desired results. The first guideline is to evaluate whether the vendor has inherent efficiencies that the client cannot replicate. Most potential outsourcing customers assume that vendors achieve tremendous economies of scale, but that may largely be a myth. The second guideline is to introduce some common vendor practices for reducing costs. Again, given a cooperative environment, the company may be able to reduce costs on their own.

7.1.1   Is the Vendor Inherently more Efficient?

The theoretical basis of economies of scale is that large-sized companies have lower average costs than small-sized companies due to mass production and labor specialization efficiencies (Leftwich & Eckert, 1984). Mass production is presumed to reduce average costs by allocating fixed costs over more units of output and by receiving volume discounts on inputs. Labor specialization is presumed to reduce costs by allowing workers to focus on tasks at which they are most adept.

Applying the economic theory of efficiency to information systems outsourcing is a messy proposition. The inherent problems of measuring efficiency once again surface. How do we know a vendor is inherently more efficient than the internal IS department? The only area of efficiency that has been adequately measured is data processing, in particular, cost per MIP. Most of the efficiency arguments, however, are more qualitative in nature. For example, vendors are assumed to have lower average hardware and software costs due to volume discounts, the sharing of software lease costs over multiple customers, and the use of standard technology platforms. On the labor specialization side, outsourcing vendors are assumed to be information systems specialists. They can allegedly design, develop, and maintain systems more efficiently because of their expertise.

An evaluation of the cases, however, reveals that the application of the economies of scale model to outsourcing vendors is often fallacious—vendors are not necessarily more efficient. The arguments and evidence, primarily qualitative in nature, are discussed below (see Table 7.3).

Mass Production Efficiency Myth 1: costs per MIP. Industry experts often report that data processing shops achieve economies of scale around 150 MIPS (Krass, 1990). Real Decisions, for example, has documented that costs per CPU minute are lowest for data centers in the 135 to 200 MIP range. Their analysis is based on data gathered and normalized from hundreds of their clients. Their evidence seems compelling: large IS shops are more efficient than smaller IS shops. However, several examples from this research suggest that small shops can be more efficient than large shops. FIRM1, FIRM8, and FIRM12 provide three examples where small shops were more efficient, as measured by cost per MIP, than large, vendor-run data centers.

FIRM1. FIRM1 operates a 28 MIP shop, yet five outsourcing

Table 7.3 *Economies of scale myths*

Mass Production Efficiency Myths:
1. Cost per MIP
2. Hardware costs
3. Software costs

Labor Specialization Efficiency Myths:
1. Access to technical talent
2. Access to business talent

companies could not underbid the internal IS department. Stanley, the Manager of Data Processing at FIRM1, claims he initiated an outsourcing evaluation because he read in the trade literature that data centers don't achieve economies of scale until the 200 MIP range. Stanley was surprised to discover that outsourcing could not save him money. When it was asked of him how he reconciled the fact that the vendors couldn't reduce his costs, he responded that he really didn't know:

> "His comment [i.e. the vendor's comment] was he had to pay operators more than I pay them. They pay systems programmers more than I can hire them for. Because they are a larger company, their overhead is higher. Now that's a salesman talking, I'm not sure I really buy that. Why could they not do it cheaper? I don't know."

FIRM8. FIRM8, which operates a 14 MIP machine, provides another example. The first time FIRM8 requested bids from five outsourcing vendors, all declined. Stephen, FIRM8's Data Center Manager, explains:

> "They went out and canvassed, I believe at that time they talked to [five vendors]. And they all came back and said that we were not a good candidate for outsourcing. Our costs were under control. We had just finished doing a data center assessment with IBM, and they rated us very high. They said for a shop this size our procedures were very tight too. And effectively they gave us a clean bill of health."

FIRM12. FIRM12 terminated an outsourcing contract with a vendor that had a very large data processing facility. The cost to rebuild his 17 MIP shop via AS400s proved less expensive than using the vendor's massive data center.

When Walter, an outsourcing consultant, was asked how costs per MIP were more expensive for large vendors than these tiny shops, he responded that (a) vendors may not manage their resources properly, or (b) vendors may not pass savings onto their customers. He stated that the average cost of a CPU minute is $6.00. Vendors, however, often charge their customers $10 or more per CPU minute. Also, customers should investigate what costs are included in the calculation. If cost per MIP is low, vendors may charge excess for other resources such as tape mounts or disk space.

Tom Blitz, President of Compass America, a company that conducts IS efficiency audits, concurred with our assessment that the theoretical relationship between size and efficiency does not hold in practice. His company studied 165 data centers ranging from 20 to 1000 MIPS, and found *no correlation in itself between size and efficiency.* He explains:

"Some small data centers outperformed others that were five times their size. There is, however, significant economy of scale. From a pure cost-efficiency point of view, a 1000 MIPS data center should be able to outperform smaller data centers. Our conclusion is that it is all a question of management."

From these cases, we witness several small shops that appear to be more efficient than larger outsourcing shops. We assert that these instances suggest that outsourcers do not necessarily have lower average costs than smaller, internally-managed IS departments. We agree with Tom Blitz that achieving theoretical economies of scale requires proper management.

Mass Production Efficiency Myth 2: hardware costs. As previously stated, economic theory purports that large companies have lower average costs than small companies partly because they receive volume discounts on inputs. The volume discount theory presumes that large companies buy in bulk and therefore receive quantity discounts. This argument extends to the outsourcing arena by assuming that outsourcing vendors buy hardware for less. As evidenced by the cases, this assumption is violated on two counts. First, many internally-managed companies receive discounts similar to outsourcing vendors. Second, very small companies may pursue hardware strategies that enable them to achieve average costs comparable to an outsourcing vendor but perhaps through difficult technology configurations.

Large outsourcing vendors do receive discounts on current hardware. However, many large companies receive similar discounts. Walter offers the following example:

"Can an outsourcing vendor buy a machine for less than FIRM7? Sure they can. I'll give you numbers that aren't exactly accurate, but a large IBM 3090 probably is in the $15 million list range. An outsourcing vendor could probably get it for $11 million. FIRM6 or FIRM7 could probably get it for about $11.5 or $12 million. Now, over a five-year period, there is not a whole lot of money being saved."

Smaller companies are often able to negotiate dirt cheap hardware leases by using older technology. The Information Systems manager at FIRM8, for example, leases an IBM 3081K for only $4000 month. He feels that smaller IS shops can contain hardware costs by renegotiating leases on dated equipment:

"And I said as long as we stay on the trailing edge of technology—and I've been pushing this concept to senior management—we have an opportunity to capitalize on cheaper computing costs."

So, IS managers can obtain hardware costs comparable to outsourcing vendors by negotiating favorable rates, using older technology or using smaller, cheaper networked technology.

Mass Production Efficiency Myth 3: software costs. The assumption that average costs decrease when fixed costs are spread over more units of output has been applied to software costs. The argument is that outsourcing vendors spread software licensing fees over multiple clients. This argument, however, is no longer valid for two reasons. First, software companies have changed the structure of their software licensing fees in response to outsourcing. Second, software companies charge clients excessive fees to transfer a license to an outsourcing vendor.

Before outsourcing came into vogue, software vendors issued site licenses to clients. This meant that a company paid a fixed fee for one copy of a software package used at a single data center site. For example, IBM typically charged their customers around $200 000 per year to operate IMS, a hierarchical database management system. It follows that the average cost per IMS transaction was lower for an outsourcer than for an internally-operated IS shop since the outsourcer spread the site licensing fee over more transactions. Software vendors such as IBM and Computer Associates, however, have changed the structure of site licensing fees in reaction to outsourcing. Rather than charge customers a fixed fee for every site, the software vendor charges based on the size of the hardware. With these new type of licenses, called group licenses, customers with bigger machines get charged more money.

The change to group licenses has seriously curtailed the outsourcing vendors' profitability. The outsourcing Account Manager at FIRM11 explains the impact on an outsourcing vendor's costs:

"[Software vendors are] thinking, 'All the times these deals are signed, the outsourcer can channel everything into one box, use one copy of the software. Therefore, we are going to lose money.' And from a business perspective, I suppose that makes sense. So what the software vendors have done is gone to group pricing. And of course, the outsourcer operates a larger box than FIRM11, so they pay more fees. . . . This has dire consequences for outsourcing deals."

In addition to the structural change, software companies are charging transfer fees to their customers who outsource. At FIRM6, for example, a software company sued FIRM6 for $500 000 for transferring the software license to an outsourcing vendor. From the software company's perspective—outsourcing reduces their revenue; the transfer fee is their way of seeking compensation.

Labor Specialization Myth 1: access to technical talent. The labor specialization myth is based on the fact that the outsourcing vendor typically hires the entire previous IS staff, so the level of expertise remains comparable. Many companies outsource to access the vendor's pool of technical talent only to find (a) they are supported by the same staff and (b) additional vendor expertise is expensive. FIRM13, FIRM9, and FIRM11 provide three examples where companies outsourced to acquire technical expertise.

FIRM13. The parts company, which subsequently was purchased by FIRM13, outsourced because they felt their IS staff did not have the technical skills to implement a new architecture. The conversion (not to mention the whole outsourcing arrangement) failed because the same people (now vendor employees) performed the installation. FIRM13's IS manager notes:

> "They [the vendor] took over all the people as they usually do, so what happens in that environment is your unqualified IS people that you had become unqualified [vendor] people."

FIRM9. FIRM9 outsourced largely to acquire vendor expertise. In this case, only half of FIRM9's IS department transferred. Since FIRM9 informed employees of the outsourcing decision early in the process, many found positions elsewhere. This was to FIRM9's benefit since the vendor supplemented the staff with other people. However, this new talent was expensive. A user from FIRM9 notes:

> "None of it is cheap. I guess there is a perception that once you have [a vendor] locked in that you have a conduit to all this expertise, but you pay."

FIRM11. FIRM11 outsourced because they felt their IS staff was incompetent. FIRM11 ended up being supported by the same staff after outsourcing, but the vendor invested significant funds for technical and customer-awareness training. So the question remains: could FIRM11 have increased the quality of the staff without the vendor?

Labor Specialization Myth 2: access to business talent. Many participants who outsourced felt a real loss of business expertise. The problem is that vendors often siphon talented employees to woo other accounts in the industry. This happened to FIRM7 and FIRM12.

FIRM7. FIRM7 was the vendor's first entrée into the petroleum industry. FIRM7 users complain that the vendor not only transferred their best employees to other accounts, they retrained the remaining staff to be more technical. A FIRM7 user explains:

> "But of the managers that we had, we lost the three best managers that were transferred. Has the caliber improved or changed radically? The nature of the people has changed. They are more technical, less user-oriented, they are more technically-oriented and less functionally-oriented, less industry-oriented. So if you were to grade them overall, yes I lost."

When Trevor, another FIRM7 participant, was asked whether the outsourcing vendor was able to achieve economies of scale in software development, he simply replied, "Rubbish."

FIRM12. FIRM12 participants also claim that business expertise has declined. FIRM12's IS manager claims talented business people are often transferred to new accounts:

> "You pay for them to learn your business, then they move those people to court other companies in your industry. They transfer skills to get new business, now the learning curve is yours to pay for again."

In summary, if a vendor submits a bid that undercuts current IS costs, the potential client should determine how the vendor has managed to reduce costs. The vendor may inherently be more efficient, but this should not be accepted without scrutiny. Furthermore, a natural cost advantage must be significant to cover a vendor's profit margin. FIRM13's IS manager warns:

> "Let's just assume that they have a certain amount of cost [that is lower]. But those guys look for a gross margin of 50 to 60%. So how can they do it cheaper?"

If the vendor does not have inherent efficiencies of scale, the potential client may decide to reduce costs on their own.

7.1.2 Can Savings be Achieved Internally?

Many participants felt that cost savings achieved by vendors could be produced internally. In particular, companies may be able to reduce costs in a number of ways: consolidate data centers, optimize current resource use, implement more controls, and/or train analysts (see Table 7.4). Each of these strategies is briefly discussed below.

Table 7.4 *Cost reduction strategies*

Consolidate Data Centers
Optimize Resource Use
Implement Cost Controls
Train Analysts

7.1.2.1 Consolidate Data Centers

One reason why vendors may offer lower costs is because they run their clients' information systems through one data center. Prior to outsourcing, companies may run multiple data centers. Since the overhead associated with machine costs and labor can be excessive, vendors consolidate data centers to reduce costs. The obvious question then is could companies consolidate data centers without outsourcing. The corporate culture may resist consolidation without considerable upper management support.

Of the thirteen cases, five companies ran or continue to run multiple data centers: FIRM7, FIRM10, FIRM4, FIRM3, and FIRM13. When FIRM7 and FIRM10 outsourced, their vendors consolidated data processing to one site. The IS department may not have had the power to consolidate data centers on their own. The CFO at FIRM10, for example, notes that the IS department could not convince the powerful operating divisions to consolidate the six data centers into one. Via outsourcing, the vendor eventually migrated all systems to one data center. A similar situation occurred at FIRM4. Their IS department had tried to consolidate three data centers into one. The operating divisions refused. Not until senior management threatened the divisions with outsourcing was FIRM4 able to consolidate and subsequently reduce costs by $22 million. FIRM3 and FIRM13 still manage multiple data centers. As international conglomerates, they run data centers in the U.S. and abroad. Service degradation is feared if users have to cross an ocean to run a program.

For more information on technical and business plans for data center consolidation, see the November 1990 edition of *I/S Analyzer* (Rochester & Douglass, 1990b).

7.1.2.2 Optimize Resource Use

Companies may also be able to reduce costs by optimizing current resource use. One outsourcing consultant said that IS managers should occasionally "spring clean" operations:

"Across the board, if I were to look at hardware, there is probably some old hardware that is around that I am paying maintenance on that we inherited from someone else, some other acquisition that we did, that we can turn around and say, 'get that out of here.' Software that nobody is using anymore. DASD space that is sitting out with files on it that haven't been used in a year and a half."

Typically, however, a formal efficiency audit is needed to supplement "spring cleaning." A number of reputable consultants will help their clients "insource"—that is, use the current IS department to achieve savings similar to those of a vendor. These consultants will recommend improvements to resource usage, controls, hardware and software purchasing practices.

Tom Blitz of Compass America discussed some of the ways a consultant can reduce costs. For example, in printing services, he reduced some of his clients' costs by $300 000 per year just by reviewing their print policy. Blitz explains,

"Many users request their printout paper to have color logos 'because we've always done it that way.' This hardly used to cost anything extra at the time when impact printers were mostly in use. With today's laser printer technique it means that the data center will have to stop the expensive laser printer, mount the new form and then start the printer again. This means lost capacity and more manual work. The outsourcer will charge extra for every form handled."

7.1.2.3 Implement Cost Controls

IS departments can decrease costs by implementing cost controls such as chargeback systems, monthly software releases, or user request prioritization. Surprisingly, many participants did not employ these rudimentary controls. Without these controls, users view IS resources as "free." With no demand restrictions, users request many services that simply are not cost-justified.

Walter, an outsourcing consultant, stated that vendors immediately take charge of costs by implementing a chargeback system:

"A chargeback system is typically the best run-time improvement there is. With a chargeback system you get a bill that shows you here's everything that you ran for that month. And if you were wasting resources, and the bill jumps as a result of that, you'd be amazed how much people reduce their costs the minute a chargeback system is implemented."

At FIRM6, for example, users would run production systems two or three times due to sloppy procedures. With a chargeback system implemented by the vendor, they postpone execution until input data are validated.

Tom Blitz, on the other hand, contends that chargeback is not enough. His printing costs example demonstrates the trouble with a chargeback philosophy. With chargeback, users are viewed as customers who pay for as much service as they want. The problem is that users do not have the technical expertise to understand how changes in their policy can significantly reduce costs. So while chargeback is a first step to decreasing costs, it is not the final step. Someone has to identify productivity improvements as a result of measuring costs per unit of service.

Another cost-saving measure is to implement monthly releases. At FIRM7, for example, users told analysts to change production code daily. Once FIRM7 outsourced, the vendor tightened controls so that changes will only be migrated to production every two months. Walter describes the situation:

> "FIRM7 is an example where people made changes to production at least once a week. And they make changes to production every time the user calls and says 'I need this fixed, I want the screen changed.' There is a tremendous amount of money to be burned up in doing that."

FIRM7's outsourcing vendor implemented a monthly release so that changes are moved into an acceptance library in 30 days and into production 30 days after that. Walter notes, "These types of mechanisms will dramatically reduce costs." Users countered, however, that the vendor also dramatically reduced service. Changes now require estimates, approvals, testing—procedures that considerably increase service delivery time.

Another cost-saving measure is to have users prioritize work requests. In many companies, the "squeaky wheel gets greased" syndrome exists where some users acquire the greatest share of IS resources by virtue of their lung-power. By requiring user managers to prioritize requests for their departments, IS will only address the most pertinent issues. In addition, users are less likely to request cosmetic or non-essential changes if they know their managers will scrutinize work requests.

7.1.2.4 Train Analysts

When companies are normally faced with financial difficulties, two services are typically slashed: travel and training. Companies reduce training because they can pinpoint the cost but not the benefits. Analyst training, however, is critical for the productivity, morale, and professionalism of an IS staff. The first thing an outsourcing vendor initiates to reduce costs is to provide technical and customer-related training to the newly transferred employees. Employees then become indoctrinated into the procedures, technical architecture and culture of the vendor. Expectations about professionalism are also established during training—which often includes grooming and professional attire requirements. Although the proposal to increase training during hard times is counter-mainstream, successful proponents may find that training increases the IS staff's productivity.

In summary, the cost-saving strategies mentioned here may all be achievable by an internal IS department. If the vendor does not enjoy an inherent efficiency advantage, "insourcing" may be more prudent since an internal IS department does not have to turn a profit. Some companies, however, may still wish to outsource for a number of reasons: the political climate of the organization's culture may prevent the IS department from initiating cost savings; the company may need the cash generated by the sale of information assets; the company may need to reduce headcount, etc. If companies decide to outsource, they need to protect their interests. The next section addresses fourteen negotiation strategies designed to balance the power between the company and their outsourcing vendor.

7.2 NEGOTIATE A CONTRACT TO ENSURE THAT EXPECTATIONS ARE REALIZED

This section starts with the assumption that the prospective client wishes to outsource with a vendor. Regardless of the reason—rational/political/financial survival—outsourcing clients must negotiate a sound contract to ensure their outsourcing expectations are realized. The negotiation strategies presented in this section should be most helpful.

The first step to a successful outsourcing arrangement is to realize that *outsourcing vendors are not partners because profit motives are not shared.* Claiming that vendors are partners is like claiming that Chrysler is a partner just because you purchase a LeBaron. Account managers at outsourcing providers are rewarded for maximizing profits, primarily by charging clients additional fees for services that extend beyond the contract (in the outsourcing parlance, these are called "excess fees"). When a customer's costs increase, so do the vendor's profits. How, then, can an outsourcing vendor be conceived of as a partner? The term "customer" is more appropriate.

The idea that outsourcing vendors are "strategic partners" may be attributed to Eastman Kodak. In 1987, Eastman Kodak outsourced almost its entire IS operations to IBM, Businessland and DEC. Vaughn Hovey, Director of Data Center Services for Kodak, told an audience of practitioners, "We think of our strategic alliances as 'partnerships' because of their cooperative and long term qualities." Kodak sealed these partnerships with little more than a gentleman's agreement. According to Hovey, Kodak rarely refers to their "six or seven page contracts."

The danger in viewing the outsourcing vendor as a partner is that the customer may sign a very loose agreement. After the agreement goes into effect, the vendor may not provide the level of service the customer expects. Instead, the vendor may refer to the written contract as the only source of obligation. Customers may subsequently be charged excess fees for services that they assumed were in the contract. One company in our study was charged a significant amount in excess fees the first month into the contract. These charges were for services they assumed were covered in the agreement. The vendor rightfully retorts that services not documented in the contract are above baseline and subject to excess fees. This does not imply that outsourcing vendors are unethical; more likely, the vendor representatives who made verbal promises are off on another sale. The remaining account manager has no recourse but to follow contract stipulations. After all, his first responsibility is to his company. Customers in this situation will have little recourse since the vendor possesses a significant amount of power over the relationship. What other information alternatives are available to the dissatisfied customer? They sold their assets, transferred leases, and transferred employees in order to enter into the arrangement.

Once potential outsourcing customers realize that vendors are running businesses and are therefore motivated to maximize profits, they can protect themselves by signing an airtight contract. *The contract is the only mechanism that establishes a balance of power in the outsourcing relationship.* Every person in this research who decided to outsource stated that the contract is the number one key to a successful outsourcing relationship. The companies most dissatisfied with outsourcing—FIRM7, FIRM12, and FIRM13—all signed contracts that dramatically favored the vendor. These contracts merely stipulated that the vendor would provide the same level of service that the company received prior to outsourcing. In contrast, participants most pleased with their outsourcing arrangements— FIRM6, FIRM8, and FIRM9—found that airtight contracts reduced the threat of opportunism. When service levels, cost structures, and penalties for non-performance are specified in the contract, the vendor becomes legally obligated to accommodate. The following paragraphs provide advice on how customers should negotiate contracts with outsourcing vendors. Although the lessons seem to favor the customer over the vendor, the true motive is to establish a balance of power that benefits both parties. Since the initial position favors the vendor (they are experts at negotiation), the customer needs to leverage his position by attending to the major lessons presented in Table 7.5.

The first lesson is to discard the vendor's off the shelf contract.

7.2.1 Discard the Vendor's Standard Contract

Vendors will likely parade their standard contract in front of their prospective clients. Janet, the Vice President and Director of IS for FIRM6, notes that this contract should be immediately discarded.

Table 7.5 *Lessons in contract negotiations*

1.	Discard the vendor's standard contract.
2.	Do not sign incomplete contracts.
3.	Hire outsourcing experts.
4.	Measure everything during the baseline period.
5.	Develop service level measures.
6.	Develop service level reports.
7.	Specify escalation procedures.
8.	Include penalties for non-performance.
9.	Determine growth.
10.	Adjust charges to changes in business volume.
11.	Select your account manager.
12.	Include a termination clause.
13.	Beware of "change of character" clauses.
14.	Take care of your people.

She, as well as other participants, feels that the key to successful outsourcing arrangements is building a site-specific contract:

> "One thing for sure: you cannot use the vendor's contract. It is too one-sided. I mean I tell people—the vendor gave us a generic contract, but we didn't use it. The problem is that all deals are so different."

The vendor's standard contract typically obligates the vendor to perform the same level of service that the company's internal IS department provides during a baseline period. These contracts, however, neither set performance standards nor include penalty clauses if the vendor fails to meet requirements.

The payment schedules in these standard contracts may also favor the vendor. For example, FIRM9's outsourcing vendor wanted FIRM9 to sign their standard contract. This contract required FIRM9 to pay the bill on the first day of the month, prior to service delivery. Richard, the IS consultant who assisted FIRM9 with their contract negotiations, explains the impact of this proposed payment schedule:

> "On FIRM9, [the outsourcing vendor] wanted it day one net 15. We got it to in arrears net 45. There was a difference in a ten-year contract, there was a difference of $8 million. So that's why [the outsourcing vendor]. . .they play those games."

So, the first lesson in contract negotiations is to discard the vendor's standard contract. Create a site-specific contract, but make sure that this contract is complete before consummating the deal.

7.2.2 Do Not Sign Incomplete Contracts

Since both parties are often anxious for the relationship to begin, the temptation to close negotiations swiftly is strong. The outsourcing vendors, in particular, may try to convince their clients to sign the contract before items are clearly specified. They assure their clients, "we'll take care of the details later." But since the vendor is not legally bound to alter the contract a posteriori, they may never agree to supplement the original contract.

FIRM7, for example, signed an incomplete outsourcing contract in January of 1989. The vendor promised to define services, service level measures and service level reports within the first six months. As of June 1991, these items remain incomplete, primarily because of the discrepancies over the contents of the baseline bundle of services. FIRM7 managers argue that certain services were understood to be covered in the contract. The vendor argues that if they were not already in the contract, then those services are subject to excess fees. This major problem could have been avoided if FIRM7 postponed the commencement date in order to complete the contract.

7.2.3 Hire Outsourcing Experts

During negotiations, the vendor uses a host of their technical and legal experts to represent their interests. These experts thoroughly understand the way to measure information services and how to protect their interests. In order to counterbalance the vendor's power, customers should hire experts to represent their interests. Participants in this research concur that experts are a critical success factor in negotiating an equitable contract. Specifically, FIRM8, FIRM6, and FIRM9 all hired outsourcing experts to assist them in their contract negotiations. Although participants admit that outsourcing experts are expensive, they believe experts will help prevent excessive above-baseline charges.

Two types of outsourcing experts are recommended—a technical expert and a legal expert. A technical expert is particularly helpful when measuring baseline services. They not only create technical measures of the customer's information resources, they are able to convert these measures to the technical idiosyncrasies of the vendor's environment. In simpler terms, technical experts convert the customer's apples to the vendor's oranges—a crucial skill that many customers do not possess. In addition, customers may feel wary about using their in-house technical staff to assist in baseline measures since many of these people may be affected by the outsourcing contract.

A legal expert familiar with outsourcing contracts is also recommended. These legal experts, who typically work in conjunction with the customer's internal legal department, ensure that the customer's wishes are adequately documented in the contract. Together, the legal expert and internal lawyer pose a formidable legal team.

As far as timing, customers will typically wish to hire a legal expert at the final stages of negotiation. A technical expert, however, is typically needed much sooner, particularly during the measurement of baseline services.

7.2.4 Measure EVERYTHING During the Baseline Period

During contract negotiations, the customer's current information services are documented during the baseline period. The baseline period becomes the yardstick that determines what services the vendor is obligated to provide to the customer. The outsourcing vendor will charge a fixed fee for delivering this bundle of services, but will charge an excess fee for services above and beyond the baseline. Therefore, customers must measure every service during the baseline period to ensure that these services will be included under the fixed fee obligation.

The consequences of not measuring services were readily apparent in this study. Participants that neglected this phase—FIRM7, FIRM12, and FIRM13—all suffered serious service problems and excess charges because they failed to measure all information services during the baseline period. Some participants assumed that their request for proposals (RPFs) documented their service needs, but RPFs are only high level descriptions of service requirements. Baseline measures must be monotonously detailed. The length of the baseline period is also an important consideration. Since service volumes typically fluctuate with the tax season, seasonal business oscillations, end-of-year processing, etc., a baseline period of six months is recommended. Typically, measures are calculated once a month for each service. For example, during March the customer may use X hours of CPU time. During April, volume may decrease or increase. At the end of the baseline period, six observations exist for each service. The customer and vendor must then establish an algorithm to determine the baseline number. Vendors often suggest averaging monthly measures, but this results in the customer exceeding baseline services 50% of the time. Perhaps a more equitable solution is to create a volume variance for each service level. The customer will not be charged an excess fee as long as volumes remain within specified ranges.

At this point, the reader may realize that comprehensive baseline measures are crucial, but still be unclear on precisely *what* services to measure and *how* to measure them. Assuming the outsourcing arrangement encompasses the entire IS department, customers should measure data processing, telecommunications, applications development, applications support, and residual services. Residual services include any services that aren't captured in the other categories such as user consultation, training, report distribution, and office moves. Each of these areas are briefly discussed below.

7.2.4.1 Data Processing and Telecommunication Services

Of all the IS service areas, participants felt that data processing and telecommunications were the easiest to measure. Most participants used the system's monitoring facilities to capture resource usage during the baseline period. In IBM environments, for example, SMF data was typically used to assess baseline data processing activity. Monitoring facilities track the number of jobs submitted, the resources used for each job (tape mounts, DASD storage, CPU minutes), turnaround time for jobs, on-line response time, and system availability. Similar reports are generated by network management systems for telecommunications.

During the baseline period, participants felt confident that their monitoring systems adequately captured their current level of processing. Resource requirements, however, vary based on the machine. Thus, a company's systems may perform significantly different on a vendor's machine. Care must be taken to convert the company's baseline activity to a comparable load on the vendor's machine. Vendors will typically develop a conversion model based on a sample set of test transactions run on their test machine. One technical expert advises customers to discard the vendor's conversion model since a vendor's test environment may vary significantly from their operating environment. The customer runs the risk of being charged excess fees if the vendor under-estimates the resources required to run the customer's systems. To avoid this risk, the customer may stipulate in the contract that the conversion model be updated after the customer's systems are run at the vendor site. (Note: That technical expert the customer should have hired by now will be most helpful during this process.)

7.2.4.2 *Applications Development and Support*

These service areas are difficult to measure since the activities are labor intensive. Participants in the study decided to use headcount as the baseline measure. Thus, if 200 analysts and programmers currently work in applications, the customer becomes entitled to 200 Full-Time-Equivalents (FTEs). Two hundred FTEs typically equate to 8000 hours worth of work a week (200 people times a 40 hour work week). Participants, however, cited four problems with this measure. First, the vendor may eliminate people and make the remaining staff work excessive hours. Gary, FIRM12's IS manager, explains the problem when the vendor reduced staff:

> "They [the remaining staff] pick up the slack so I still get my 1000 hours so contractually I couldn't do anything about it. The programmers, so they have to pick up more hours, they are tired, sick. They make mistakes."

Second, several participants complained that the quality of the analysts and programmers diminished. Vendors siphoned their best employees from the account to attract other customers. Third, non-productive hours are included in the FTE hours such as vendor group meetings and analyst training. Fourth, the FTE does not provide a measure of productivity, merely hours worked. Since the vendor charges for hours that exceed the FTE, customers suspect that the vendor's employees exaggerate project estimates.

These service problems, however, cannot be blamed on the vendor. They are free to hire, fire, and assign staff any way they see fit. If the customer wants control over headcounts, hours worked, project estimates, and staff quality, perhaps they should not have outsourced applications development in the first place.

7.2.4.3 Residual Services

In full blown outsourcing arrangements, companies often neglect to measure many services because (a) they are not reflected in current IS budgets, (b) they are not currently monitored or measured, and/or (c) customers assume they fall within other service areas. For example, many times users ask in-house analysts to help them set up their printers, use the phone system, recommend products, etc. The analysts usually respond without documenting or charging users for these favors. However, if the customer does not document and measure these services, the vendor will not include them in the baseline.

Residual services include such items as disaster recovery testing, environmental scanning for new hardware and software, micro-computer support (purchase decisions, installation, training repair), office relocation services such as rewiring and node changes, storage management to balance cost and performance trade-offs, teleconferencing support, etc. As evidenced by these examples, many residual services are difficult to measure. How do you measure intangible items such as advice, courteous service, and environmental scanning? In most cases, these services can only be measured during the baseline period by maintaining service logs. Since outsourcing decisions often cause a degradation in morale, management may fear that IS employees might ignore or sabotage the measurement effort. Therefore, some companies assigned their users to maintain the service logs during the base period.

7.2.5   Develop Service Level Measures

Some may question why service level measures need to be developed since the baseline period allegedly covered this issue. The answer is simple: the customer or vendor may wish to add, combine, improve, or delete measures. Thus, baseline measures merely provide a yardstick for what the vendor's obligations will be during the arrangement. For every service that the vendor is expected to provide, a service level measure should unequivocally express the level of required service.

During this phase of contract negotiations, participants warn that vendors will try to manipulate measures in their favor. At FIRM7, for example, the vendor attempted to dilute measures in two ways. First, they tried to dodge accounting for 100% of services. Second, the vendor tried to manipulate the laws of probability in their favor. Both these issues are discussed below.

7.2.5.1   *Specify 100% Service Accountability*

Measures typically require vendors to deliver a certain amount of work in a certain period of time. For example, vendors may agree to process 90% of all service requests within 3 days. The customer, however, may never know what happens to the remaining 10% of the service. This 10% may be serviced very late or never at all. Despite the fact that 10% of the work may never be accounted for, vendors technically meet their service level requirements.

The best way to avoid services falling through the proverbial cracks is to specify 100% service accountability. For example, if the vendor agrees to process 90% of all service requests in 3 days, then make an additional requirement that specifies the remaining 10% must be completed within a set period of time, e.g. 5 days. The client should require that exceptions be fully documented and reported.

7.2.5.2   *Know the Basic Laws of Probability*

Vendors may also dilute measures by exploiting some simple laws of probability. At FIRM7, for example, the vendor finally agreed to deliver 95% of a particular service within the agreed upon time frame. FIRM7's consultants agreed to the measure, as long as the service was delivered correctly. The vendor countered with a proposal to implement two measures. The first measure specified that 95% of the service is completed by the target date. The second measure specified that 95% of the service will be accurate. By proposing two measures, the vendor attempted to dilute the service level since the probability of the service being delivered on time *and* accurate is only roughly 90%.

7.2.6   Develop Service Level Reports

During outsourcing negotiations, companies may spend a significant amount of time developing measures, then fail to require the vendor to report on these measures. Vendors may tell their clients that their standard reports address their measures, but this assertion may be untrue.

One participant, for example, complained that the vendor's standard reports only indicate the volume of service performed. For instance, the vendor's security request report indicated "100 ACF2 rules were implemented this month." This report does not specify how many security changes were requested or the average turn-around time for the requests. According to the contract, the vendor was meeting service levels. Users, however, complain that some security requests took 17 days to fill. Imagine waiting over two weeks before accessing a needed dataset.

Service level reports should document the agreed upon service level, the service performance for the current time period, exception reporting for missed measures, and a trend analysis of the performance from previous reporting periods. Beware that vendors may charge customers for the creation of these reports. The investment is well worth it—how can service level measures be monitored without service level reports?

7.2.7   Specify Escalation Procedures

Customers realize that IS is often a volatile business—there are bound to be occasional events that prevent the vendor from meeting a service level measure. In some instances, the customer may even be at fault. Thus, in addition to the service level reports, the customer and vendor must agree upon problem escalation procedures.

Typically, the vendor will request that fault (customer or vendor) be determined for each missed measure. This protects the vendor's interests—since they are contractually bound to meet measures, they should not be punished for customer errors. Perhaps a bipartisan committee will determine blame for missed measures. Granted, this task is repulsive to most; as professionals we want to fix problems not fix blame. However, the reality is that dollars may be exchanged as a result of a missed measure.

Services may be divided into critical versus non-critical categories to prevent micro-management. For non-critical measures, such as analyst training hours, perhaps the vendor may miss this measure once or twice a year. For critical services, such as on-line availability, the customer may require immediate reporting, problem resolution within a specified period of time, and perhaps even a cash penalty.

7.2.8 Include Cash Penalties for Non-performance

In cases of severe service degradation, the customer may insist on cash compensation. FIRM6, for example, charges a penalty for failure to meet end user response time, system availability, and batch delivery deadlines for critical systems. Customers may also wish to escalate cash penalty amounts with frequency. For example, the first occurrence may result in a penalty of $25 000. Another occurrence for the same service within a specified time period may cost the vendor $50 000, and so on.

Participants that specified cash penalties in their contracts hope that they will never need to enact the penalty clause. Jack, the CFO at FIRM10, notes that penalty clauses do not fully compensate the customer. Rather, the purpose of penalty clauses is to ensure that the vendor's senior management will attend to service level problems:

> "You don't get total reimbursement for your lost profit and your lost cash. But you do have a penalty that is significant to [the outsourcing vendor] and gets their attention. Our penalty is in the $100 000 range up to $1 million. So it's not enough to compensate us for the downtime, but it will certainly get their attention. It will get somebody fired. You know it will get to the top layers within [the outsourcing vendor]."

Thus, cash penalties motivate the vendor to perform, although they do not necessarily fully compensate the customer for the consequences of sub-standard service.

7.2.9 Determine Growth Rates

Most outsourcing contracts include a growth rate where the customer gets a certain amount of growth for free. The reasoning is that the cost of a unit of processing decreases every year, so the customer deserves to share the benefits of price/performance improvements. The problem, however, is that the vendor understands growth rates much better than the senior executives with which they negotiate. The customer is warned that if growth is under-estimated, they may be charged excess fees in the future.

The following example will illustrate the problem. The vendor may convince the customer that their growth rate is 5% to 6% per year, based on IS budget increases. The vendor then offers to provide a 6% increase in resource requirements (MIPS, storage, tapes) free of charge. To a customer unfamiliar with the intricacies of IS (such as the CFO or CEO), this deal seems appealing. However, in actuality, the resource requirements may be growing at 10% to 20% since the IS department is able to exploit price/performance improvements. During the outsourcing arrangement, the customer will either pay extra for resource growth above 6% or they will curtail growth.

7.2.10 Adjust Charges to Changes in Business

Customers should also include a clause for severe volume fluctuations caused by acquisitions, mergers or sale of business units. In cases of a sale of a business unit, the customer may specify a major reduction in the fixed fee expense. The vendor, however, may insist for several months notice to allow ample time to redirect resources. The customer may also want the vendor to promptly accommodate mergers or acquisitions. The vendor may insist, again, on advanced notice. In addition, the vendor may insist on charging the customer a transition fee for the volume adjustment.

7.2.11 Select your Account Manager

FIRM11's contract negotiators insisted on one truly unique feature: they specified the name of the account manager in the contract. Paul, FIRM11's Controller, had so much faith in Lawrence, one of the vendor's account managers, that he demanded that Lawrence manage the arrangement. Lawrence is indeed a special character; as a previous outsourcing customer, he was once the vendor's most vocal critic, often complaining about services and fees. The vendor finally hired him "to shut him up." Paul feels Lawrence's background as an outsourcing customer will prevent the threat of opportunism. Paul's choice was wise; after one and one half years with the vendor, Paul has never been charged an excess fee. Although Paul's contract seems weak in other areas (lack of service measures, penalty clauses), his utter trust in Lawrence compensates for legal loopholes.

7.2.12 Include a Termination Clause

Most lawyers will insist that a termination clause be included in the contract. This clause protects both parties, since the desire to terminate by one party will severely affect the other party. Either party may need to terminate because of bankruptcy or sale of the company. In addition, the customer may wish to terminate because of failure to provide services. Most contracts require either party to notify the other within a specified time period, such as three months. Failure to give adequate notice may result in a severe penalty charge.

The customer, however, will typically require more than three months to find an alternative to meet their information needs. Negotiation with another vendor may require six months; rebuilding an internal IS department may require a year or more. In addition, the customer needs the vendor's assistance to transfer systems to an alternative site. Therefore, vendor assistance should be specified as a requirement for termination—regardless of the initiating party.

7.2.13 Watch Out for "Change of Character" Clauses

Another weakness of several outsourcing contracts is the "change of character" clause. This provision states that the customer will be charged for any changes in functionality. This clause has triggered several disputes. At FIRM7, for example, the vendor wanted to charge FIRM7 for changing their word processing software. The vendor argues that a change in software represents a change of character since this new product was not supported during the baseline period. FIRM7 argues that this is not a change of character since the function—word processing—has not changed, only the software.

At FIRM7, personal computers is another point of contention. Their contract says that the vendor will service all personal computers for a fixed price. However, the number of computers has doubled since 1989, and many PCs are now connected to LANs. The vendor claims that LAN technology is a "change in character," whereas FIRM7 claims it's only a difference in technology. In addition, the outsourcing vendor wants to charge $X for each additional PC supported. FIRM7 contends that "volumes do not equal costs." In other words, doubling the number of PCs does not require double the cost to support them.

In sum, customers should carefully specify what changes will trigger an excess charge and what changes will be included in the baseline fee.

7.2.14 Take Care of your People

The discussion so far has concentrated on protecting the interests of the customer. (We have assumed vendors are capable of protecting their own interests.) The collective term "customer," however, excludes many of the organization's people. In particular, the IS employees will be dramatically affected by the outsourcing decision. Companies have a social responsibility to treat these people fairly; that includes informing them of the decision as soon as possible and helping them secure positions elsewhere.

In typical outsourcing arrangements, the vendor will hire the majority of IS employees for a one-year trial basis. This allows the employees to prove themselves to the vendor before the vendor commits to lifetime employment. The vendor may also request performance ratings for each analyst from the customer. If the customer views outsourcing as an opportunity to eliminate low performers, they may be tempted to share this information. However, customers should examine the ethical implications carefully since a person's career is at stake. Furthermore, the customer may be pleasantly surprised to find that low performers in one culture may thrive in another culture.

7.3 CONCLUSION

The lessons presented in this section were targeted for practitioners yet to face outsourcing decisions. The lessons were extracted to allow practitioners outside of the research study to learn from the participants' victories and mistakes. In particular, the reader was warned not to outsource merely because vendor bids were more desirable than internal IS bids. Rather, the prospective client should pause and ask: why is the vendor's bid better? Could we achieve these results on our own? If not, how do we ensure that the vendor keeps their promises? To answer these questions, the reader was given some guidelines for assessing vendor efficiency, reducing IS costs, and negotiating a sound contract.

8
Summary

This final chapter addresses the question: What overall lessons can we learn from the successes and failures of practitioners who have already evaluated the outsourcing alternative? Seven lessons that contribute to our understanding of the motivation, processes and consequences of IS outsourcing evaluations are summarized below.

Lesson 1: Public information sources portray an overly optimistic view of IS outsourcing

The overall lesson learned from scrutinizing public information sources is that these sources often portray an overly optimistic view of outsourcing. Three reasons were identified to explain the optimism. First, reports are made during the honeymoon period when clients first sign an outsourcing contract. At this point, the client and vendor possess high outsourcing expectations. Second, public sources only report projected savings instead of actual savings. Therefore, the preponderance of literature that suggests that outsourcing can save 50% on IS costs is largely based on expectations. Public sources neglect to report that some outsourcing clients are charged exorbitant excess fees for above baseline measures. Third, public reports under-represent outsourcing failures because few companies wish to advertise a mistake. Therefore, the literature misrepresents the spectrum of outsourcing experiences by focusing only on the success stories.

This research revealed several findings that are absent from public information sources. First, outsourcing is not a panacea for IS problems. Several participants suffered severe service degradation and paid significant excess charges that negated expected savings.

These outsourcing failures warn others that outsourcing vendors are not partners because the profit motive is not shared. Second, outsourcing may be a viable alternative, but successful outsourcing relationships require substantial contract negotiations. The negotiation process may take six months or more to adequately measure services and to capture service expectations in an excruciatingly detailed contract.

As a final note on public information sources, optimistic IS trends are not limited to outsourcing—exaggerated claims are symptomatic of other practices. For example, the use of information technology for competitive advantage received ample press coverage in the past decade. However, when pressed to cite companies that truly strategically employ IT, the same examples surface: American Airlines, American Hospital Supply, Merrill Lynch. Therefore, practitioners should be wary that public information sources are not necessarily representative.

Lesson 2: Outsourcing appears to be a symptom of the problem of demonstrating the value of IS

In the participating companies, an overwhelming majority of senior managers viewed their IS functions as cost burdens. As such, IS managers could not appeal to effectiveness or strategic significance to justify their existence. Instead, they must somehow demonstrate efficiency. However, IS managers have difficulty demonstrating efficiency because overhead accounts camouflage IS's contribution, meaningful measures elude the majority of IS services, increases in user demand burden the IS manager to request more and more resources, and IS professionals command high salaries that cannot be tied to profitability.

In the outsourcing context, we saw that the IS manager's inability to demonstrate value was tied to outsourcing evaluations in several ways. First, IS managers may use outsourcing evaluations to demonstrate efficiency by showing that outsiders cannot provide a cheaper service. Second, IS managers may use outsourcing evaluations to justify resource requests. By bundling the resource request with an outsourcing evaluation, the IS manager "proves" that his request is cost-justified. Third, IS managers may use outsourcing to demonstrate their commitment to corporate objectives. By sacrificing part of their IS kingdom for the good of their company, IS managers demonstrate that they are good corporate citizens. These are just a few examples how IS managers struggle to overcome senior management's view of IS as a cost vortex.

The larger problem of demonstrating efficiency must be addressed. Several factors that seem correlated with demonstrated value are the IS accounting structure, reporting level of the IS manager, use of IS to support corporate strategies, top management support, and some measures (however pitiful) of effectiveness.

Tom Blitz of Compass America believes that senior managers have poor impressions of IS because they judge a variable output with a fixed budget. He explains:

> "Many IT budgets are regarded as a fixed overhead in the company and are reviewed only on the level of total cost, not on unit cost. Most industries are reviewed on cost per unit such as cost per nut or bolt, cost per engine produced, per bumper produced, etc., or cost per checking transaction in a bank, cost per insurance claim handled, cost per airline seat-revenue-mile, etc."

Thus, IS should develop measures based on cost per unit. Without these measures, IS managers are caught in a squeeze between meeting increased user demand and requirements to keep budgets fixed.

Lesson 3: Organizational members may initiate outsourcing for reasons other than cost efficiency

Participants identified a variety of motives for initiating outsourcing decisions: react to the efficiency imperative, acquire or justify additional resources, react to the positive outsourcing media reports, reduce uncertainty, eliminate a burdensome function and enhance credibility. A host of theories can be used to interpret these intentions. From a rational perspective, participants responded to the efficiency imperative. However, since actual IS efficiency is ethereal, participants reacted to their perceptions of efficiency. From a political perspective, members initiated outsourcing to promote their self-interests at the expense of others. From a garbage-can perspective, members did not proactively make outsourcing decisions but rather reacted to popular IS management trends. From a bureaucratic stance, members wished to avoid decision-making since risk-taking behavior is not rewarded. In summary, the interpretation of the participants' outsourcing experiences extends far beyond the economic rationale purported in the trade literature—costs are but one reason why participants considered outsourcing.

Lesson 4: An outsourcing vendor may not be inherently more efficient than an internal IS department

Many practitioners assume that outsourcing vendors are inherently more efficient due to economies of scale. The theory of economies of scale states that large-sized companies achieve lower average costs than small-sized companies due to mass production and labor specialization efficiencies. In the outsourcing arena, however, the applicability of the economies of scale model may be questioned. First, small shops may have lower costs per MIP than large shops by employing older technology, offering below market wages, and maintaining tight controls and procedures. Second, a vendor's hardware discount advantage is negligible in many instances. Third, changes in software licensing agreements diminish a vendor's advantage. Fourth, labor expertise is largely a myth since clients are usually supported by the same staff that transitioned to the vendor.

Lesson 5: The internal IS department may be able to achieve similar results without vendor assistance

When vendors submit bids that indicate savings, companies may question whether they can achieve similar results without vendor assistance. If the vendor is not inherently more efficient, perhaps the company can reduce its own IS expenses through data center consolidation, resource optimization, chargeback implementation, and other sundry methods.

Lesson 6: If a company decides to outsource, the contract is the only mechanism to ensure that expectations are realized

When some companies decide that outsourcing is the preferred mechanism for achieving IS objectives, they often like to view their vendors as partners. This assumption, however, is flawed. Vendors are not partners because profit motives are not shared—remember, a dollar out of the client's wallet is a dollar in the vendor's wallet. An outsourcing contract is the only way to ensure an equitable balance of power. Service level measures, arrangements for growth, penalties for non-performance and other contract provisions must be stipulated prior to outsourcing commencement.

Lesson 7:   The metaphor that IS is merely a utility is misguided

Chapter 2 presented some practitioner statements that compared the entire IS department to electricity, cafeterias, fruit stands, and laundry services. These metaphors are based on the assumption that IS services are homogeneous. . .one unit of IS service is equal to any other. The problem with this metaphor is it ignores the idiosyncratic nature of an organization's information needs. Close communication between the organization and IS must occur to accurately relay requirements. As utility users, we typically do not call the power company to communicate our complicated changing business needs. As IS users, we do. So, how is an IS department like electricity?

If the utility metaphor is at all appropriate, perhaps it should be restricted to data processing and telecommunications. These functions are inherently more capital intensive and less labor intensive than applications development, applications support, end user support and IS management. Even then, one might question the prudence of farming out the data center. Unlike true utilities, regulatory bodies do not monitor and control vendor prices.

In summary, it is hoped that practitioners yet to face outsourcing decisions will find this research relevant and insightful. The concrete examples presented from participants' actual experiences should challenge conventional assumptions about IS outsourcing. If the research has led to any one key message it is that above all else, one cannot outsource the management of IS.

References

Allen, R., Madison, D., Porter, L., Renwick, P., and Mayes, B., "Organizational Politics: Tactics and Characteristics of Its Actors," *California Management Review*, Vol. 22, 1, 1979, pp. 77–83.

Allison, G., *Essence of Decision*, Little, Brown & Company, Boston, 1971.

Ambrosio, J., "Outsourcing at Southland: Best of Times, Worst of Times," *Computerworld*, Vol. 25, 12, March 25, 1991.

Anthes, G., "HUD set to Outsource IS," *Computerworld*, Vol. 24, 49, December 3, 1990, pp. 1, 119.

Anthes, G., "Perot wins 10-year Outsourcing Deal," *Computerworld*, Vol. 25, 14, April 8, 1991, pp. 96.

Blair, D., "I Survived Outsourcing," *CIO*, Vol. 3, 10, July 1990, pp. 20–24.

Bowen, D., and Jones, G., "Transaction Cost Analysis of Service Organization-Customer Exchange," *Academy of Management Review*, Vol. 11, 2, 1986, pp. 428–441.

Brown, B., and Eckerson, W., "Kodak Turns Nets over to IBM and DEC; Farming out Net Operations can Trigger Staffing Issues," *Network World*, Vol. 7, 3, January 15, 1990, pp. 1, 4, 61, 63.

Bucher, R. "Social Process and Power in a Medical School," Mayer, B. (ed.), *Power in Organizations*, Vanderbilt University Press, Nashville, Tennessee, 1970, pp. 3–48.

Burrell, G., and Morgan, G., *Sociological Paradigms and Organizational Analysis*, Heinemann, Portsmouth, New Hampshire, 1988.

Caswell, D., "Outsourcing: A Brave New World," *Canadian Insurance/Agent & Broker*, Vol. 96, 1, January 1991, pp. 20–21.

Crane, K., "Often, The Best Nuggets Aren't in the Written Reports," *Computerworld*, Vol. 24, 16, April 16, 1990, pp. 71–73.

Cyert, R., and March, J., *A Behavioral Theory of the Firm*, Prentice-Hall, Englewood Cliffs, New Jersey, 1963.

Cyert, R., Simon, H., and Trow, D., "Observation of a Business Decision," *Journal of Business*, Vol. 29, 4, 1956, pp. 237–248.

DeMuth, J., "Outsourcing a Data Center Raises Pros and Cons," *Savings Institutions*, Vol. 111, 4, April 1990, pp. 60–61.

Dorn, P., "Selling One's Birthright," *Information Week*, Issue 241, October 16, 1989, p. 52.

Eckerson, W., "Pan Am's Outsourcing Plan Grounded by Chapter 11, *ComputerWorld*, Vol. 8, 27, July 8, 1991, pp. 2, 67.

Eckerson, W., "Changing User Needs Drives Outsourcing," *Network World*, Vol. 7, 27, July 2, 1990, pp. 1, 47.

Emerson, R., "Power-Dependence Relations," *American Sociological Review*, Vol. 27, 1962, pp. 31–41.

French, J., and Raven, B., "The Basis of Social Power," *Studies in Social Power*, Cartwright, D. (eds), University of Michigan, Ann Arbor, 1959, pp. 150–167.

Gallant, W., Interview, January 18, 1991.

Gallant, W., and McGuire, D., presentation to the University of Houston's Information Systems Research Center, January 22, 1991.

Gardner, E., "Going On-line with Outsiders," *Modern Healthcare*, July 15, 1991, pp. 35–47.

(a) Gillin, P., "EDS Rides Outsourcing to Riches," *Computerworld*, Vol. 24, 42, October 15, 1990, pp. 113, 117.

(b) Gillin, P., "Sharper Image: EDS in the 90s," *Computerworld*, Vol. 24, 40, October 1, 1990, p. 79.

Green, C., Lacity, M., and Hirschheim, R., *Information Systems Productivity: Support of Existing Application Systems*, University of Houston, Information Systems Research Center white paper series, Spring, 1990.

Griesinger, D., "The Human Side of Economic Organization," *Academy of Management Review*, Vol. 15, 3, July 1990, pp. 478–499.

Hackman, J., "Power and Centrality in the Allocation of Resources in College Universities," *Administrative Science Quarterly*, Vol. 30, 1985, pp. 61–77.

Hamilton, R., "Kendall Outsources IS Chief," *Computerworld*, Vol. 23, 46, November 13, 1989, pp. 1, 4.

Hammersmith, A., "Slaying the IS Dragon with Outsourcery," *Computerworld*, Vol. 23, 38, September 18, 1989, pp. 89–93.

(a) Hennart, J.F., "The Transaction Costs Theory of Joint Ventures: An Empirical Study of Japanese Subsidiaries in the United States," *Management Science*, Vol. 34, 4, April 1991, pp. 483–497.

(b) Hennart, J.F., "Control in Multi-National Firms: The Role of Prices and Hierarchy," *Management International Review*, Vol. 31, 1991, pp. 71–96.

Hesterly, W., Liebeskind, J., and Zenger, T., "Organizational Economics: An Impending Revolution in Organizational Theory?" *Academy of Management Review*, Vol. 15, 3, July 1990, pp. 402–420.

Hickson, D., Hinings, C., Lee, C., Schneck, R., and Pennings, J., "A Strategic Contingencies' Theory of Intraorganizational Power," *Administrative Science Quarterly*, Vol. 16, 2, June 1971, pp. 216–229.

Hill, C., "Cooperation, Opportunism, and the Invisible Hand: Implications for Transaction Cost Theory," *Academy of Management Review*, Vol. 15, 3, July 1990, pp. 500–513.

Hinings, C., Hickson, D., Pennings, J., and Schneck, R., "Structural Conditions of Intraorganizational Power," *Administrative Science Quarterly*, Vol. 19, 1, March 1974, pp. 22–44.

Hopper, M., "Rattling SABRE—New Ways to Compete on Information," *Harvard Business Review*, Vol. 68, 3, May–June 1990, pp. 118–125.

Horwitt, E., "Signet Signals Outsourcing Vendors," *Computerworld*, Vol. 24, 50, December 10, 1990, p. 2.

Hovey, V., presentation to the University of Houston's Information Systems Research Center, January 22, 1991.

Huber, G., "The Nature of Organizational Decision-Making and the Design of Decision Support Systems," *MIS Quarterly*, June 1981, pp. 1–10.

Huff, S., "Outsourcing of Information Services," *Business Quarterly*, Vol. 55, 4, Spring, 1991, pp. 62–65.

Kass, E., "EDS Sprouts Wings," *Information Week*, Issue 259, February 26, 1990, pp. 12–13.

Kass, E., "EDS Shifts To The Fast Lane," *Information Week*, Issue 268, April 30, 1990, pp. 30–34.

Kass, E., and Caldwell, B., "Outsource Ins, Outs," *Information Week*, Issue 260, March 5, 1990, p. 14.

Kay, S., "Joining an Outsourcing Team," *Computerworld*, Vol. 23, 50, December 11, 1989, p. 112.

Kelleher, J., "The Dollars and Sense of Outsourcing: Sometimes a Great Notion," *Computerworld*, Vol. 24, 2, January 8, 1990, pp. 76–77.

Krass, P., "The Dollars and Sense of Outsourcing," *Information Week*, Issue 259, February 26, 1990, pp. 26–31.

Leavitt, H., "Some Effects of Certain Communication Patterns on Group Performance," *Journal of Abnormal and Social Psychology*, Vol. 46, 1, January 1951, pp. 38–50.

Leavitt, H., "Applied Organizational Change in Industry," *Handbook of Organizations*, Rand McNally, Chicago, 1965.

Leftwich, R., and Eckert, R., *The Price System and Resource Allocation*, Chicago, Dryden Press, 1985.

Leinfuss, E., "IS Staffs Can Win When Outsourcers are Employers," *Computerworld*, Vol 25, 38, September 23, 1991, p. 80.

Lieberman, M., "Determinants of Vertical Integration: An Empirical Test," *The Journal of Industrial Economics*, Vol. XXXIX, 5, September 1991, pp. 451–466.

Lowry, S., "Bargain and Contract Theory in Law and Economics," *Journal of Economic Issues*, Vol. 1, 12, 1976.

Lucas, H., "Organizational Power and the Information Services Department," *Communications of the ACM*, Vol. 27, 1, January 1984, pp. 58–65.

Luthans, F., and Davis, T., "An Ideographic Approach to Organizational Behavior Research: The Use of Single Case Experimental Designs and Direct Measures," *Academy of Management Review*, Vol. 7, 3, July 1982, pp. 380–391.

Malone, T., "Modeling Coordination in Organizations and Markets," *Management Science*, Vol. 33, 10, October 1987, pp. 1317–1332.

Malone, T., Yates, J., and Benjamin, R., "Electronic Markets and Electronic Hierarchies," *Communications of the ACM*, Vol. 30, 6, June 1987, pp. 484–497.

March, J., and Simon, H., *Organizations*, John Wiley, New York, 1958.

Marx, K., *Selected Writings in Sociology and Social Philosophy*, translated by Bottomore, T., McGraw-Hill, New York, 1964.

Marx, K., *Grundrisse: Foundations of the Critique of Political Economy*, translated by Nicolaus, M., Penguin, Harmondsworth, 1973.

Marx, K., *Capital: A Critique of Political Economy*, translated by Frowkes, B., Penguin, Harmondsworth, Vols. 1–3, 1976.

Mason, T., *Perot*, Dow Jones-Irwin, Homewood, Illinois, 1990.

McClintock, C., Brannon, D. and Maynard-Moody, S., "Applying the Logic of Sample Surveys to Qualitative Case Studies: The Case Cluster Method," *Administrative Science Quarterly*, Vol. 24, 4, December 1979, pp. 612–629.

McCormick, J., "Outsourcing Action," *Information Week*, Issue 337, September 10, 1991, pp. 84, 88, 92.

(a) McManus, J. (ed.), "Fortune 500: Largest U.S. Manufacturing Companies," *Fortune*, Vol. 123, 8, April 22, 1991, pp. 279–336.

(b) McManus, J. (ed.), "Fortune 500: Largest U.S. Service Companies," *Fortune*, Vol. 123, 11, June 3, 1991, pp. 254–286.

McMullen, J., "New Allies: IS and Service Suppliers," *Datamation*, Vol. 36, 5, March 1, 1990, pp. 42–51.

Mechanic, D., "Sources of Power in Lower Participants in Organizations," *Administrative Science Quarterly*, Vol. 7, 3, December 1962, pp. 349–364.

Mensching, J., and Adams, D., *Managing an Information System*, Prentice-Hall, Englewood Cliffs, New Jersey, 1991.

Morgan, W., and Gladyszewski, S., "Outsourcing: The Great Debate," *Computerworld*, Vol. 23, 50, December 11, 1989, pp. 69–74.

Morse, P., "Big Business in Outsourcing," *ComputerData*, Vol 15, 1, January 1990, p. 23.

O'Leary, M., "The Mainframe Doesn't Work Here Anymore," *CIO*, Vol. 6, 6, June 1990, pp. 27–35.

Oltman, J., "21st Century Outsourcing," *Computerworld*, Vol. 24, 16, April 16, 1990, pp. 77–79.

Perrow, C., "Departmental Power and Perspective in Industrial Firms," in *Power in Organizations*, Zald, M. (ed.), Vanderbilt University Press, Nashville, Tennessee, 1970, pp. 59–89.

Perrow, C., *Complex Organizations*, Random House, New York, 1986.

Pettigrew, A., *The Politics of Organizational Decision-Making*, Tavistock Publications, London, 1973.

Pfeffer, J., *Organizational Design*, AHM Publishing, Arlington Heights, Illinois. 1978.

Pfeffer, J., *Power in Organizations*, Pitman Publishing, Marshfield, Massachusetts, 1981.

Pfeffer, J., and Salanick, G., "Organizational Decision Making as a Political Process: The Case of A University Budget," *Administrative Science Quarterly*, Vol. 19, 2, June 1974, pp. 135–151.

Pfeffer, J., Salancik, G., and Leblebici, H., "The Effect of Uncertainty on the Use of Social Influences in Organizational Decision Making," *Administrative Science Quarterly*, Vol. 21, 2, June 1976, pp. 227–245.

Pisano, G., "The R&D Boundaries of the Firm: An Empirical Analysis," *Administrative Science Quarterly*, Vol. 35, 1, March 1990, pp. 153–176.

(a) Quinn, J., Doorley, T., and Paquette, P., "Beyond Products: Service-Based Strategy," *Harvard Business Review*, Vol. 68, 2, March/April 1990, pp. 58–68.

(b) Quinn, J., Doorley, T., and Paquette, P., "Technology in Services: Rethinking Strategic Focus," *Sloan Management Review*, Vol. 31, 2, Winter 1990, pp. 79–87.

Radding, A., "The Ride is no Bargain if You Can't Steer," *Computerworld*, Vol. 24, 2, January 8, 1990, pp. 67, 70–72.

Ricoeur, P., *Conflict of Interpretations*, Northwestern University Press, Evanston, 1974.

Robins, J., "Organizational Economics: Notes on the Use of Transaction

Cost Theory in the Study of Organizations," *Administrative Science Quarterly*, Vol. 32, 1, March 1987, pp. 68–86.

(a) Rochester, J., and Douglass, D. (eds). "Taking An Objective Look at Outsourcing," *I/S Analyzer*, Vol. 28, 8, September 1990, pp. 1–16.

(b) Rochester, J., and Douglass, D. (eds). "Consolidating Multiple Data Centers", *I/S Analyzer*, Vol. 28, 11, November 1990, pp. 1–18.

Rogers, E., *Diffusion of Innovations*, 3rd ed., Free Press, New York, 1983.

Rothfeder, J., and Coy, P., "Outsourcing: More Companies are Letting George Do it," *Business Week*, No. 3181, October 8, 1990, p. 148.

Salanick, G., and Pfeffer, J., "Uncertainty, Secrecy, and the Choice of Similar Others," *Social Psychology Quarterly*, Vol. 41, 3, September 1978, pp. 246–255.

Saunders, C., and Scamell, R., "Intraorganizational Distributions of Power: Replication Research," *Academy of Management Journal*, Vol. 25, 1, March 1982, pp. 192–200.

Saunders, C., and Scamell, R., "Organizational Power and the Information Services Department: A Reexamination," *Communications of the ACM*, Vol. 29, 2, February 1986, pp. 142–147.

Simon, H., *Administrative Behavior*, The Free Press, New York, 1976.

Singer, C., "Life After Facilities Management," *Computers in Healthcare*, Vol. 11, 6, June 1990, pp. 29–33.

Stagner, S., "Corporate Decision Making: An Empirical Study," *Journal of Applied Psychology*, Vol. 53, 1969, pp. 1–13.

Thurow, L., *Dangerous Currents*, Vintage Books, New York, 1983.

Tushman, M., "A Political Approach to Organizations: A Review and Rationale," *Academy of Management Review*, Vol. 2, 2, April 1977, pp. 206–216.

Walker, G., and Poppo, L., "Profit Centers, Single-Source Suppliers, and Transaction Costs," *Administrative Science Quarterly*, Vol 36, 1, March 1991, pp. 66–87.

Walsh, J., and Seward, J., "On the Efficiency of Internal and External Corporate Control Mechanisms," *Academy of Management Review*, Vol. 15, 3, July 1990, pp. 421–450.

Ward, B., "Hiring Out: Outsourcing is the New Buzzword in the Management of Information Systems," *Sky Magazine*, Vol. 20, 8, August 1991, pp. 37–45.

Weber, M., *The Theory of Social and Economic Organization*, translated by Henderson, A. and Parsons, T., Free Press, Glencoe, Illinois, 1947.

Weber, M., *The Methodology of the Social Sciences*, Free Press, Glencoe, Illinois, 1949.

Welsh, M., and Slusher, E., "Organizational Design as Context for Political Activity," *Administrative Science Quarterly*, Vol. 31, 3, September 1986, pp. 389–402.

Wilder, C., "Setting an IS Standard," *Computerworld*, Vol. 23, 16, April 17, 1989, pp. 67–68.

(a) Wilder, C., "Outsourcing: Fad or Fantastic?" *Computerworld*, Vol. 24, 1, December 25, 1989/January 1, 1990, p. 8.

(b) Wilder, C., "How IBM, Perot lost out," *Computerworld*, Vol. 24, 47, November 19, 1990, p. 112.

Wilder, C., and Margolis, N., "Outsourcing's Hidden Cost Bite," *Computerworld*, Vol. 24, 39, September 24, 1990, pp. 1, 12.

Wilder, C., "Bend Me, Shape Me," *Computerworld*, Vol. 24, 52–53, December 24, 1991–January 1, 1991, p. 14.

Williamson, O., *Markets and Hierarchies: Analysis and Antitrust Implications. A Study in the Economics of Internal Organization*, The Free Press, New York, 1975.

Williamson, O., *Markets and Hierarchies*, The Free Press, New York, 1975.

Williamson, O., "Transaction Cost Economics: The Governance of Contractual Relations," *Journal of Law and Economics*, Vol. 22, 2, October 1979, pp. 233–261.

Index

Index compiled by Annette J. Musker